THE THEORY OF
COMMITTEES AND
ELECTIONS

THE THEORY OF
COMMITTEES AND
ELECTIONS

BY

DUNCAN BLACK, M.A., Ph.D.

Emeritus Professor of Economics in the
University College of North Wales

CAMBRIDGE

AT THE UNIVERSITY PRESS

1971

CAMBRIDGE UNIVERSITY PRESS
Cambridge, New York, Melbourne, Madrid, Cape Town, Singapore,
São Paulo, Delhi, Dubai, Tokyo

Cambridge University Press
The Edinburgh Building, Cambridge CB2 8RU, UK

Published in the United States of America by Cambridge University Press, New York

www.cambridge.org
Information on this title: www.cambridge.org/9780521141208

First published 1958
Reprinted 1963, 1968, 1971
This digitally printed version 2010

A catalogue record for this publication is available from the British Library

ISBN 978-0-521-04262-8 Hardback
ISBN 978-0-521-14120-8 Paperback

IN MEMORIAM
M.B.

CONTENTS

PART II

HISTORY OF THE MATHEMATICAL THEORY
OF COMMITTEES AND ELECTIONS (EXCLUDING
PROPORTIONAL REPRESENTATION)

PREFACE

THIS book or some related work has occupied me spasmodically over rather a long period, in fact ever since I listened to the class lectures of Professor A. K. White on the possibility of forming a pure science of Politics. After an earlier version of Part I had failed to obtain publication in 1947, some chapters appeared as articles, and I am obliged to the editors of the journals mentioned below for permission to reprint this material, sometimes in a modified form.

When I first attempted publication I was unacquainted with the earlier history of the theory, and, indeed, did not even know that it had a history; and the later additions to the book have largely been by way of writing the present Part II. This historical section does not include the important recent work, *Social Choice and Individual Values* (1951), of Professor Kenneth J. Arrow; but it does include all the mathematical work on committees and elections appearing before the middle of this century which has come to my notice, although the last item in it is dated 1907. No doubt there is much important material which I have failed to see.

The theorizing of the book grew out of a reading of the English political philosophers and of the Italian writers on Public Finance. At a very early stage I was helped to find the general lines of development by discussion with my colleague Professor Ronald H. Coase on his view of the nature of the firm; and later talks with Dr R. A. Newing did much to clear my ideas on some of the mathematical issues. Dr Newing suggested to me the use of a matrix notation which, some years afterwards, I discovered had already been employed by Rev. C. L. Dodgson (Lewis Carroll).

Dodgson's pamphlet *A Discussion of the Various Methods of Procedure in Conducting Elections* is reproduced by courtesy of the Library of the University of Princeton in which is the only known copy, and his pamphlet *A Method of Taking Votes on More Than Two Issues* and 'The Cyclostyled Sheet' by courtesy of the Bodleian Library, Oxford. At Dodgson's old college of Christ Church, Dr T. B. Heaton, Professor J. O. Urmson and Mr Geoffrey Bill were helpful in a number of ways; and I have been permitted to quote from the minutes of the Governing Body of the college and also from the 'Vere Bayne Memorandum Book' which is the property of the Senior Common Room. It was a pleasure to correspond with Miss F. Menella Dodgson who has enabled me to quote two entries from the diaries of Lewis Carroll, which, owing to their specialized interest, had been excluded from the published version.

The Académie des Sciences permitted access to its minutes in connexion with the work of Borda and Condorcet.

The University of Wales has added to my already great obligations to it by a generous grant towards publication, made by its Press Board.

D.B.

BANGOR,
August 1956

ACKNOWLEDGEMENTS

I am indebted to the editors for permission to incorporate, wholly or in part, material which has already appeared as articles in the following journals.

'On the Rationale of Group Decision-Making', *Journal of Political Economy*, February 1948.

'Un approccio alla teorìa delle decisioni di comitato', *Giornale degli Economisti*, May–June 1948.

'The Decisions of a Committee Using a Special Majority', *Econometrica*, July 1948.

'The Elasticity of Committee Decisions with an Altering Size of Majority', *Econometrica*, July 1948.

'The Elasticity of Committee Decisions with Alterations in the Members' Preference Schedules', *South African Journal of Economics*, March 1949.

'The Theory of Elections in Single-Member Constituencies', *Canadian Journal of Economics and Political Science*, May 1949.

'Some Theoretical Schemes of Proportional Representation', *Canadian Journal of Economics and Political Science*, August 1949.

PART I

THE THEORY OF COMMITTEES AND ELECTIONS

CHAPTER I

A COMMITTEE AND MOTIONS

Scope of the work. The present book will present the logic of committee decisions and of elections, for an election is a species of committee.

Most of the book presupposes no knowledge of Mathematics* beyond simple arithmetic, but at the same time it makes use of a mathematical mode of reasoning and the student who is acquainted with Mathematics will be at a considerable advantage. The unmathematical reader is advised to omit chapter v and to skip freely at times in the others. Likewise the reader who is not acquainted with Economics should omit chapters XIII and XIV.

DEFINITIONS. By a *committee* we will mean any group of people who arrive at a decision by means of voting. The voters or members of the committee may be situated in one room, as in the case of the committee meeting of a sports club, or they may be scattered over an area, as in the election of a member of parliament.

The committee will be choosing either a motion or a candidate. The theory will first be developed in relation to a committee which is choosing one out of the various motions which are put forward on a particular topic; the extension of the theory to the case of an election will be obvious.

A *motion* we define as any proposal before a committee which it may adopt or reject by a method of voting.

It is accepted in practice that the motions between which a vote is taken should propose courses of action which are alternative to

---

* Throughout the book subjects of study are denoted by capital letters and the material studied is given a small letter. For example, the subject Politics is distinguished from politics, the phenomena which it studies.

one another; or, as we may say, they must relate to the same topic. This requirement is met by the chairman having the duty to refuse any amendment which is irrelevant to the original motion before the committee. As Erskine May says of House of Commons procedure, 'It is an imperative rule that any amendment must be relevant to the question on which the amendment is proposed.'

The members of the committee may, of course, hold different opinions on whether a particular motion is relevant to the matter under discussion, and the chairman's decision, or a vote of the committee, may be called on to decide the relevance of particular motions. The principle involved is clear, and while the decision reached in any particular case may not be logically unassailable, it will settle the practical question of which motions are to be put against each other in a vote.

We may take it then that in our theory, as in real life, the motions put forward and to be winnowed by voting are alternatives to one another, the adoption of one precluding the adoption of any other.

The representation of motions. We will suppose that in the committee with which we are dealing, m motions have been put forward $(m \geqslant 1)$, and we will denote them by $a_1, a_2, ..., a_m$ respectively.*

Another way of denoting these motions will be by the m points named $a_1, a_2, ..., a_m$ on a horizontal straight line (Fig. 1).

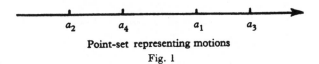

Point-set representing motions

Fig. 1

Sometimes the only difference between one motion and another will relate to the size of a particular quantity, e.g. the committee may be fixing the wage rate of a group of workmen, and the motions may be that the workmen be paid £10, £10. 10s., etc. Here the obvious representation is by means of a measurable variable. We may measure wage per week along the horizontal axis and represent the motion that the wage should be £10 by the point marked £10, and so on. The correspondence between

---

* The philosophical justification of this step is discussed in chapter III below.

a particular motion and the number concerned is then quite plain (Fig. 2).

Sometimes for purposes of theoretical development it will be convenient to suppose that the number of motions before a committee becomes increased indefinitely; and it will be as if an infinite number of motions, each one of them a definite motion, were before the committee to be voted on. For instance, in the case of the above committee we might suppose that every wage rate that could possibly be named, lying between £10 a week and £12 a week, was before the committee. Then all these motions could be represented by points on the horizontal axis lying between £10 and £12. To every motion there would correspond a point on the axis.

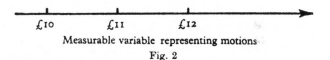

Measurable variable representing motions
Fig. 2

The motion a_0. In the usual committee procedure, if only a single motion has been put forward it will be put to the vote of the members for acceptance or rejection. If it obtains the necessary majority of votes it becomes the decision of the committee; if it fails to secure the necessary majority, the decision of the committee in rejecting it is that, for the present, things are to remain as they are. It is as if the original motion had been put against another motion to the effect 'that this committee take no further action in the matter', or 'that the existing state of affairs remain unchanged'. Thus the minimum number of motions as between which this kind of committee can be called upon to choose is two, a motion which suggests some change in the existing state of affairs, and the implicit motion 'that the existing state of affairs remain unchanged'.

When, in a committee of this type, two motions have been put forward by members, these would first be reduced by a process of voting to a single motion; and then, if no further amendments were forthcoming, the surviving motion would be put to the meeting for acceptance or rejection. This would be equivalent to placing it against the further motion 'that the existing state of affairs remain unchanged'. And in general this type of committee

B

procedure always adds one to the number of motions actively put forward by the members.

Since it comes into operation so frequently and is always in effect the same motion, we will denote the motion 'that the existing state of affairs remain unchanged' by a_0.

The same motion would often be introduced in the procedure of a committee which was selecting one from among a number of applicants for a post. By a process of voting a single applicant would be selected; but if any member of the committee were in doubt as to whether this applicant was of sufficient merit to hold the post, the chairman would certainly grant a further vote to accept or reject the candidate, and would often hold the further vote without being asked to do so. This would be equivalent to putting the motion 'that this candidate be elected' against the motion 'that the existing state of affairs continue unchanged'. The same motion as before is called into play.

But in parliamentary or local-government elections the candidate who gets the stipulated majority over his opponents automatically becomes elected. The voters do not receive the further option that they return no member.

CHAPTER II

INDEPENDENT VALUATION

The first mode of representation. We will name the n members of our committee by the capital letters A, B, C, ...

We will assume that each member of the committee ranks the motions put forward in some definite order of preference, whatever that order may be; for example, if there are four motions denoted by a_1, a_2, a_3, a_4 before a committee, the member A may prefer a_2 to any of the others, may be indifferent as between a_3 and a_4, and may prefer either of them to a_1.

If so, A's valuation of the motions can be represented by the schedule of preferences on the left-hand side of Fig. 3, in which a_2 stands highest, a_3 and a_4 next highest, each at the same level, and a_1 lowest. And similar scales could be drawn for other members of the committee with a_1, ..., a_4 appearing in some definite order on each scale, though the ordering of the motions may be different on the scale of each member.

We are here using the theory of relative valuation of orthodox Economic Science. The only points which have significance on the directed straight line representing a member's schedule of preferences are those at which motions are marked, and his scale really consists of a number of points placed in a certain order in relation to each other. No significance attaches to the distance between the points on the scale, and any two scales would be equivalent on which the motions occurred in the same order.

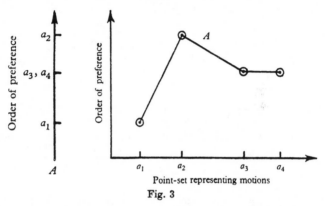

Fig. 3

When a member values the motions before a committee in a definite order, it is reasonable to assume that, when these motions are put against each other, he votes in accordance with his valuation, i.e. in accordance with his schedule of preferences. Thus the member A would be assumed to vote for a_2 when it was put in a vote against a_1; or if a_3 were put against a_4—since he is indifferent between the two and it would be irrational for him to support either against the other—he would be assumed to abstain from voting.

The second mode of representation. A member's preferences as between the different motions may also be shown by denoting the motions put forward by particular points on a horizontal axis, while we mark relative level of preference along the vertical axis. For instance, the same set of valuations of the individual A is shown in the right and left parts of Fig. 3. The only points in the diagram having significance are those for the values a_1, a_2, a_3, a_4 on the horizontal axis, corresponding to the motions actually put forward. We have joined these points standing at various levels of preference by straight-line segments, but this is done merely to assist the eye, since the curve is to be taken as imaginary except at the four points. In this diagram, as in the case of the preference schedule, it is only the relative heights of different points which have meaning, not their absolute heights.*

When we are dealing with a vertical schedule of preferences we place the member's name under it, and when we use a two-dimensional representation we place his name alongside the corresponding curve.

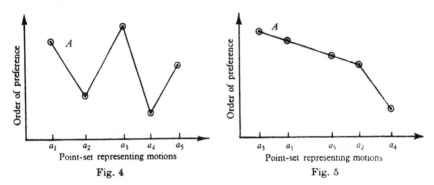

Fig. 4   Fig. 5

Shapes of preference curves. The shape of a member's preference curve will depend on the order in which the motions are ranged on the horizontal axis. For example, when five motions a_1, a_2, a_3, a_4, a_5 are put forward, the scale of preferences of the member A in regard to these motions may be represented either by Fig. 4 or by Fig. 5. The one diagram transforms into the other when we alter the ordering of the points forming the base, from a_1, a_2, a_3, a_4, a_5 to a_3, a_1, a_5, a_2, a_4.

When m motions have been put forward, the number of significant diagrams that can be drawn to represent a given preference scale will be $m!$, corresponding to the number of ways in which it is possible to arrange m points in order on a horizontal line. In any diagram the number of straight-line segments joining the points by which level of preference is expressed will be $(m-1)$. And if we designate the slope of any such segment as being up, down or horizontal, the maximum number of changes of direction that $(m-1)$ segments can show will be $(m-2)$. For example, in Fig. 4

---

* See Frank H. Knight, *Risk, Uncertainty and Profit*, pp. 68–70.

there are five motions and there are three changes of direction in the segments joining the points on the member's preference scale: the gradient of the first segment is downwards and of the second upwards, giving one change of direction; the gradient of the third segment is opposite to that of the second, giving a second change of direction; and there is another change of direction between the third and fourth segments, giving three changes in all. In Fig. 5, on the other hand, there is no change of direction, the gradient of each connecting straight-line segment being downwards.

When we are representing the preference scale of only a single member, it will always be possible to choose an ordering of the points to represent motions on the horizontal axis such that the resulting preference curve becomes fairly simple in shape, e.g. consisting of straight-line segments all either down-sloping or horizontal. But if we wish to represent the preference curves of several members on the same diagram, we may find that an ordering of the motions on the horizontal axis which simplifies the shape of the preference curve of one member, complicates the shape of the curve for one or more of the other members.

We will refer to a curve which is either always upward-sloping, or always downward-sloping, or always horizontal, or which is upward-sloping to a particular point and downward-sloping beyond that point (i.e. ∩-shaped), as being a single-peaked curve. On this definition *a single-peaked curve is one which changes its direction at most once, from up to down.*

With some given groups of schedules of the vertical sort, it will be possible, when we represent them by two-dimensional diagrams, to find an ordering of the points on the horizontal axis to represent motions that leaves all of the members' curves single-peaked; while with other given groups of schedules it will not be possible to find an ordering of the points on the axis which leaves all of the curves as simple as this in shape. For example, with the group of schedules of Fig. 6, if the points to represent motions on the horizontal axis are arranged in the order a_3, a_1, a_4, a_2 (or in the reverse order a_2, a_4, a_1, a_3), all of the members' curves become single-peaked, as seen in Fig. 7; whereas with the group of schedules of Fig. 8, no ordering of the points on the axis can be found which gives us single-peaked curves for the three members of the committee. In fact the preference curve of the member G can never be single-peaked.

We will refer to the point on the horizontal axis corresponding to the highest point on a single-peaked preference curve as the *optimum* for the member concerned. It corresponds to the motion which he prefers to any of the others put forward.

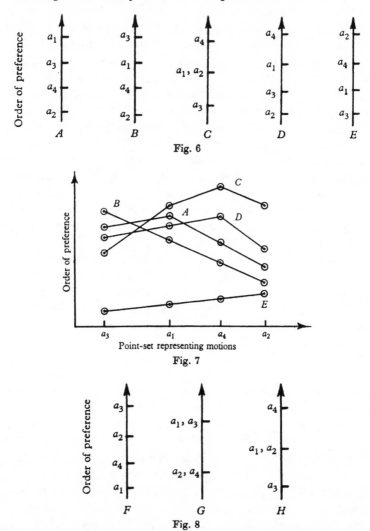

Fig. 6

Fig. 7

Fig. 8

The occurrence in practice of two shapes of preference curves. While in practice a member's preference curve may be of any shape whatever, there is reason to expect that, in some important practical problems the valuations actually carried out will tend to take the form of isolated points on single-peaked curves. This would be particularly likely to happen if the committee were considering different possible sizes of a numerical quantity and choosing one size in preference to the others. It might, for example, be reaching a decision with regard to the price of a product to be marketed by a firm, or the output for a future period, or the wage rate of labour, or the height of a particular tax, or the legal school-leaving age, and so on.

In such cases the committee member, in arriving at an opinion on the matter, will often try initially to judge which size is for him the optimum. Once he has arrived at his view of the optimum size, the further any proposal departs from it on the one side or the other, the less he will favour it. The valuations carried out by the member would then take the form of points on a single-peaked or ∩-shaped curve.

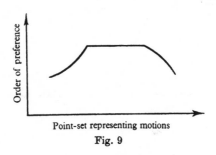

Point-set representing motions

Fig. 9

Another case likely to be of frequent occurrence in practice—especially, again, where the committee is selecting a particular size of a numerical quantity—is that in which the valuations carried out by a member take the form of points on a single-peaked curve with a truncated top. Such a case would arise when the individual feels uncertain as to which of two or more numerical quantities proposed represents his optimum choice. He cannot discriminate in choice between (say) two of these numerical quantities; but the further the proposal made falls below the lower of these values, or the higher it rises above the larger of them, the less he esteems the motion concerned (cf. Fig. 9).

Single-peaked curves emphasized in our treatment. In the present book we shall devote a considerable amount of attention to the case in which an ordering for the points on the horizontal axis can be found such that all of the members' preference curves are single-peaked. There are two advantages to be gained from this. The first is that when all the members' curves are single-peaked we have some kind of insight into their attitudes to the topic under discussion; we can see the optimum for the various members concerned and we know that the further a motion departs to the right (or to the left) of a member's optimum, the less he desires that that motion should be adopted. We have some understanding of the data of the problem, and we can have some appreciation of the significance for the committee members of the decision which is reached. The other reason for working largely in terms of single-peaked curves is that this class of curves allows a geometrical treatment which is comparatively simple.

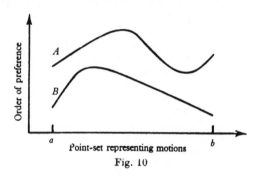

Fig. 10

In addition to single-peaked curves we shall consider a few curves of other types and then give an arithmetical treatment which will apply to curves of all shapes.

The supposition of an infinite number of motions. In practice in any committee never more than a few motions are put forward on any one topic. We may suppose, however, that an infinite number of motions are put forward and that each member of the committee values each of these motions in relation to every other. For instance, in Fig. 10 any point in the segment ab of the horizontal axis may be taken to represent a motion and the preference curves of the members A and B taken to be given by the curves shown, of which one is single-peaked and the other less regular in shape. Both curves must extend over the same range of the horizontal axis.

[10]

Part of our theory will be developed in terms of smooth curves of this sort, each of which is supposed to be significant at all points on it. But the treatment we give, it will be found, would still apply even though each of the curves concerned were to be significant at only two or more points, corresponding say to the motions a_h, a_k, ...

A shape of curve which cannot occur. If a member's preferences can be represented by points on a vertical straight line, then as between any two motions he has a definite attitude of preference or indifference. It follows that his preference curve cannot bend back on itself as ⊂ or ⊃ ; and in any representation his preference curve must be a single-valued function of the variable (motions).

CHAPTER III

CAN A MOTION BE REPRESENTED BY THE SAME SYMBOL ON DIFFERENT SCHEDULES?

The possible objections considered seriatim. So far as I can see, the main objection to the symbolism we have used would be that it represents a motion by the same symbol on the schedules of different individuals. This might be objected to on any or all of the following grounds:

(a) A motion states a proposed course of action. Now, it may be urged, epistemologists accept that before any statement can be understood it must be taken up by the mind into a system of judgements; and this system of judgements, because of differences in native make-up and differences in past history, can be the same for no two minds. Not even the simplest sentence can bear the same meaning for different people.

Thus a motion will have different meanings for different people. The meanings that different members take from a motion may be sometimes fairly similar, and at other times may diverge widely. But if the meanings are different for different people, can the same symbol be used on their schedules?

(b) Nor, it may be said, is there identity in the stuff by which the meaning of the motion is conveyed: for the motion must have been made orally or in writing; if in writing, the black marks on paper read by each person would be different; if made orally, the sound waves heard by each member would be different, and, because of differences in aural apparatus, would be heard differently. Are we entitled, then, to use a single symbol to denote the motion?

(c) The motives leading different people to support one motion against another may be either fairly similar, or, quite possibly, vastly different. One may support a motion for the most altruistic of reasons while another supports it because he expects it to favour his own particular interests.

(d) The effects expected to result from the adoption of any motion will inevitably be different for different people, and the differences will tend to become greater the more important or the more complex the proposal made. For example, different people expect very different consequences from the election of a given person to the Presidency of the United States.

The most important of these objections are (a) and (b), and our reply to them is that the same objections would apply in other instances where the legitimacy of the use of a single symbol to denote an object is generally accepted. Thus the novel *The Fountain*, and the poem *In Memoriam*, if they have been read by you and me, will have been read in different books, possibly in different editions. There is no identity of letterpress. And their meanings will have been different for our two minds. Or you may have read the poem while I have not, though both of us know that it is a longish poem written by Tennyson on the death of a friend. The point is that although the meaning of *In Memoriam* is very different for you and me, the same title can be used to denote the same thing for each of us without any logical difficulties arising. Indeed, if we did not use the same title, or the same symbol, to denote what we both accept as being the same thing, the difficulties which would arise would be most considerable.

Similarly, if I point to a chair in the room and speak of 'that chair' to a friend, although our positions are different and we get different views of it, and although our eyesight may be very different, nevertheless 'that chair' is a symbol with which neither of us finds fault, because there is a sufficient overlap between the meanings which we both attribute to it.

Exactly the same principle is in operation when we use the symbol a_1, say, to denote a motion. It is the overlap of meaning which the motion has for the different minds of the different members that enables us to use a single symbol.

To reply further to (a)—which we judge to be the objection that deserves the most serious consideration—and also to (c) and (d), we may fall back on the analogue of Economics. Here it would be accepted that if a person is confronted with the choice between an apple, a pear and a nut, and he prefers the apple to the pear and the pear to the nut, then his scale of valuations can be represented as in Fig. 11. This is merely the simplest instance of the mode of representation on which the whole of Economic Science is based; no one has managed to stir up doubts as to its validity and it has been used by a host of investigators in different countries for the last eighty years. Its validity must, we think, be accepted.

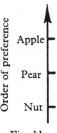

Fig. 11

Now in our economic analogue, the person who is valuing the apple, the pear and the nut may have a very imperfect knowledge of the objects being valued. The apple may be sound or unsound, or the nut may be of a kind that he has never tasted. Or it may be second-hand cars that he is valuing, or some patent medicine, or the services of a doctor or a lawyer; people may be practically unacquainted with the things they are valuing and bidding for; their judgements may be mistaken or foolish; but the technique of Economics still works and enables us to examine how the price of the goods or the receipts of the doctor or lawyer is determined. The technique of demand and supply is still available when the commodity for sale is the tickets in a sweepstake, where the buyers have little notion of their true chances of winning, or where the commodity offered is the ordinary shares of a company whose profits lie in the future and can only be guessed at by buyers and sellers alike.

It is not, therefore, a requirement of Economics that the people concerned should be fully acquainted with the commodity that they buy and sell. No more is it a requirement for the same technique to apply in Politics, that each person should take the same meaning from the motions put forward in the committee with which we are dealing.

Next let us consider objection (c), that different people may prefer the motion a_1 to the motion a_2 from quite different motives, and that this may invalidate our mode of representation. But in dealing with the person's preference for an apple over a pear and over a nut, we used this type of representation without considering for a moment what his motive was. Motive is one of the aspects of choice which is abstracted by Economics and similarly it can be abstracted in the theory of committees. This particular objection is not likely to give the slightest trouble to anyone acquainted with Economics.

The objection (d), that different people expect quite different consequences to result from the adoption of the motion a_1, say, is in no better case. In Economics we do not ask what consequences the person expects to result from eating the apple; and it is extraneous to the theory of committees to ask what a person's expectations are in regard to the consequences of the adoption of any motion.

These are the main objections which may be brought against the symbolism we use. Certainly they raise difficult questions in the theory of knowledge, as indeed do all similar queries that may arise in any branch of mathematical science. But there seems to be no doubt that the symbolism we use is valid.

CHAPTER IV

A COMMITTEE USING A SIMPLE MAJORITY: SINGLE-PEAKED PREFERENCE CURVES

A quite general theorem. The following will hold whatever the shapes of the members' preference curves may be:

THEOREM. *At most, only a single motion can get a majority over every other.*

Let us assume that two motions, a_h and a_k say, can each get a simple majority over every other. Then a_h can get a simple majority over a_k and a_k can get a simple majority over a_h, which is absurd. Hence at most only one motion can get a simple majority over every other.

An illustration of the subsequent argument. We will assume that in a committee m motions are put forward (m finite or infinite) and that an ordering can be found for the points to represent these motions on the horizontal axis, such that the members' preference curves become single-peaked.

To show the method of reasoning employed we will give an arithmetical example. Fig. 12 shows the preference curves of the five members of a committee. Only part of each curve has been drawn, and the curves are supposed to extend over a common range of the horizontal axis. We name the members' optima $O_1, O_2, \ldots$, in the order of their occurrence as we move from left to right along the horizontal axis.

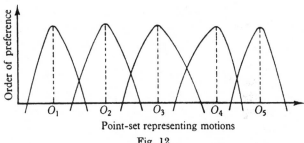

Point-set representing motions

Fig. 12

Then if a_h is put against a_k (where $a_h < a_k \leqslant O_1$), the preference curve of each member—irrespective of what its precise shape may be—is up-sloping from a_h to a_k; and a_k, standing at a higher level of preference on the curve of each member, will get a 5:5 (5 out of 5) majority against a_h. If a_h is put against a_k (where $a_h < a_k \leqslant O_2$), at least four members—viz. those with optima at or above O_2— will have preference curves which are up-sloping from a_h to a_k; and a_k will get at least a 4:5 majority against a_h. If $a_h < a_k \leqslant O_3$, a_k will get at least a 3:5 majority against a_h. And similar relations hold for motions corresponding to values above O_3. If two values above O_3 are placed against each other in a vote, the nearer of the two values to O_3 will get a majority of at least 3:5 against the other.

If a value a_h (where $a_h < O_3$) is put against a value a_k (where $a_k > O_3$), before we could find which of the values would win in a vote, we would have to draw the complete preference curve for each member, find whether a_h or a_k stood higher on the preference curve of each member and count up the votes cast for a_h and a_k. But even though a value below the median optimum O_3 should defeat all values to the left of itself, and should defeat some of the values above O_3, this would be without significance, because what

[15]

we will look for in the following paragraphs is a value which can defeat *every* other by at least a simple majority. Now we notice that the preference curves of at least three members are down-sloping from O_3 leftward, and the preference curves of at least three members are down-sloping from O_3 rightward. Therefore O_3 can defeat any other value in the entire range by at least a simple majority. And we have already seen that this can be true at most of only a single value.

The general proof. To establish the general theorem we must distinguish between the case in which the number of members in the committee is odd and that in which it is even. We will assume that in the event of a tie in the voting, one member of the committee, the chairman, has the right to a casting vote.

THEOREM. *When there are n members in a committee, all of whose curves are single-peaked, and n is odd, the value $O_{\frac{1}{2}(n+1)}$ can get at least a simple majority against every other, and it is the only value which can do so.*

When n is even, if the chairman's optimum is at $O_{\frac{1}{2}n}$ or lower, the value $O_{\frac{1}{2}n}$ can get a simple majority against every other, and it is the only value which can do so; or if the chairman's optimum is at $O_{\frac{1}{2}n+1}$ or higher, the value $O_{\frac{1}{2}n+1}$ can get a simple majority against every other.

We will treat these three cases separately.

(i) When n is odd, the middle or median optimum will be the $\frac{1}{2}(n+1)$th; and in Fig. 13 this optimum, the one immediately below and the one immediately above, are shown.

Now suppose $O_{\frac{1}{2}(n+1)}$ were placed against any lower value, say, $a_h\ (a_h < O_{\frac{1}{2}(n+1)})$. Since $\frac{1}{2}(n+1)$ members have optima at or above $O_{\frac{1}{2}(n+1)}$, as we move from left to right, from a_h to $O_{\frac{1}{2}(n+1)}$, at least $\frac{1}{2}(n+1)$ curves are up-sloping, namely, those of members with optima at or to the right of $O_{\frac{1}{2}(n+1)}$. At least $\frac{1}{2}(n+1)$ members prefer $O_{\frac{1}{2}(n+1)}$ to a_h and, in a vote against a_h, $O_{\frac{1}{2}(n+1)}$ will get a majority of at least $\frac{1}{2}(n+1):n$, and this is sufficient to give it at least a simple majority. Therefore $O_{\frac{1}{2}(n+1)}$ can get at least a simple majority over any lower value against which it is put. Similarly, it can get at least a simple majority against any higher value. Thus it can get a simple majority against any other value which can be proposed. By the initial theorem of this chapter, it is the only value which can do so.

(ii) Let n, the number of members in the committee, be even. Fig. 14 shows the two middle optima, $O_{\frac{1}{2}n}$, $O_{\frac{1}{2}n+1}$, and the two neighbouring optima $O_{\frac{1}{2}n-1}$, $O_{\frac{1}{2}n+2}$; and we take it that the chairman, who in the event of a tie has the right to a casting vote, is a member whose optimum lies at $O_{\frac{1}{2}n}$ or lower.

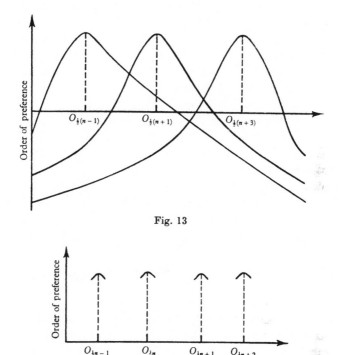

Fig. 13

Fig. 14

In these circumstances $O_{\frac{1}{2}n}$ will be able to defeat any lower value, a_h, say $(a_h < O_{\frac{1}{2}n})$: for $(\frac{1}{2}n+1)$ members have optima at or above $O_{\frac{1}{2}n}$; and at least $(\frac{1}{2}n+1)$ preference curves will be up-sloping as we move from left to right from a_h to $O_{\frac{1}{2}n}$. At least $(\frac{1}{2}n+1)$ members will vote for $O_{\frac{1}{2}n}$ against a_h, and this is sufficient to give $O_{\frac{1}{2}n}$ a simple majority.

If $O_{\frac{1}{2}n}$ is put against any higher value a_k $(a_k > O_{\frac{1}{2}n})$, since there are $\frac{1}{2}n$ optima at or below $O_{\frac{1}{2}n}$, the preference curves of at least $\frac{1}{2}n$ members will be down-sloping from $O_{\frac{1}{2}n}$ to a_k, and $O_{\frac{1}{2}n}$ will get at least $\frac{1}{2}n$ votes against a_k, i.e. will at least tie with a_k. In the event

[17]

of a tie $O_{\frac{1}{2}n}$ will defeat a_k with the aid of the chairman's casting vote because, by hypothesis, his optimum is situated at or below $O_{\frac{1}{2}n}$ and his preference curve must be down-sloping from $O_{\frac{1}{2}n}$ to a_k.

Thus when the chairman's optimum is situated at or below $O_{\frac{1}{2}n}$, $O_{\frac{1}{2}n}$ will be able to get at least a simple majority against any other value which may be proposed. And it is the only value which can do so.

(iii) Similarly, when n, the number of members in the committee, is even, and the chairman's optimum is at or above $O_{\frac{1}{2}n+1}$, it can be shown that $O_{\frac{1}{2}n+1}$ will be able to get at least a simple majority against every other value.

DEFINITION. That motion, if any, which is able to obtain a simple majority over all of the other motions concerned, is the *majority motion*. Similarly in an election, that candidate, if any, who is able to obtain a simple majority over each of the others, is the *majority candidate*.

CONVENTION. When n, the number of members, is odd, let us denote $O_{\frac{1}{2}(n+1)}$ by $O_{\text{med.}}$. When n is even and the chairman's optimum is at $O_{\frac{1}{2}n}$ or lower, let us denote $O_{\frac{1}{2}n}$ by $O_{\text{med.}}$; or when the chairman's optimum is at $O_{\frac{1}{2}n+1}$ or higher, let us denote $O_{\frac{1}{2}n+1}$ by $O_{\text{med.}}$.

Then the results we have arrived at can be summarized as follows:

THEOREM. *If the members' curves are single-peaked, $O_{\text{med.}}$ will be able to get a simple majority over any of the other motions $a_1, ..., a_m$ put forward.*

A similarity and a contrast. This theorem presents a striking analogy with the central principle of Economics—that showing how price is fixed by demand and supply. The theorem states that the motion which will defeat any other put forward becomes determinate as soon as the position of the median optimum becomes determinate. No matter in what manner the preference curves or optima of the other members move about, provided the location of the median optimum $O_{\text{med.}}$ remains unchanged, this motion will defeat any other. The analogy with Economics is that, in the determination of price in a market, price remains unchanged so long as the point of intersection of the demand and supply curves is fixed and given, irrespective of how these curves may alter their shapes above and below that point. Or, in the version

[18]

of the theory due to Böhm-Bawerk,* which brings out the point very clearly, price remains unaltered so long as the 'marginal pairs' of buyers and sellers and their price attitudes remain unchanged.

But the analogy exists only between the two theories; there is a marked difference in the materials to which they relate. In the case of the market, when the price of a commodity is being determined, a series of adjustments on the part of the consumers will bring into existence a state of affairs in which this commodity, and all others which they purchase, will have the same significance at the margin for each consumer. If one consumer values 1 lb. of tea at 3 lb. of sugar, so will every other consumer of these commodities. This is one of the several grand harmonies running through the material of economic life, a harmony by which no one who understands it can fail to be impressed—and by which the economists of the last generation were perhaps over-impressed. In the material of committee decisions (or of political phenomena in general), on the other hand, no such grand harmony exists. The possibility of the persistence of disharmony and discord is as striking in the one case as is the certainty of harmony in the other.

The transitive property. *When the members' preference curves are single-peaked, if a_1 can defeat a_2 in a vote, and a_2 can defeat a_3, then a_1 can defeat a_3.*

This can be shown by considering the orderings of the points a_1, a_2, a_3 in relation to $O_{\text{med.}}$. The total number of orderings of the four points a_1, a_2, a_3, $O_{\text{med.}}$ on a straight line, is the same as the number of permutations of the four letters by which the points are denoted, that is, $4! = 24$. In six of these permutations $O_{\text{med.}}$ will be in the last place, in six in the third place, etc.

(i) When $O_{\text{med.}}$ is the last in order, five of the six arrangements possible are incompatible with the condition that a_1 defeats a_2 and a_2 defeats a_3; these arrangements are $a_2 a_3 a_1 O_{\text{med.}}$, $a_3 a_1 a_2 O_{\text{med.}}$, $a_1 a_3 a_2 O_{\text{med.}}$, $a_2 a_1 a_3 O_{\text{med.}}$ and $a_1 a_2 a_3 O_{\text{med.}}$. The only ordering of points fulfilling the conditions of the problem is that of Fig. 15. In this case the proof that a_1 can defeat a_3 is obvious.

(ii) By symmetry, when $O_{\text{med.}}$ occupies the first place, a_1 can defeat a_3.

(iii) When $O_{\text{med.}}$ occupies the third place in the order of points, the three arrangements $a_2 a_3 O_{\text{med.}} a_1$, $a_1 a_3 O_{\text{med.}} a_2$, $a_1 a_2 O_{\text{med.}} a_3$ are

* *The Positive Theory of Capital*, edited by W. Smart, pp. 208–9.

C

incompatible with the conditions assumed. For example, when the order is $a_2a_3O_{med.}a_1$ it would be impossible that a_2 should defeat a_3.

The three arrangements compatible with the condition that a_1 beats a_2 and a_2 beats a_3, are $a_3a_1O_{med.}a_2$, $a_3a_2O_{med.}a_1$ and $a_2a_1O_{med.}a_3$. In the first of these the proof that a_1 defeats a_3 is obvious.

Proof for the case when the order of points is $a_2a_1O_{med.}a_3$ can be given as follows (see Fig. 16).

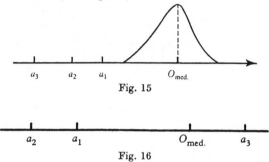

a_3 a_2 a_1 $O_{med.}$

Fig. 15

a_2 a_1 $O_{med.}$ a_3

Fig. 16

The members who vote for a_2 against a_3 are all members with optima lying below a_2, possibly some with optima lying in the range a_2a_1 and possibly some with optima lying in the range a_1a_3.

But all members with optima below a_2, and all with optima in the range a_2a_1, prefer a_1 to a_3; and all of the members with optima in the range a_1a_3, who prefer a_2 to a_3, must *a fortiori* prefer a_1 to a_3. Hence against a_3, a_1 can get at least as many votes as can a_2. Hence a_1 can defeat a_3.

Proof when the order of the points is $a_3a_2O_{med.}a_1$ can be given in the same way.

Hence in all cases where $O_{med.}$ occupies the third place in the order of the points, the theorem holds good.

(iv) By symmetry, the theorem is true when $O_{med.}$ occupies the second place in the order.

(v) The only other positions possible for the three points a_1, a_2, a_3, are those in which a_1 or a_2 or a_3 coincides with $O_{med.}$.

If a_2 coincides with $O_{med.}$, a_1 cannot defeat a_2; if a_3 coincides with $O_{med.}$, a_2 cannot defeat a_3. If a_1 coincides with $O_{med.}$, the theorem clearly holds.

All possible cases are covered by (i)–(v) above, and in all cases the theorem is true.

[20]

An *extension of the transitive property* is that *if a_1 can defeat a_2, a_2 can defeat a_3, ..., and a_{r-1} can defeat a_r, then a_1 can defeat a_r.*

It follows from the transitive property that a_1 can defeat a_3. By hypothesis a_3 can defeat a_4. Hence a_1 can defeat a_4. By successive applications it follows that a_1 can defeat a_r.

The types of committee procedure (α), (β) and (γ), with some examples and a theorem. The type of committee procedure almost universally used in practice may be described as follows:

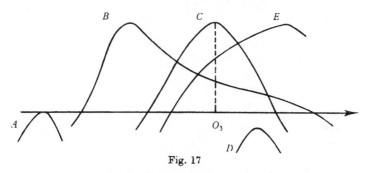

Fig. 17

Procedure (α). In this two tests are applied.

Test (i). Every motion put forward must enter the voting process at some stage, and whenever a motion is defeated by a simple majority it is eliminated from further consideration.

Test (ii). The motion that passes test (i) is put in a final vote for acceptance or rejection, and, for adoption, must obtain at least a simple majority.

It follows from the preceding that if the curves are single-peaked the value which passes test (i) is $O_{\text{med.}}$. And it is the value adopted provided it can get a simple majority against a_0.

It is often convenient in the geometrical treatment to draw the preference curve of each member so as to intersect the horizontal axis in those values, if any, as between which and a_0 he is indifferent. Then if $O_{\text{med.}}$ lies under a majority of curves, if need be taking into account the chairman's casting vote, it will be the value adopted. If $O_{\text{med.}}$ should lie under a minority of curves, the committee's decision will be a_0.

EXAMPLE 1. Given that the preference curves of the five members of a committee, drawn so as to intersect the horizontal axis in those values, if any, as between which and a_0 the member is indifferent, are as in Fig. 17. The curves are single-peaked and are supposed to extend over a common range of the horizontal axis. What will be the decision of the committee?

The member A is indifferent as between a_0 and what for him is the optimum among the motions $a_1, ..., a_m$ put forward. The member D prefers a_0 to any of the motions put forward.

The motion corresponding to the value O_3 can get a simple majority against any of the motions put forward, $a_1, ..., a_m$. It lies under three curves and so can get a majority of $3:5$ (3 out of 5) against a_0. On procedure (α), therefore, O_3 will be the value adopted.

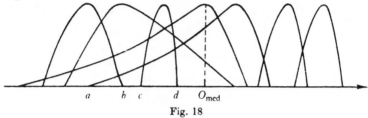

Fig. 18

A committee might choose to follow a procedure different from the usual one. Let us suppose that a committee adopts the procedure specified as follows:

Procedure (β). Test (i). Those motions are to be selected which are able to get a simple majority against the proposal that the existing state of affairs remain unchanged, i.e. against a_0.

Test (ii). Of the motions, if any, which pass the first test, that one is to be selected which is able to get a simple majority against all of the others. If no motion satisfies this test, a_0 is to be adopted.

It can be seen that if no motion can pass the first test then the committee's decision is a_0; and that if $O_{\text{med.}}$ is one of the values which pass the first test, it is bound to become the decision of the committee. In each of these cases procedure (β) yields the same result as procedure (α) would have done.

EXAMPLE 2. With the curves of Fig. 17, the committee decision, if it follows procedure (β), is O_3.

The other cases that can arise are covered by the following two propositions:

Proposition. If the first test in procedure (β) gives one or more sets of values, all of which lie on the same side of $O_{\text{med.}}$, then that value which is situated nearest to $O_{\text{med.}}$ will be the committee's decision.

For example, let the curves shown in Fig. 18 be drawn so as to intersect the horizontal axis in those values as between which and a_0 the members are indifferent, a, b, c and d being among such points of intersection. Then all points within the ranges ab, cd can get a simple majority over a_0, and no other values of the variable can do so.

The next significant point on the axis below d can easily be shown to defeat any lower value. Hence this point can pass the

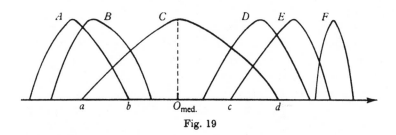

Fig. 19

second as well as the first test on procedure (β), and so becomes the decision of the committee.

In this instance, had the committee followed procedure (α), $O_{med.}$ would have been selected by test (i) and rejected when placed against a_0 in test (ii). Procedure (β) may, therefore, furnish one of the motions a_1, ..., a_m as the decision, where procedure (α) would give the decision a_0.

Proposition. Let test (i) *in procedure* (β) *yield one or more sets of values below $O_{med.}$ which can defeat a_0, and one or more sets of values above $O_{med.}$ which can defeat a_0. Of the values below $O_{med.}$ which pass test* (i), *select that which lies nearest to $O_{med.}$; and of the values above $O_{med.}$ which pass the test, again select that which lies nearest to $O_{med.}$. Then whichever of this pair of values gets a majority over the other will become the decision of the committee.*

We will indicate the lines of the general proof. In Fig. 19 let the curves be drawn so as to intersect the horizontal axis in the values as between which and a_0 the members are indifferent; a, b, c, d are among such points. It is given that the chairman's curve is C.

The only values to pass test (i) are those lying within the ranges ab and cd, the end-points in each case being excluded.

The first significant point on the axis below b can get a majority against any lower value; and the first significant point on the axis above c can get a majority against any higher value.

If the first significant point below b can get a majority against the first significant point above c, by the transitive property it will also be able to get a majority against any point on the axis above c. Hence, of the values which are able to pass test (i), it will be able to defeat all those lower and all those higher than itself. It will, therefore, become the decision of the committee.

A corresponding conclusion holds if the first significant point above c is able to defeat the first significant point below b.

A procedure of great theoretical interest is the following:

Procedure (γ). Test (i). All the motions are put forward before voting takes place, and every motion is put against every other. That motion, if any, is selected which is able to get a simple majority over every other.

Test (ii). The motion selected by the first test is put against a_0 for acceptance or rejection.

Unless a motion can both pass the first test and defeat a_0, a_0 is the decision of the committee.

It should be noticed that procedures (α) and (β) do not suppose the motions $a_1, \ldots, a_m$ to be put forward before voting takes place, whereas procedure (γ) does require this.

EXAMPLE 3. With the preference curves of Fig. 17, O_3, corresponding to the median optimum, can defeat every other of the motions $a_1, \ldots, a_m$ put forward. It lies under three curves and so can defeat a_0. Hence O_3 is the decision when the committee follows procedure (γ).

EXAMPLE 4. With the curves of Fig. 18, O_4 passes test (i) but is defeated by a_0 at test (ii); and a_0 is the decision of the committee.

THEOREM. *If, in relation to all of the motions concerned $a_1, \ldots, a_m$ and a_0, the members' curves are single-peaked, then whether the committee follows procedure (α) or (β) or (γ) its decision will be $O_{\text{med.}}$.*

This follows since $O_{\text{med.}}$ can get a simple majority against any motion against which it is put. It may be, of course, that $O_{\text{med.}}$ is the motion a_0; and the existing state of affairs will then remain unchanged.

It should also be observed that the assumption that an ordering can be found for the motions $a_1, \ldots, a_m$ and a_0 on the horizontal axis, such that the members' curves become single-peaked, is more restrictive than the assumption that single-peaked curves exist for the motions $a_1, \ldots, a_m$. One more motion, a_0, is involved, and although single-peaked curves may exist for the motions $a_1, \ldots, a_m$, they may not exist for $a_1, \ldots, a_m$ and a_0.

CHAPTER V

A COMMITTEE USING A SIMPLE MAJORITY:
OTHER SHAPES OF PREFERENCE CURVES

1. Curves either single-peaked or single-peaked with a plateau on top

Some examples. We pointed out in chapter II that a curve likely to occur in practice was the single-peaked curve with a plateau on top, and we now consider this case.

It may be that when the curves of the members of the committee are either single-peaked or single-peaked with a plateau on top, the median curve will be found to be a single-peaked curve,

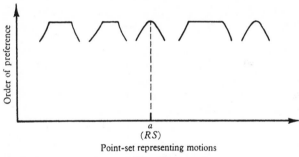

Point-set representing motions

Fig. 20

as in Fig. 20. The value a would be able to get a simple majority against every other, because there are five members in the committee and three curves down-sloping from a leftward and three down-sloping from a rightward. (In this and each of the diagrams that follow we have marked the range within which the majority motion must lie RS.)

In Fig. 21 the majority motion, either a or b, would become determinate as soon as we knew which member was chairman.

In Fig. 22 there is a distinct median item, the plateau C. Leftward from a three curves are down-sloping and rightward from b three curves are down-sloping. Any point in the range ab is able to get a majority over any point outside this range. If the chairman is A or B the value a can get a simple majority over every

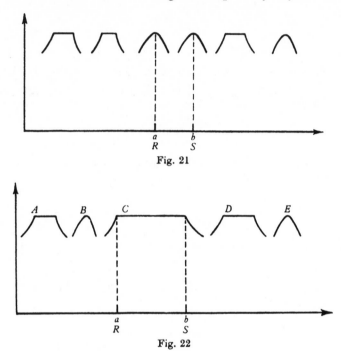

Fig. 21

Fig. 22

other value; if the chairman is D or E the value b can get a simple majority over every other. If C is the chairman, he is indifferent as between all points in the range ab, and there is no reason in the data of the problem why he should support any point in this range against another. If, however, he does support some value in the range against other points in it, that value will be able to get a simple majority against every other.

When, instead of a single median curve, there are several overlapping peaks and plateaus, we first isolate the range within which any majority motion must lie. To do this we determine the point, a say, up to which just over half of the curves ($\frac{1}{2}(n+1)$ of the curves for n odd, $\frac{1}{2}n + 1$ of the curves for n even), are up-sloping, as we move from left to right; and then the point, b say, beyond which just over half of the curves are falling as we move from left to right. The majority motion, if any, must lie in *ab*.

Next we count the number of curves which are down-sloping and up-sloping over each segment of *ab*, and in this way narrow down the range within which the majority motion, if any, must lie. We give some examples.

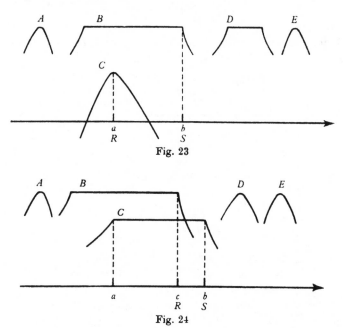

Fig. 23

Fig. 24

In Fig. 23 there are three curves up-sloping to the point *a*, and three curves down-sloping from the point *b* onwards. If *A* or *C* is chairman, *a* will be the majority motion; if *D* or *E* is chairman, *b* will be the majority motion. If *B* is chairman we cannot say whether any majority motion exists, but if it does it must lie in the range *ab*.

In Fig. 24 there are five members in the committee and the preference curves of three of them are up-sloping to the point *a*, and the curves of three of them are down-sloping after the point *b*. The majority motion, if any, must lie in *ab*. Over the range *ac*, two members are indifferent as between the various values, and two curves are up-sloping as we move from left to right. The value *c*, therefore, would defeat any other value in *ac*. Over the range cb, two curves are down-sloping, two up-sloping and one horizontal. Thus the majority motion, if any, must lie in cb. If A or B is chairman, c will be the majority motion. If C is chairman we get the same kind of indeterminacy as in the above example. If D or E is chairman, b is the majority motion.

In the committee of Fig. 25, with six members, four curves are up-sloping to a and four down-sloping beyond b. The majority motion, if any, must lie in ab.

Over the range ac, two curves are horizontal, three up-sloping from left to right and one down-sloping. Hence the point c would defeat any other point in ac. The majority motion, if any, must therefore lie in cb.

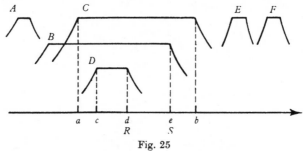

Fig. 25

In the range cd, three curves are horizontal, two are up-sloping from left to right and one is down-sloping. Hence the point d would defeat any other point in cd and the majority motion, if any, must lie in db.

In the range de, two curves are horizontal, two are up-sloping from left to right and two are down-sloping. Points in de will tie with each other in a vote.

In the range eb, one curve is horizontal, two curves are up-sloping from left to right and three are down-sloping. Hence the point e would defeat any other point in eb.

The majority motion, if any, therefore, must lie in de.

It is seen from the diagram that any point in de could in fact get a majority against any point lying outside. If the chairman is A or D, d is the majority motion; if the chairman is E or F, the majority motion is e; if the chairman is B or C, the result, on the data given, is indeterminate.

The theory. We now investigate in a more general way the properties of such a group of curves.

Let us define the point a as being the last point, as we move from left to right, up to which at least an absolute majority ($\frac{1}{2}(n+1)$ for n odd, $\frac{1}{2}n+1$ for n even) of the curves are rising; and the point b as being the first point, as we move from left to right, at which at least an absolute majority of the curves become down-sloping.

Then in virtue of the curves being either single-peaked or being single-peaked with plateaus on top, each curve which is up-sloping to a must be up-sloping from the beginning of the range to a. Hence a can get an absolute majority against any lower point.

Similarly, b can get an absolute majority against any higher point.

Within the range ab, as we move from left to right, the curves may be up-sloping, down-sloping or horizontal. If no curves are horizontal, the range ab must either contract to a single point, corresponding to the optimum value for a single-peaked curve, which is able to obtain an absolute majority against every point in the entire range; or else it must be defined by the two optimum values for single-peaked curves, one occurring at a and the other at b. These cases virtually fall under the treatment of the preceding chapter and need not be separately considered here.

Let us suppose that, within ab, some curves are horizontal. Let there be h curves which are horizontal as, moving from left to right, we approach the point a. And we will suppose that, in the particular instance, there is a bare majority of up-sloping curves at a and a bare majority of down-sloping curves at b. If so, the number of down-sloping curves at a, for n odd, is

$$n - \tfrac{1}{2}(n+1) - h = \tfrac{1}{2}(n-1) - h.$$

The number of down-sloping curves at b is $\frac{1}{2}(n+1)$.

Hence as we move from a to b, the number of curves which change over from being either horizontal or up-sloping, to become down-sloping, is $\frac{1}{2}(n+1) - \{\frac{1}{2}(n-1) - h\} = 1 + h$.

For n even the corresponding result is $2 + h$.

If we suppose that, moving from right to left, as we approach the point b, k curves are horizontal and a bare majority up-sloping, the similar result is obtained that as we move from b to a, the number of curves that change over from horizontal or up-sloping to down-sloping is $1 + k$ for n odd, or $2 + k$ for n even.

These results may be used to plot the point a or the point b, once the other has been obtained.

Within the range ab, no point is able to get an absolute majority against every other, but at most a relative majority, because it is not until, moving from a, we reach the point b, that an absolute majority of the curves are sloping in one direction.

Proposition. If the point H, lying anywhere in the entire range of the variable, can defeat a value G lying to the left of H $(G < H)$, then it can defeat any value G' lying to the left of G $(G' < G)$.

Let us suppose that between H and G, $f(f \geqslant 0)$ curves are horizontal and g curves down-sloping, then against G the point H gets $g : n - f - g$ votes, and by hypothesis this gives it a majority. But between H and G', the g curves which had been down-sloping between H and G must continue down-sloping since they correspond to peaks or plateaus which lie at or to the right of H; and the f curves which had been horizontal between H and G must be either horizontal or down-sloping between H and G'. Hence H when put against G' can get at least $g : n - f - g$ votes, i.e. can get a majority.

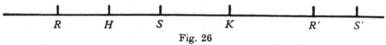

Fig. 26

Similarly, if H can defeat any value K lying to the right of H $(K > H)$, it can defeat any value K' lying to the right of K $(K' > K)$.

Proposition. At most there is a single range of values (RS), each one of which is able to get a majority against all points lying outside that range.

Let us suppose that there are two such ranges RS and $R'S'$, with an intervening range between. Then if H lies in RS it can get a majority against K (Fig. 26), and therefore against any point in $R'S'$. That is, values in $R'S'$ cannot get a majority against all other points and RS is the only such range.

Thus the majority motion, if it exists, must lie in a range RS, each point of which is able to get a (relative or absolute) majority against all values on either side of the range.

THEOREM. *Such a range (or point) RS exists.*

Let a be the point up to which an absolute majority of the curves are up-sloping, and b the point beyond which an absolute majority of the curves are down-sloping. It is possible that one of these points may lie at an extremity of the range, or both may lie at the extremities.

We need only consider the case where, within the range ab, one or more horizontal curves occur, since the theorem is obviously true for the other cases.

At a there is a preponderance of up-sloping curves, at b of down-sloping curves. But, as we move from a to b, the number of curves changing over from up-sloping to horizontal or down-sloping, or from horizontal to down-sloping, continually increases. It follows that the change-over from a preponderance of up-sloping to a preponderance of down-sloping curves must occur either at a single point (RS), or else there must be a region (RS) in which the up-sloping curves and down-sloping curves are equal in number and beyond which down-sloping curves are in the preponderance.

Thus in all cases such a point or range RS must exist.

The transitive property. *For a group of curves, all of which are either single-peaked or single-peaked with plateaus on top, if a_1 can defeat a_2 in a vote and a_2 can defeat a_3, then a_1 can defeat a_3.*

At most one of the points concerned can lie in RS, since no point in this region can obtain a majority over any other.

Proof can be given in the same way as for single-peaked curves in the preceding chapter, by considering the possible orderings of the points a_1, a_2, a_3 in relation to the region RS.

For the ordering of points of Fig. 15 where the point $O_{\text{med.}}$ is replaced by the point or region RS, every curve that is down-sloping between a_1 and a_2 continues down-sloping between a_1 and a_3. Hence, since a_1 can defeat a_2, it can also defeat a_3.

When the ordering of the points is $a_2 a_1 (RS) a_3$, the proof already given for the case of single-peaked curves holds without alteration (cf. Fig. 16).

The *extension of the transitive property* will also hold, namely, that *if a_1 can defeat a_2, a_2 can defeat a_3, ..., and a_{r-1} can defeat a_r, then a_1 can defeat a_r.*

EXAMPLE. For the group of sixteen curves shown in Fig. 27, nine curves are up-sloping to a and one is horizontal as we approach a. The point b, therefore, corresponds to the third down-turn of a curve after we have passed the point a.

Within the range RS, two curves are horizontal, seven down-sloping and seven up-sloping. The majority motion, if any, must therefore lie in RS. If the chairman is one of the six members A or the member C, R will be the majority motion; if he is one of the five members E or the two members F, S will be the majority motion. If he is the member B or the member D, the result will be indeterminate.

If desired, the motion a_0 can be brought explicitly into the discussion in the same way as in chapter IV.

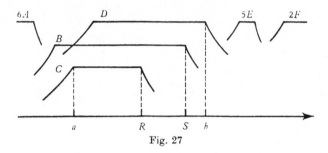

Fig. 27

2. Other classes of curves

Defining the curves. Let us suppose that the preference curves of the members take the form of multi-peaked curves or of curves consisting of peaks and plateaus. The highest peak or the highest plateau on a curve may occur at any point of the range.

Taking first the case in which n is odd, let the highest peak on a curve, or, if this is higher, the highest plateau on a curve count as one, and let these summits be numbered 1, 2, ..., n in the order in which they occur, as we move from left to right. And let us suppose that when this has been done, the $\frac{1}{2}(n+1)$th peak or plateau turns out in fact to be a peak. Name the value of the variable corresponding to it $O_{\frac{1}{2}(n+1)}$.

Through $O_{\frac{1}{2}(n+1)}$ draw a perpendicular to the horizontal axis. Then provided that a curve whose highest peak or whose highest plateau occurs to the left of $O_{\frac{1}{2}(n+1)}$, is never as high in the range above $O_{\frac{1}{2}(n+1)}$ as it is at the point $O_{\frac{1}{2}(n+1)}$, and provided that a curve whose highest peak or whose highest plateau occurs to the right of $O_{\frac{1}{2}(n+1)}$, is never as high in the range below $O_{\frac{1}{2}(n+1)}$ as it is at the point $O_{\frac{1}{2}(n+1)}$, then $O_{\frac{1}{2}(n+1)}$ will be able to defeat any value which can be proposed against it (cf. Figs. 28 and 29 in illustration).

Proof. Let one such value to be proposed against $O_{\frac{1}{2}(n+1)}$ be a_h, say, where $a_h < O_{\frac{1}{2}(n+1)}$. When $O_{\frac{1}{2}(n+1)}$ is put against a_h, $O_{\frac{1}{2}(n+1)}$ must stand higher on the curves of at least $\frac{1}{2}(n+1)$ members, namely, the members whose highest peaks or highest plateaus lie at or

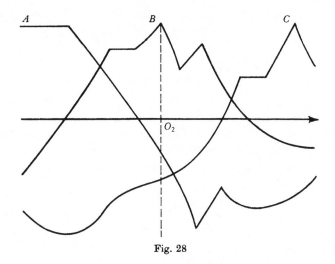

Fig. 28

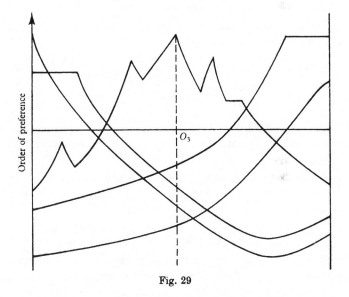

Fig. 29

above $O_{\frac{1}{2}(n+1)}$. At least $\frac{1}{2}(n+1)$ members, therefore, will vote for $O_{\frac{1}{2}(n+1)}$ against a_h, and $O_{\frac{1}{2}(n+1)}$ will get a majority. That is, $O_{\frac{1}{2}(n+1)}$ will be able to defeat any value lower than itself.

Similarly, it can be shown to defeat any value higher than itself.

Hence $O_{\frac{1}{2}(n+1)}$ can defeat any other value in the entire range and it is the only value which can do so.

In the case where n is even, let us suppose that when the highest peaks and plateaus on the curves are numbered in the order of their occurrence, it is found that the $\frac{1}{2}n$th is a peak occurring at $O_{\frac{1}{2}n}$, and that the highest peak or plateau on the curve of the chairman occurs at or below $O_{\frac{1}{2}n}$. And let us suppose that each curve whose highest peak or plateau occurs to the left of $O_{\frac{1}{2}n}$, is higher at $O_{\frac{1}{2}n}$ than at any value above it, and each curve whose highest peak or plateau occurs to the right of $O_{\frac{1}{2}n}$, is higher at $O_{\frac{1}{2}n}$ than at any value below it. Then $O_{\frac{1}{2}n}$ will be able to get at least a simple majority over every other value in the range.

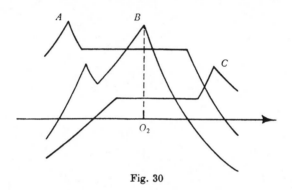

Fig. 30

Proof. The requirements stated ensure that in comparison with any lower value, $O_{\frac{1}{2}n}$ stands higher on at least $\frac{1}{2}n + 1$ curves and so is able to get a simple majority against it.

Similarly, in comparison with any higher value, $O_{\frac{1}{2}n}$ stands higher on at least $\frac{1}{2}n$ curves and on the scale of preferences of the chairman, and so again can get a majority.

Thus $O_{\frac{1}{2}n}$ can get a majority over any other value in the range.

If, when the peaks and plateaus are numbered, $O_{\frac{1}{2}n+1}$ is a determinate value corresponding to the occurrence of a peak, and the highest peak or plateau on the chairman's curve occurs at or above $O_{\frac{1}{2}n+1}$, the corresponding proposition can be stated.

EXAMPLE 1. In Fig. 28 the curve A satisfies the condition that its height at O_2 is greater than at any value to the right of this; the curve B satisfies the condition of being a median peak; and the curve C is higher at O_2 than at any value to the left of this. The three curves, therefore, satisfy all the requirements named, and O_2 is able to get a majority over any other value in the range.

EXAMPLE 2. In Fig. 29, O_3 can defeat all other values in the range, since the curves satisfy all the requirements.

EXAMPLE 3. In Fig. 30 the curve A is as high on the plateau at some values of the variable greater than O_2, as it is at the point O_2, and so fails to meet the requirements. The same is true of C. A consequence of the requirements stated, indeed, is that the median peak cannot be overlapped by any plateau.

CHAPTER VI

A COMMITTEE USING A SIMPLE MAJORITY: ANY SHAPES OF PREFERENCE CURVES, NUMBER OF MOTIONS FINITE

The matrix. In the preceding chapters we have supposed the members' preference curves to be of certain restricted shapes. Now we remove all restrictions on the shapes of the preference curves, but suppose the number of motions put forward to be finite.

To deal with this case we use a voting matrix* whose construction can be seen from an example. Let the group of schedules with which we are dealing be that of Fig. 31. Then construct a table in which the columns and rows are named (see the matrix shown) a_1, a_2, a_3, a_4, these being the motions before the committee. This table will consist of 4×4 cells, (a_1, a_1), (a_1, a_2), (a_1, a_3), ..., where the first letter used in naming a cell is that at the left-hand end of the row in which the cell appears, and the second letter is that at the top of the column in which the cell appears. Now divide up each cell (a_h, a_k) into two parts, and place in the left-hand side of the cell the number of votes for a_h when it is placed against a_k, and in the right-hand side of the cell the number of votes for a_k. For example, we see from the schedules that a_1 put against a_2 would get 3 votes and a_2 would get 2 votes; and the entries made in the cell therefore are $(3, 2)$. The other cells are filled up in the same way, except (a_1, a_1), (a_2, a_2), (a_3, a_3), (a_4, a_4)

---

* I am indebted to Dr R. A. Newing for suggesting the use of a matrix notation. Later I discovered that this notation had already been employed by Rev. C. L. Dodgson in 1876.

D

along the main diagonal. Since it would be senseless to put a_1 against a_1, etc., in each of these cells we enter a zero.

All the cells of the matrix can be filled up in the manner described, but a simple relationship holds between the two halves of the matrix, above and below the diagonal, which enables us to reduce the labour. Take any cell on the main diagonal, the cell (a_h, a_h), say, containing a zero. The first cell in the row to the right

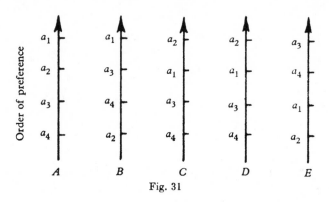

Fig. 31

Matrix for Fig. 31

(against)

(for)		a_1	a_2	a_3	a_4
	a_1	0	(3, 2)	(4, 1)	(4, 1)
	a_2	(2, 3)	0	(3, 2)	(3, 2)
	a_3	(1, 4)	(2, 3)	0	(5, 0)
	a_4	(1, 4)	(2, 3)	(0, 5)	0

Fig. 32

of it will be (a_h, a_{h+1}); and the first cell in the column below (a_h, a_h) will be (a_{h+1}, a_h). Now if the entries in the cell (a_h, a_{h+1}) are, say (p, q), those in the cell (a_{h+1}, a_h) must be (q, p), since the two cells give the same information in the reverse order. Similarly, the figures in the cell (a_{h+2}, a_h) will be those in the cell (a_h, a_{h+2}) in the reverse order, and so on. That is, the figures in the cells in any column below the diagonal can be got 'by reflexion' in the diagonal of the figures in the cells of the row to the right of the diagonal (cf. Fig. 33). This practically halves the work of constructing the matrix.

Obviously a_0, the motion 'that no change be made', can also be introduced into the matrix; and for uniformity we will always place a_0 at the end of the top row of the matrix and at the foot of the left-hand column (see Fig. 35).

This example also illustrates how to deal with cases of indifference as between motions. The three members with the first scale are indifferent as between a_1 and a_2 and vote for neither against the other. Collecting votes from the other scales, we see that

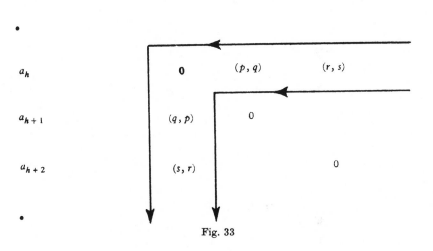

Fig. 33

5 *plus* 7 members vote for a_1 and 2 vote for a_2. The figures in the cell (a_1, a_2) are therefore $(12, 2)$. The other cells are filled up likewise.

Some important properties of the voting matrix are as follows.

It is always a square matrix, the number of columns being equal to the number of rows.

If the number of columns or rows—one of them corresponding to a_0 and each of the others corresponding to the other motions put forward—is $m + 1$, the number of cells in the matrix, including the diagonal cells, is $(m + 1)^2$. There are $m + 1$ cells on the main diagonal, each containing a zero, so that, excluding these, the number of cells is $(m + 1)^2 - (m + 1) = m(m + 1)$.

Since the lower part of the matrix can be got by reflexion of the upper part in the diagonal, the number of cells showing a majority must always be equal to the number showing a minority; and the number of cells showing a tie in the voting must be even.

When we deduct the sum of the numbers in the cell (a_h, a_k) from the total number of members, we obtain the number of members who are indifferent as between a_h and a_k. This property sometimes affords a check on the arithmetic.

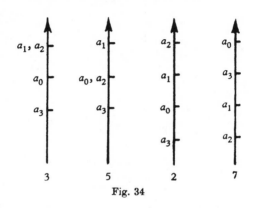

Fig. 34

Matrix for Fig. 34

(against)

(for)		a_1	a_2	a_3	a_0
	a_1	0	(12, 2)	(10, 7)	(10, 7)
	a_2	(2, 12)	0	(10, 7)	(5, 7)
	a_3	(7, 10)	(7, 10)	0	(0, 17)
	a_0	(7, 10)	(7, 5)	(17, 0)	0

Fig. 35

The valuations of the individual, as expressed in his schedule of preferences, can also be put in the form of a matrix.

An example illustrating the use of the matrix. For the group of schedules of Fig. 34 we see from the corresponding matrix that, if the committee follows the ordinary procedure, it will adopt the motion a_1 as its decision. Because the motion a_1 must enter the voting process at some stage and when it does it will defeat any other motion that it is put against—by 12 votes for to 2 against if it meets a_2, and by 10 votes for to 7 against if it meets a_3. When a_1 is finally put to the meeting for acceptance or rejection—i.e. is put against a_0—there will be 10 votes in favour of accepting a_1

and 7 votes against. Hence a_1 will become the decision of the committee.

Cyclical majorities. We now come to one of the most surprising and disconcerting features of the theory of committees: for a given group of schedules there may be no motion which is able to get a simple majority over each of the others. For example, Fig. 36 shows the scales of preferences of the three members A, B and C of a committee, in relation to the three motions a_1, a_2 and

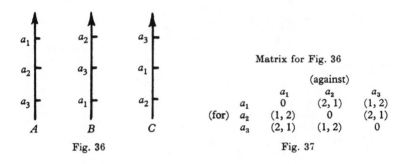

Fig. 36

Matrix for Fig. 36

		(against)		
		a_1	a_2	a_3
(for)	a_1	0	(2, 1)	(1, 2)
	a_2	(1, 2)	0	(2, 1)
	a_3	(2, 1)	(1, 2)	0

Fig. 37

a_3 which have been put forward. We see, either directly from the scales or from the corresponding matrix, that

a_1 would defeat a_2 but would be defeated by a_3,

a_2 would defeat a_3 but would be defeated by a_1,

a_3 would defeat a_1 but would be defeated by a_2.

No one of the three motions could get a simple majority over each of the others.

The valuations of each member of the committee as between the motions put forward are complete and are transitive, but the *majorities* of the committee are *cyclical*. In the instance given the *cyclical majority* may be denoted by $a_1 a_2 a_3 a_1$, any of these motions being able to get a majority against the motion next following: a_1 can defeat a_2, a_2 can defeat a_3, a_3 can defeat a_1, ...

A theorem and some illustrations. In the ordinary committee procedure a motion enters the voting once and remains before the committee until such time as it is defeated by one of the others; and, where a cyclical majority exists, the decision arrived at will depend on the order in which the motions enter the voting.

[39]

THEOREM. *When the ordinary committee procedure is in use, the later any motion enters the voting, the greater its chance of adoption.*

If the motion in question is able to get a simple majority over every other (including a_0), it will be adopted as the decision of the committee whether it enters the voting soon or late.

If the motion in question, a_h say, is unable to get a simple majority over each of the motions a_p, a_q, a_r, ..., the later a_h enters

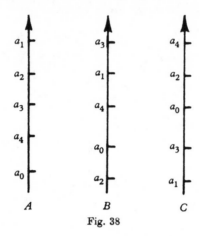

A   B   C

Fig. 38

Matrix for Fig. 38

		(against)				
		a_1	a_2	a_3	a_4	a_0
	a_1	0	(2, 1)	(1, 2)	(2, 1)	(2, 1)
	a_2	(1, 2)	0	(2, 1)	(1, 2)	(2, 1)
(for)	a_3	(2, 1)	(1, 2)	0	(2, 1)	(2, 1)
	a_4	(1, 2)	(2, 1)	(1, 2)	0	(3, 0)
	a_0	(1, 2)	(1, 2)	(1, 2)	(0, 3)	0

Fig. 39

the voting, the greater is the chance that all of the motions a_p, a_q, a_r, ... will already have been eliminated, and the greater the chance of a_h being adopted.

The principle involved is that the later a motion enters the voting, the fewer are the obstacles it has to cross, and the greater its likelihood of passing over them.

EXAMPLE 1. Given the schedules of preference of Fig. 38 and given also that the motions enter the voting in the order a_1, a_2, a_3, a_4, a_0, which will be the motion adopted?

We see by looking in each case to the appropriate cell in the matrix, that the course of the voting is as follows:

when a_1 is put against a_2, a_1 wins,

when a_1 is put against a_3, a_3 wins,

when a_3 is put against a_4, a_3 wins,

when a_3 is put against a_0, a_3 wins.

When the motions enter the voting in this order, the motion selected is a_3.

EXAMPLE 2. The data as in Fig. 38 but voting on the motions in the order a_2, a_3, a_1, a_4, a_0.

From the matrix it is seen that a_1 is the motion adopted.

EXAMPLE 3. The same data but the motions voted on in the order a_1, a_3, a_2, a_4, a_0.

From the matrix it is seen that a_4 is the motion adopted.

EXAMPLE 4. The same data but voting on the motions in the order a_1, a_4, a_3, a_2, a_0.

From the matrix it is seen that a_2 is the motion adopted.

Thus any of the motions a_1, a_2, a_3, a_4 may be adopted, provided the motions are called for voting in a suitable order.

The use of the matrix when the committee follows the procedure (α) or (β) or (γ). In the following examples we take a committee for which there is a given group of preference schedules and show the results of the voting according as the committee follows procedure (α) or (β) or (γ) described on pp. 21–4 above.

EXAMPLE 5. Given the group of schedules of Fig. 40.

Procedure (α). To see the consequences of test (i) in the voting we look to the submatrix got by excluding the row a_0 and the column a_0. This shows that a_3 is able to get a simple majority over each of the other motions a_1, a_2, a_4. It is bound to enter the voting at some stage in test (i), and when it does it will defeat any motion against which it is put. Test (i) will therefore select a_3.

At test (ii), we see from the cell (a_3, a_0) that a_3 will again obtain a majority and will be the decision adopted.

Procedure (β). We get the result of the first test from the column a_0. This shows that each of the motions except a_1 can pass the first test.

For the second test the result is given by the submatrix from which the rows and columns a_1, a_0 are excluded. Of the three motions a_2, a_3 and a_4 which had passed the first test, a_3 can gain a simple majority over each of the others and becomes the decision.

Procedure (γ). We get the result of the first test from the matrix, by excluding the row a_0 and the column a_0. The first test chooses a_3, which is able to get a majority over each of the other motions a_1, a_2, a_4. The result of the second test, got from the cell (a_3, a_0), is to adopt a_3.

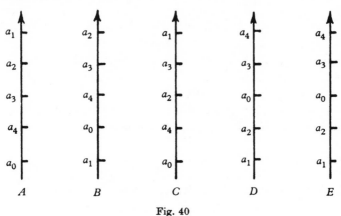

Fig. 40

Matrix for Fig. 40

		(against)				
		a_1	a_2	a_3	a_4	a_0
	a_1	0	(2, 3)	(2, 3)	(2, 3)	(2, 3)
	a_2	(3, 2)	0	(2, 3)	(3, 2)	(3, 2)
(for)	a_3	(3, 2)	(3, 2)	0	(3, 2)	(5, 0)
	a_4	(3, 2)	(2, 3)	(2, 3)	0	(5, 0)
	a_0	(3, 2)	(2, 3)	(0, 5)	(0, 5)	0

Fig. 41

EXAMPLE 6. Given the group of schedules of Fig. 42.

Procedure (α). Test (i) selects a_1 and test (ii) adopts a_0.

Procedure (β). Test (i) selects a_2 and, as this is the only motion to enter test (ii), it is adopted.

Procedure (γ). Test (i) selects a_1 and test (ii) adopts a_0.

Various theorems. In procedure (α), that ordinarily followed by committees, when m motions $a_1, \ldots, a_m$ are put forward, $(m-1)$ votes will be held at test (i), whereas on procedure (γ) all the motions must be put forward beforehand and the number of votes

[42]

held at test (i) is the number of ways of choosing two things out of m, i.e. $\frac{1}{2}m(m-1)$.

THEOREM. *If all of the motions $a_1, \ldots, a_m$ are put forward beforehand, and if one of them is able to obtain a majority over each of the others, this motion will also be selected if only $(m-1)$ votes are held* (in the manner of test (i) of the ordinary committee procedure).

Let us suppose that when $\frac{1}{2}m(m-1)$ votes are held and every motion is placed against every other, the motion a_h can obtain a simple majority over every other. Now when only $(m-1)$ votes

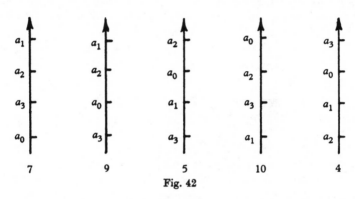

Fig. 42

Matrix for Fig. 42

(against)

		a_1	a_2	a_3	a_0
	a_1	0	(20, 15)	(21, 14)	(16, 19)
(for)	a_2	(15, 20)	0	(31, 4)	(21, 14)
	a_3	(14, 21)	(4, 31)	0	(11, 24)
	a_0	(19, 16)	(14, 21)	(24, 11)	0

Fig. 43

are held, each motion must still enter into the sequence of votes, and it will continue in the voting until it is defeated. Thus the motion a_h must enter the voting at some point, and when it does it will defeat every motion against which it is put. It will, therefore, be the motion which emerges from the sequence of $(m-1)$ votes.

THEOREM. *Given that if $\frac{1}{2}m(m-1)$ votes are held among the motions $a_1, \ldots, a_m$, and that if members vote in accordance with their schedules of preference the majority motion will be a_h, then it is not*

[43]

possible for any member or group of members, by voting contrary to their schedules of preference, to convert any other motion into the majority motion.

Let us suppose that some members who prefer a_k to a_h attempt to make a_k the majority motion. But when these members vote directly in accordance with their preference scales they already support a_k against a_h. The only members who, by voting contrary to their scales of preference, could give a_k a majority over a_h, would be those who have a_k lower on their scales than a_h; and it is against their interest to do so.

It would be possible, however, for a number of members to vote so that no motion obtained a simple majority over every other. If, for example, a number of members voted against a_h when it was placed against some value which stood lower on their scales, a_h might be defeated. At most, therefore, a group of voters would have it in their power to convert the situation into one in which no motion got a majority over every other.

THEOREM. *When the ordinary committee procedure is in use, it may be open to one or more of the members to bring into existence a decision more favourable to themselves by voting otherwise than in accordance with their schedules of preference.*

To establish this it is enough to provide a single instance. First we do so for a case in which the members' curves are single-peaked. In Fig. 44 the members' optima are O_1, ..., O_5, and the abbreviated diagram is consistent with the group of schedules shown alongside.

If the members voted directly in accordance with their schedules, the decision adopted would be the median optimum O_3. But if, say, the first vote were taken between O_2 and O_3, and if either D or E voted for O_2, O_3 would be eliminated. And if, after that, the members voted directly in accordance with their schedules, O_4 would be the motion adopted. Thus D or E, by voting at one stage contrary to his schedule of preferences, would be able to alter the decision in his own favour.

As a further example let us take the group of schedules of Fig. 36. When the members vote directly in accordance with their schedules, if in the initial vote a_1 is put against a_2, a_2 is eliminated. When a_1 is put against a_3, a_3 wins.

If, however, instead of voting directly in accordance with his schedule of preferences, A in the first vote had supported a_2

[44]

against a_1, a_2 would have gone to the second vote and would have defeated a_3. Since a_2 stands higher on his schedule of preferences than a_3, by voting in this way A would have altered the decision in his favour.

The preceding theory has assumed that members vote directly in accordance with their schedules of preference. We know from experience that people do not invariably do so; and now we have

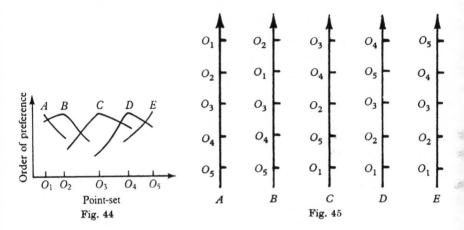

Fig. 44

Fig. 45

Matrix for Figs. 44 and 45, if the members vote directly in accordance with their schedules

		(against)				
		O_1	O_2	O_3	O_4	O_5
	O_1	0	(1, 4)	(2, 3)	(2, 3)	(2, 3)
	O_2	(4, 1)	0	(2, 3)	(2, 3)	(3, 2)
(for)	O_3	(3, 2)	(3, 2)	0	(3, 2)	(3, 2)
	O_4	(3, 2)	(3, 2)	(2, 3)	0	(4, 1)
	O_5	(3, 2)	(2, 3)	(2, 3)	(1, 4)	0

Fig. 46

shown that when the ordinary committee procedure is in use, it may be against their interest to do so. In this case, therefore, the theory may sometimes fail to correspond to reality. But the restriction on its applicability from this source is probably not very significant.

We will recur to this general topic of voting contrary to one's schedule of preferences in discussing the work of Borda, Laplace and Dodgson (see below, pp. 182, 218, 232–3 and 237–8).

CHAPTER VII

CYCLICAL MAJORITIES*

The term 'cyclical majority' and a series of propositions.
Condorcet was the first to show that it was possible for the results
of voting to take some such form as

$$a_1 \text{ beats } a_2, \quad a_2 \text{ beats } a_3, \quad a_3 \text{ beats } a_1,$$

and dealt extensively with these 'contradictory cases' as he called
them. At a later date, Dodgson, working over the theory, also
discovered this possibility and referred to the majorities in an
instance like this as being 'cyclical', the motions 'forming the
cycle $a_1 a_2 a_3 a_1$'. Since no actual logical contradiction is involved,
Condorcet's term is unsatisfactory, while Dodgson's aptly de-
scribes the facts, and we will retain it. Instances of such cycles
have already been given.

In the following propositions we assume that no ties occur in the
voting, these having been removed, if need be, by the use of the
chairman's casting vote.

Proposition 1. *The minimum number of motions in a cycle is
three.*

For suppose only two motions a_1 and a_2 to be involved, the cycle
being $a_1 a_2 a_1$. This would mean a_1 beats a_2, a_2 beats a_1, which is
impossible.

Proposition 2. *The designation of a cycle may begin and end with
any given motion in the cycle.*

For example, in the cycle $a_1 a_2 a_3 a_1$, a_1 defeats a_2, a_2 defeats a_3
and a_3 defeats a_1; and we may equally well designate these facts by
$a_2 a_3 a_1 a_2$ or $a_3 a_1 a_2 a_3$.

Proposition 3. *If a motion exists which is able to defeat every other
then it cannot form part of a cycle.*

To form part of a cycle a motion must be defeated by at least
one of the other motions in the cycle; and this is not true of the
majority motion.

Proposition 4. *When a majority motion exists, there may still be
one or more cycles among the other motions.*

* This chapter is under considerable obligation to the Rev. C. L. Dodgson's
paper *A Method of Taking Votes on More than Two Issues* (1876), which is reprinted in the appendix.

This is easiest shown by constructing examples.

Proposition 5. *If certain of the motions before a committee form a cycle and another motion, a_r say, defeats one of the motions in the cycle and is defeated by another, then it must be possible to enlarge the cycle so as to include a_r.*

Let us suppose that the initial cycle is $a_1 a_2 a_3 \ldots a_1$, and that a_1 defeats a_r. Try fitting a_r into the cycle in the position after a_1. Now either a_r defeats a_2, giving a cycle containing a_r; or else a_2 defeats a_r, in which case we can try fitting a_r into the cycle in the position after a_2. But since by hypothesis a_r defeats at least one motion in the cycle, a stage must be reached at which a_r defeats the motion that follows it; and then a_r fits into the cycle.

Proposition 6. *There cannot be more than one motion, a_h say, which is defeated by every other motion; and if there is such a motion a_h, it cannot be part of any cycle.*

If there is a motion a_h which is defeated by all of the others, at most there can be a single motion a_k, which is defeated by all of the others except one, namely, a_h; and a_k cannot be part of any cycle.

If there are two such motions a_h and a_k, at most there can be a single motion a_l which is defeated by all of the other motions except two, namely, a_h and a_k; and a_l cannot form part of a cycle; and so on.

Let us suppose that the motion a_h scores no majority against any of the others. Then every other motion scores at least one majority, namely, that over a_h; so that at most one motion can score no majorities.

If the motion a_k scores only this majority over a_h, then it is defeated by each of the other motions; and each of these other motions must score at least two majorities, namely, those over a_h and a_k; and so on.

Next it is clear that a_h cannot be part of any cycle, since it does not defeat any motion. Nor can a_k be part of a cycle, because the only motion which could follow it in the cycle would be a_h, which defeats no other motion; and so on.

This proposition sometimes enables us to eliminate certain motions from consideration, when we are examining for the existence of cycles.

Proposition 7. *If no majority motion exists which is able to defeat each of the others, there must be at least a single cycle among the motions.*

Reject any motion a_h which is defeated by all of the others, any motion a_k which is defeated by all of the others except a_h, and so on (see Proposition 6).

When we have done this we must be left with three or more motions, because if there were only two, a_p, a_q say, one would be able to defeat the other and a_h, a_k, ... in addition, giving us a majority motion; and by hypothesis there is no such.

Let the series of motions which remain be $a_r, a_s, a_t, ..., a_u$. Since they do not form part of the series $a_h, a_k, ...,$ each of these remaining motions must defeat at least one of the others. And since there is no majority motion, each of these motions $a_r, a_s, a_t, ..., a_u$ must be defeated by at least one of the others.

Now let us begin with any motion, a_s say, and take a motion it defeats, a_r say, and arrange them $a_s a_r ...,$ placing each before a motion which it defeats. Then since each of these motions is able to defeat at least one of the others, a stage must be reached when we are able to include one of the motions which has occurred earlier in the chain, either when we reach the last of the motions to be taken from the series $a_r, a_s, a_t, ..., a_u$ or before then. That is, at least one cycle must exist among the motions $a_r, a_s, a_t, ..., a_u$.

DEFINITIONS. Two or more cycles which have at least one motion in common will be termed *intersecting cycles*.

Two cycles which can have no motion in common will be termed *necessarily non-intersecting cycles*.

Proposition 8. Necessarily non-intersecting cycles exist.

We can use Proposition 5 to help to construct examples of this kind.

Proposition 9. If two (intersecting) cycles have one motion in common, it must be possible to form a cycle which includes all of the motions from both cycles.

Let the cycles be, say, $a_1 a_2 a_3 ... a_1$ and $a_1 a_4 a_5 ... a_1$, with the motion a_1 in common.

Then either a_2 defeats a_4, in which case we get the cycle $a_1 a_2 a_4 a_5 ... a_1$; or else a_4 defeats a_2 in which case we get the cycle $a_1 a_4 a_2 a_3 ... a_1$.

That is, it must be possible to increase one of the cycles by the motion in the other that follows their common term. When this has been done the cycles have a new common term; and it must be possible to increase one or other of them in the same way. The process only comes to an end when all of the motions in one of the cycles have been used up, i.e. when a cycle has been formed which includes all of the motions in the two original cycles.

The proposition can be extended to the case of three or more intersecting cycles.

Proposition 10. *If two cycles are necessarily non-intersecting, every motion in one of these cycles must be able to get a simple majority over every motion in the other.*

Let the cycles be $a_1a_2a_3a_4 \ldots a_1$ and $a_5a_6a_7a_8 \ldots a_5$, respectively. Proof consists of two parts.

(against)

		a_1	a_2	a_3	a_4	a_5	a_6	a_7	a_8	a_9
	a_1	0	(M)	(m)	(M)	(M)	(M)	(m)	(m)	(m)
	a_2	(m)	0	(M)	(M)	(M)	(M)	(m)	(m)	(m)
	a_3	(M)	(m)	0	(M)	(M)	(M)	(m)	(m)	(m)
	a_4	(m)	(m)	(m)	0	(M)	(m)	(M)	(M)	(M)
(for)	a_5	(m)	(m)	(m)	(m)	0	(M)	(M)	(M)	(M)
	a_6	(m)	(m)	(m)	(M)	(m)	0	(M)	(M)	(M)
	a_7	(M)	(M)	(M)	(m)	(m)	(m)	0	(M)	(m)
	a_8	(M)	(M)	(M)	(m)	(m)	(m)	(m)	0	(M)
	a_9	(M)	(M)	(M)	(m)	(m)	(m)	(M)	(m)	0

Fig. 47

First, let one of the motions a_5, a_6, a_7, a_8, ..., defeat one of the motions a_1, a_2, a_3, a_4, ..., say a_5 defeat a_1. Then a_5 must also defeat $a_2, a_3, a_4, \ldots$. For suppose that a_5 were defeated by a_3, say. Then we could form the cycle $a_5a_1a_2a_3a_5$, and (Proposition 9), a cycle containing all of the motions a_1, a_2, a_3, a_4 ... and a_5; but, by hypothesis, the two cycles can have no motion in common. Hence if a_5 defeats a_1, it must also defeat every motion in the cycle of which a_1 is part.

Secondly, if a_5 defeats a_1, so also must $a_6, a_7, a_8, \ldots$. For suppose that a_7, say, were defeated by a_1. Then we could form the cycle $a_5a_1a_7a_8 \ldots a_5$; and again we would have two intersecting cycles. But, by hypothesis, this is not possible; and a_7 also must defeat a_1.

Hence, every motion in the one cycle must either defeat, or be defeated by, every motion in the other cycle.

Alternatively, the proposition is obviously true in virtue of Proposition 5.

Proposition 11. *If there are three cycles which are necessarily non-intersecting, every motion in the first may be able to defeat every motion in the second, and every motion in the second may be able to defeat every motion in the third, and yet every motion in the third cycle may* be able to defeat every motion in the first. *Or, as we may say, there may be cycles among cycles.*

An example of this is shown in the matrix of Fig. 47, where the cycles are $a_1a_2a_3a_1$, $a_4a_5a_6a_4$ and $a_7a_8a_9a_7$ respectively, where M denotes a majority and m a minority. Each of the motions a_1, a_2, a_3 defeats each of the motions a_4, a_5, a_6; a_4, a_5, a_6 defeat

a_1	a_2	a_3	a_7	a_8	a_9	a_4	a_5	a_6
a_2	a_3	a_1	a_8	a_9	a_7	a_5	a_6	a_4
a_3	a_1	a_2	a_9	a_7	a_8	a_6	a_4	a_5
a_4	a_5	a_6	a_1	a_2	a_3	a_7	a_8	a_9
a_5	a_6	a_4	a_2	a_3	a_1	a_8	a_9	a_7
a_6	a_4	a_5	a_3	a_1	a_2	a_9	a_7	a_8
a_7	a_8	a_9	a_4	a_5	a_6	a_1	a_2	a_3
a_8	a_9	a_7	a_5	a_6	a_4	a_2	a_3	a_1
a_9	a_7	a_8	a_6	a_4	a_5	a_3	a_1	a_2
A	B	C	D	E	F	G	H	I

Fig. 48

Table showing the ratio

$$\frac{\text{total number of cases in which a majority decision exists}}{\text{total number of possible cases}}$$

(The members are assumed never to be indifferent as between motions.)

Number of motions	Number of members					
	1	2	3	4	5	...
2	$\dfrac{2}{2}$	$\dfrac{4}{4}$	$\dfrac{8}{8}$	—	—	—
3	$\dfrac{6}{6}$	$\dfrac{36}{36}$	$\dfrac{204}{216}$	—	—	—
4	$\dfrac{24}{24}$	$\dfrac{1056}{1056}$	—	—	—	—
5	$\dfrac{120}{120}$	$\dfrac{14400}{14400}$	—	—	—	—
...	—	—	—	—	—	—

Fig. 49

a_7, a_8, a_9; and yet a_7, a_8, a_9 defeat a_1, a_2, a_3. This matrix would apply in the case of a committee of nine members $A, ..., I$, whose schedules in relation to the motions $a_1, ..., a_9$, are as in Fig. 48.

The proportion of cyclical majorities. For a committee with n members and m motions, the total number of different possible groups of schedules is given by the total number of possible arrangements of $a_1, ..., a_m$ on the scales of the members.

[50]

It would be of interest to know in what fraction of all the possible cases one motion is able to get a simple majority against each of the others as n and m vary, and in what fraction the majorities are cyclical. Had we been able to do so, we would have calculated the figures for Fig. 49 giving these fractions (and also for the case in which the members may be indifferent as between various motions); but we have been unable to derive the general series which would enable us to make the calculations for the table and have entered only a few figures in the cells.

If the general series could be derived it would almost certainly show that for a committee with a given number of members, the proportion of cases in which there is no majority decision increases rapidly with an increase in the number of motions. (See also pp. 173–4 below.)

(See also pp. 173–4 below.)

CHAPTER VIII

WHEN THE ORDINARY COMMITTEE PRO-CEDURE IS IN USE THE MEMBERS' SCALES OF VALUATION MAY BE INCOMPLETE

Description of the usual procedure. Nearly all committees whose members meet together in a room to put forward proposals and vote on them follow the procedure (α), defined above on p. 21, and we will therefore examine this case somewhat more closely.

In this procedure a proposal, known as the original motion, is put forward on some topic. If a second proposal, known as an amendment to the original motion, is put forward, the original motion and the amendment will be placed against each other in a vote after discussion, the amendment being taken first. The survivor of this vote (either the original motion or the amendment) is known as the 'substantive motion', and members are then free to propose further amendments. There may be a sequence of amendments put forward, followed by a sequence of votes.

In our definition of procedure (α), we spoke of motions and made no use of the terms original motion, substantive motion or amendment.

E

The conditions required for our theory to apply. A misconception that should be guarded against is that the type of theory given above will not apply to the ordinary committee procedure because, it is (wrongly) supposed, it assumes the motions to be put forward before the voting begins. The theory, it will be found, applies even though the motions are put forward one after another in time, and even though the third motion is not put forward until after one of the first two motions has been eliminated in a vote, and so on.

What our theory does assume in dealing with the ordinary committee procedure is that the preference curves of all members of the committee can be represented by straight-line schedules (or the alternative two-dimensional diagrams), and *this presupposes both that the valuations of each member of the committee are transitive and that he values each motion in relation to every other.*

Now it may be that these assumptions are not fulfilled, because the motions are in fact put forward one after another, and all of the earlier motions, except one, are eliminated before the next motion is put forward. At the end of the process some motions will have met in a vote while others have not. When the motion a_h, say, is placed against the motion a_k, each member of the committee is challenged by the vote to carry out an evaluation of a_h in relation to a_k, and we may take it that the one stands in relation to the other in some definite order of preference or indifference, on his scale. If, on the other hand, the motions a_h and a_i, say, never meet in a vote, no challenge is made to evaluate the one in relation to the other. The member may in fact carry out such an evaluation or he may not. The assumption made by the schedules we have drawn, however, is that he does carry out an evaluation as between every such pair of motions.

Elaborating the conditions under which our theory will not apply. We here examine some of the possibilities.

(i) If a single motion, a_1 say, comes before a committee, the vote to accept or reject it is equivalent to putting it against a_0, and each member will carry out an evaluation of a_1 in relation to a_0. The relative positions of the two motions on his scale of preferences will be determinate and the theory applies.

(ii) If two motions a_1 and a_2 are put forward, they will be placed against each other in a vote, and whichever wins, a_1 say, will be put against a_0. This necessitates that each member should evaluate

a_1 in relation to a_2, and a_1 in relation to a_0; but he need not evaluate a_2 in relation to a_0. A straight-line schedule (or two-dimensional diagram) amounts to taking it that three valuations are made by each individual concerned. In fact at least two are made, but not necessarily three.

In half the number of cases which can arise it will be possible to make a definite inference as to the complete scale of preferences of the person concerned, provided we are willing to assume that his

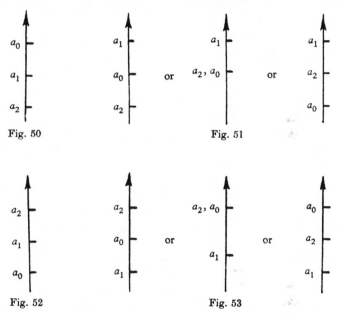

Fig. 50   Fig. 51

Fig. 52   Fig. 53

valuations are transitive. If he votes for a_1 against a_2, we know that a_1 will be above a_2 on his scale of preferences. If he then votes for a_0 against a_1, we know that his complete scale of preferences must be as in Fig. 50, a_0 being above both a_1 and a_2. But if, after voting for a_1 against a_2, he then votes for a_1 against a_0, his preference scale, so far as the information at our disposal goes, might be any of the three forms shown in Fig. 51.

Similarly, if a member votes for a_2 against a_1, and then votes for a_1 against a_0, we can infer that his scale of preferences must be as shown in Fig. 52. But if, after voting for a_2 against a_1, he then supports a_0 against a_1, his scale of preferences can only be inferred to be one of the three shown in Fig. 53.

(iii) When three motions are put forward, let us suppose that the order in which they are voted on is a_1 against a_2, a_2 winning; a_2 against a_3, a_3 winning; a_3 against a_0, either a_3 or a_0 winning. If a particular member of the committee has in each of these votes supported a_2, a_3 and a_0, respectively, we can say that a_0 stands above a_3 on his scale, a_3 above a_2 and a_2 above a_1; and, assuming his valuations to be transitive, we know his scale of preferences completely. If a second member in the three votes has supported a_1, a_2 and a_3, respectively, we again know his scale completely; on it a_1 stands highest, a_2 second highest, a_3 third highest and a_0 lowest. If a third member in the three votes has supported a_2, a_2 and a_3, respectively, we have:

$$a_2 \quad\text{and}\quad a_2 \quad\text{and}\quad a_3$$
$$a_1 \qquad\qquad a_3 \qquad\qquad a_0.$$

From this we can deduce the relative positions of a_2, a_3 and a_0 as being

$$a_2$$
$$a_3$$
$$a_0$$

and we know that a_1 occurs below a_2; but whether a_1 lies between a_2 and a_3, at the same height as a_3, between a_3 and a_0, at the same height as a_0, or lower than a_0, we cannot tell.

Indeed, it is quite possible that this third member has not in fact carried out an evaluation of a_1 in relation to either a_3 or a_0; the votes held would not challenge his mind to make any such valuation. Drawing a schedule, on the other hand, supposes him to have carried out each of these valuations.

(iv) As a further example let us take the case of a committee in which the motions a_1, a_2, a_3 and a_0 are put to the vote in the order a_1 against a_2, a_1 winning; a_1 against a_3, a_1 winning; a_1 against a_0, either a_1 or a_0 winning. And let us suppose that in these three votes a particular member has each time supported a_1 against the opposing motion. The information we have about his scale can be stated as

$$a_1 \quad\text{and}\quad a_1 \quad\text{and}\quad a_1$$
$$a_2 \qquad\qquad a_3 \qquad\qquad a_0$$

The motion a_1 stands higher on his scale than any of the others, but we do not know the relative order of a_2, a_3 and a_0.

Conclusion. When a committee follows the ordinary procedure, the scales of preferences of its members may be less complete than is assumed in the foregoing theory. If desired, a theory could be constructed which assumed that the members valued in relation to each other only such motions as met in a vote. But such a theory would tell us nothing beyond what is obvious to commonsense and would be of negligible interest.

It should also be borne in mind, as pointed out earlier, that when the matter under consideration by a committee relates to a measurable variable, the members' scales of preferences are much more likely to be complete.

CHAPTER IX

WHICH CANDIDATE OUGHT TO BE ELECTED?

The assumptions. Which candidate ought to be elected in a single-member constituency *if all that we take into account* is the order in which each of the electors ranks the various candidates? The most reasonable answer, I think, is that that candidate ought to be elected who, on the whole or on the average, stands highest on the electors' schedules of preferences.

At the very outset of the argument we try to move from the *is* to the *ought* and to jump the unbridgeable chasm between the universe of science and that of morals. Some discussion of this step should be given, even though it does no more than point out the assumptions under which the jump is made.

We assume that, in a constituency which is to elect a single member, we know the order in which the candidates are ranked on the schedule of preferences of each elector. If the electors had only been allowed to cast a single vote and the record of this was all the information at our disposal, inevitably, I think, we would have to conclude that the candidate most deserving of election was the one with the greatest number of first-preference votes. As against this, however, our assumption will be that each elector expresses his ranking of all the candidates in the field, and that we have this record of the electors' attitudes.

We do not ask whether the people with the legal right to vote have also the moral right; and since we raise no question on this matter we really will be assuming that they have the moral right. If, however, in any problem relating to actual circumstances we were provided with definite information as to which classes had received the franchise, their moral entitlement would be one of the factors that would need to be considered. We assume also that we have no information as to the moral worth either of voters or of candidates, and that the plans and objectives of the candidates are likewise unknown. And lastly and most important, we assume that no effects, either good or bad, will be produced on party structure or on cabinet government by the method of election adopted.

These assumptions, it will be seen, would be much more readily fulfilled in the election of one among several candidates to a business or academic post, than in any parliamentary or municipal election. When the assumptions are borne in mind there will at any rate be less scepticism about the legitimacy of the first step in the argument, involving though it does the transition from the *is* to the *ought*. The principle that we have enunciated holds good only under the very special conditions that we envisage.

Granted these assumptions we might offer a proof of the principle by *reductio ad absurdum*. With only the information that we suppose, it would be more reasonable to elect the candidate who, on the average, stands highest on the electors' schedules of preferences, rather than the candidate who stands second highest. It would be more reasonable to elect the candidate who stands second highest rather than third highest, and so on. This establishes the position that we have adopted.

That no one candidate is necessarily 'best'. Let us accept it, then, that the candidate who ought to be elected is the one who stands highest on the average on the electors' schedules of preferences. Even so this will not necessarily, nor even usually, point to a particular candidate. The candidate picked out will depend on how we reckon who stands highest on the average. We know from Statistics that at least three types of average are in common use and that other measures of 'the' average can easily be constructed. A change from one definition of average to another equally valid definition may lead to a change in the answer given in the problem of elections—in the same way as the answer in any other statistical problem changes according as we reckon the average as the arithmetic mean or median or mode. If so, however far we carry the present line of reasoning we will not be able to pick out a single candidate who is necessarily the best candidate to represent any given constituency. Indeed, it will be impossible in principle ever to specify such a candidate—for the very reason that it is impossible to prove that, say, the arithmetic mean is superior as a measure of average to the mode or median. Still, we know that any one of these, as of certain other measures, has good claims to be considered a *satisfactory* indicator of central or average tendency. We therefore expect that there will be not one but several satisfactory answers; and we go on to suggest three different answers to this problem as to which candidate it is that voters on the average hold to be superior to the others.

The Condorcet criterion. The criterion of standing highest on the average in the electors' preferences which, in the main, we would accept, is one which was first proposed by Condorcet;* the majority candidate who, in a direct vote against them, would defeat each of the others, can be taken as standing higher than the others on the voters' schedules of preferences. There would be the corollary that, where he exists, such a candidate ought to be elected. Certainly this criterion appeals to our sense of symmetry; and the connexion between mathematical symmetry and what is ethically right may be closer than has been recognized.

The Condorcet criterion where there is no majority candidate. The main weakness of the Condorcet criterion is that when there is no majority candidate it leaves the election undecided. If the election is of the type where people register their votes and then disperse, a decision must necessarily be arrived at even though there is no majority candidate, and so the Condorcet criterion must be supplemented by some other.

If the electors are still gathered in the same room when the results show the absence of any majority candidate, or if they can be got to reassemble, they may be asked to vote again and some of them may alter their voting schedules. It may be that at this second vote a majority candidate will emerge and be elected. In justification of this procedure—where it is possible to carry it out —it can be said that at the second vote the electors will have more knowledge than they had at the first, because (a) they now know better the attitudes of their fellow-electors and this may (quite legitimately) affect their own ranking of the candidates; and (b) in

* Cf. below, pp. 166-76.

order to enable the Condorcet criterion to work and select a candidate, some of the voters may (quite legitimately) alter the order in which they place the candidates. We can see no reason why this should not be done if the physical conditions under which the election is held permit it.

Another way of dealing with the difficulty would follow the ingenious suggestion of the Rev. C. L. Dodgson,* that if in the initial vote there is no majority candidate, the chairman, or in our case perhaps the presiding officer, should indicate which candidate would be selected with the smallest amount of change in the voting schedules of the electors; and if the electors concerned are willing to make these changes, this candidate should be chosen.

Either of these courses would extend the number of cases in which the Condorcet criterion would select a candidate; and whether or not we want one of them to be adopted will depend on the degree of trust that we place in the Condorcet criterion itself, by comparison with other criteria.

Our own attitude to the Condorcet criterion. The considerations in favour of the Condorcet criterion are those we have stated—that it is one way of defining which candidate stands highest on the average on the electors' schedules; that it ensures that if one candidate would be able to defeat each of the others in a vote, then he will be elected; and that it appeals, perhaps via mathematical symmetry, to our sense of justice. The reasons may not seem overwhelmingly convincing, but we are moving in a region where all considerations are tenuous and fine-spun; and the claims of the Condorcet criterion to rightness seem to us much stronger than those of any other.

At the same time in particular examples one may doubt whether the candidate chosen by the Condorcet criterion is the best to elect. For instance, Fig. 54 shows the scales of 15 voters, of whom 7 regard O_1 as the optimum candidate, while the Condorcet criterion would choose the candidate O_8, whom only one voter ranks first. It is certainly open to doubt whether in this instance the Condorcet criterion chooses the most appropriate candidate. (We give another example to the same effect on pp. 60–1.)

Our own position is that our faith in the Condorcet criterion is stronger than in any other, but it is not an unqualified faith. For

---

* The full procedure is described in *A Method of Taking Votes on More than Two Issues* (1876), § 1, v–viii, pp. 225–6 below.

this reason, as well as for reasons of practical convenience, we would not recommend an additional vote with a reapplication of the Condorcet criterion in those cases where the criterion fails to select a candidate, except where the decision to be taken is one of the utmost importance. Instead, we would use the Condorcet criterion and then, in cases where there was no majority candidate, supplement it by the use of some further criterion which, though less trustworthy, would make a definite choice. We will first enter into some technicalities about this further criterion.

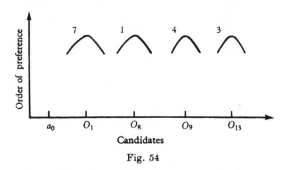

Fig. 54

The Borda criterion. Let us suppose that there are four candidates a_1, a_2, a_3, a_4, and that the elector A ranks them in the order shown in Fig. 55. Then it would be reasonable, Borda suggests,* to give a_2 a mark of zero, a_4 one mark, a_1 two marks and a_3 three marks; and when we have attributed marks in this way to the candidates on account of their placings on the schedules of all the voters, *to elect that candidate who has scored the highest total mark*. The aim again is to pick out that candidate who stands highest on the whole or on the average, on the schedules of the electors.

This scheme can be translated into terms of the voting matrix. We see that the mark given to a candidate on account of his placing on any schedule is equal to the number of candidates above whom he is placed on that schedule; e.g. in Fig. 55, a_3 is higher than three candidates and gets 3 marks. When we take into account the schedules of all the voters, the total mark scored by a candidate will be equal to the sum of the votes this candidate would get if he were placed against each of them in turn. To illustrate from the schedules

a_3

a_1

a_4

a_2

A

Fig. 55

* Cf. below, pp. 157–9.

of Fig. 56, the candidate a_1 scores in all $2 \times 5 + 3 \times 7 + 2 \times 9 = (10 + 21 + 18) = 49$ marks. But in the matrix this must be equal to the 12 votes that a_1 would get against a_2, as seen on the left-hand of the cell (a_1, a_2), *plus* the 16 that a_1 would get against a_3, *plus* the 21 that he would get against a_4. The sum of these figures on the left-hand of the cells is placed at the end of the row a_1 in the column headed Borda count; and the figures for the other candidates have been placed at the end of the rows concerned. This criterion will elect the candidate with the highest Borda count.

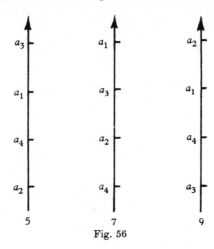

Fig. 56

Matrix for Fig. 56

| | (against) | | | | Borda |
	a_1	a_2	a_3	a_4	count
a_1	0	(12, 9)	(16, 5)	(21, 0)	49
a_2	(9, 12)	0	(9, 12)	(16, 5)	34
(for) a_3	(5, 16)	(12, 9)	0	(12, 9)	29
a_4	(0, 21)	(5, 16)	(9, 12)	0	14

Fig. 57

In some circumstances the candidate picked out by the Borda count would seem to have a stronger claim to election than the candidate who would be selected on the Condorcet criterion. For example, in Fig. 58, a_3, the majority candidate, is only able to get the slender margin of one vote against each of the others; whereas the candidate a_2, although beaten by a_3 by a single vote, nevertheless defeats each of the other candidates and gets the decisive majority of $33:2$ against a_1, whom a_3 only defeats by $18:17$. Clearly it is relevant to take into account the size of majorities (or minorities) that would be scored by a candidate if he were put against each of the others singly, and the Borda criterion does this.

Adjustment of the Borda count for cases of indifference. It was shown by Borda* that the same result is obtained by using the simple scale we have mentioned, 0 marks for a lowest place on

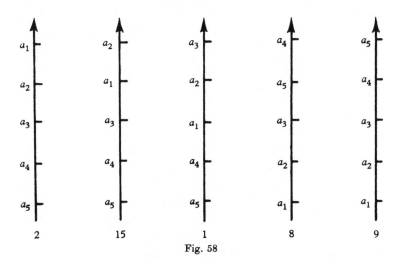

Fig. 58

Matrix for Fig. 58

		(against)					Borda
		a_1	a_2	a_3	a_4	a_5	count
	a_1	0	(2, 33)	(17, 18)	(18, 17)	(18, 17)	55
	a_2	(33, 2)	0	(17, 18)	(18, 17)	(18, 17)	86
(for)	a_3	(18, 17)	(18, 17)	0	(18, 17)	(18, 17)	72
	a_4	(17, 18)	(17, 18)	(17, 18)	0	(26, 9)	77
	a_5	(17, 18)	(17, 18)	(17, 18)	(9, 26)	0	60

Fig. 59

a schedule, 1 for a second lowest place, 2 for a third lowest place, ..., and by the more general scale of giving a marks for a lowest place, $(a+b)$ for a second lowest place, $(a+2b)$ for a third lowest place, ... We now use this more general scale to get a method of dealing with cases in which voters rank candidates at the same level of preference.

* See below, pp. 157–8.

[61]

In Fig. 60 let us give a candidate 1 mark for each candidate above whom he is placed on A's scale, and deduct 1 mark for each candidate below whom he is placed. Thus a_2 gets 3 marks, a_4 gets $2-1=1$ mark, a_3 gets $1-2=-1$ mark and a_1 gets -3 marks. This conforms to Borda's scheme of giving a for a lowest place and b for each additional notch of the scale above the lowest, when we put $a=-3$ and $b=2$.

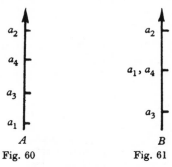

A   B

Fig. 60   Fig. 61

To extend this principle to the cases in which candidates are ranked at the same level on some of the schedules, let us give a credit of 1 mark to a candidate for each candidate above whom he stands on the schedule of any voter, a discredit of *minus* 1 mark for each candidate below whom he is placed, and a zero credit for each candidate with whom he is bracketed equal. In Fig. 61 a_2 will receive 3 marks, a_3 will receive -3 marks and a_1 and a_4 will each get $1-1+0=0$ marks. The mark scored by any candidate, reckoned in this way, will be referred to as his adjusted Borda count.

To translate into terms of the matrix, we observe that this scheme of marking gives to a candidate, a *plus* mark equal to the total number of candidates above whom he is placed on all of the schedules, and a *minus* mark equal to the total number of candidates below whom he is placed on the schedules. His *plus* mark can be got by adding the figures on the left-hand of the cells in the appropriate row, and his *minus* mark by adding the figures on the right-hand of these cells. For the matrix of Fig. 63 the adjusted Borda count of a_1 is $11+16+18-22-17-15=-9$; i.e. in all the separate votes against the other candidates, there would be 9 more votes against him than for him; and similarly for the other candidates.

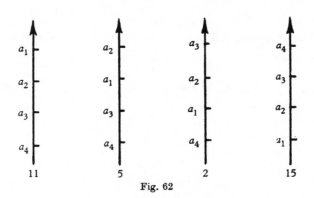

Fig. 62

Matrix for Fig. 62

		(against)				Borda count	Adjusted Borda count
		a_1	a_2	a_3	a_4		
	a_1	0	(11, 22)	(16, 17)	(18, 15)	45	−9
(for)	a_2	(22, 11)	0	(16, 17)	(18, 15)	56	13
	a_3	(17, 16)	(17, 16)	0	(18, 15)	52	5
	a_4	(15, 18)	(15, 18)	(15, 18)	0	45	−9

Fig. 63

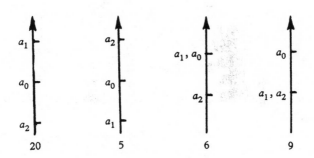

Fig. 64

Matrix for Fig. 64

		(against)			Borda count	Adjusted Borda count
		a_1	a_2	a_0		
	a_1	0	(26, 5)	(20, 14)	46	27
(for)	a_2	(5, 26)	0	(5, 35)	10	−51
	a_0	(14, 20)	(35, 5)	0	49	24

Fig. 65

[63]

We see that in this example the ranking of the candidates in accordance with the adjusted Borda count is the same as that given by the Borda count itself—as indeed is necessarily the case if no candidates are bracketed equal on the voters' schedules.

Whether or not candidates are bracketed equal, the sum of the figures in the column of the adjusted Borda count must add up to zero.

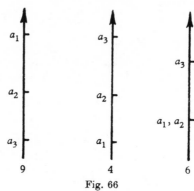

Fig. 66

Matrix for Fig. 66

		(against)			Borda count	Adjusted Borda count
		a_1	a_2	a_3		
	a_1	0	(9, 4)	(9, 10)	18	4
(for)	a_2	(4, 9)	0	(9, 10)	13	−6
	a_3	(10, 9)	(10, 9)	0	20	2

Fig. 67

Some examples comparing the choices of the Borda and Condorcet criteria.

EXAMPLE 1. In the matrix of Fig. 65 the numbers in the different cells add up to different figures, and this shows that voters sometimes bracket candidates at the same level. The appropriate form of the Borda count is the net suplus of the *plus* over the *minus* votes for each candidate. The adjusted Borda count and the Condorcet criterion select the same candidate a_1, whereas the unadjusted Borda count selects a_0 and would make no election.

EXAMPLE 2. In the matrix of Fig. 67 the unadjusted Borda count and the Condorcet criterion select the same candidate a_3, whereas the adjusted Borda count selects a_1.

EXAMPLE 3. In the matrix for Fig. 68 there is no majority candidate and the Borda count and adjusted Borda count rank the candidates quite differently; their first choices are a_1 and a_2 respectively.

A voter does not measure the relative merits of the candidates in terms of marks. We will recount later,* in some detail, certain arguments which have been put forward in support of the Borda criterion. These arguments imply that the voter gives some sort of merit rating to the various candidates, e.g. ranks the first candidate as being perhaps twice as good as the second candidate, four times as good as the third candidate, four-and-a-half times as

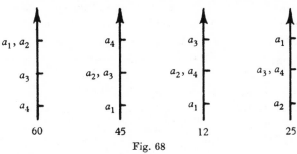

Fig. 68

Matrix for Fig. 68

		(against)				Borda count	Adjusted Borda count
		a_1	a_2	a_3	a_4		
(for)	a_1	0	(25, 57)	(85, 57)	(85, 57)	195	24
	a_2	(57, 25)	0	(60, 37)	(60, 70)	177	45
	a_3	(57, 85)	(37, 60)	0	(72, 45)	166	−24
	a_4	(57, 85)	(70, 60)	(45, 72)	0	172	−45

Fig. 69

good as the fourth, etc. Our criticism is that in fact no merit rating of this kind exists; and if this is so, no possible justification for the Borda criterion can be got along these lines.

This would be true not only of the particular scale of marking which Borda adopts, namely, a, $(a+b)$, $(a+2b)$, ... (where $b > 0$) for a lowest, second lowest, third lowest, ... place, but of *any* other scale of marking, e.g. a, ac, ac^2, ... (where $a > 0$, $c > 1$) for all voters, or even a, ad, ade, ... (where $a > 0$, $d > 1$, $e > 1$) for one voter, f, fg, fgh, ... (where $f > 0$, $g > 1$, $h > 1$) for another voter, etc., for a lowest, second lowest, third lowest place, and so on.

The justification of the Borda criterion. If we know that one candidate, a_h say, has a higher Borda count than some other

* See below, pp. 157–9 and 180–4.

candidate a_k, so far as this goes it implies that a_h has a stronger claim to election than a_k. It is possible that on a number of other tests which might be applied (e.g. the single vote, voting by elimination, etc.) a_k would be found to have a stronger claim to election than a_h. But the significance of the Borda criterion is considerable; it takes into account the position of all of the candidates on the scales of all of the voters, and in this respect is mathematically more satisfactory than the single vote or the method of elimination. It gives the total number of votes that a candidate would get if placed against each of the other candidates in turn, and it provides one of the possible valid definitions of which candidate stands highest on the whole on the voters' schedules. It seems to us to have more in its favour than any other criterion, apart from that of Condorcet; and in cases where no majority candidate exists, we shall make use of the Borda criterion.

Use of the Condorcet criterion supplemented by the Borda criterion. Our own suggestion would be that in an election about which the only information we possess is the group of schedules of the voters, the Condorcet criterion should first be used to pick out the majority candidate if there is one; and if no majority candidate exists, that candidate should be chosen who has the highest Borda count (or if candidates are ranked at the same level on some of the schedules, the candidate should be chosen who has the highest adjusted Borda count).

This scheme has certainly got the considerable practical advantage that the voting matrix drawn up in connexion with the Condorcet criterion can also be used to furnish the Borda counts.

CHAPTER X

EXAMINATION OF SOME METHODS OF ELECTION IN SINGLE-MEMBER CONSTITUENCIES

The Condorcet criterion will be used. We explained in the last chapter that our view is that in a single-member constituency the best candidate to elect is that candidate, if any, who in a direct vote against each of the others would be able to get at least a simple majority over them; and that if no majority candidate exists, the best to elect is that candidate who stands highest on the average on the schedules of the electors, as judged by the Borda count.

In the present chapter we examine whether some of the commoner methods of election necessarily select the majority candidate, where one exists. It is obvious that our examination can only be of the formal, mathematical aspect of a method of election and some aspects which are perhaps not less important will go unexamined. These will include the effect that a method of election

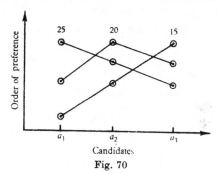

Fig. 70

Matrix for Fig. 70

		(against)		
		a_1	a_2	a_3
	a_1	0	(25, 35)	(25, 35)
(for)	a_2	(35, 25)	0	(45, 15)
	a_3	(35, 25)	(15, 45)	0

Fig. 71

has on the quality of the candidates who present themselves, the extent to which it enables the voters to acquaint themselves better with the candidates and to form a more just opinion of them, and the effect that it has in giving the electors a greater or smaller degree of interest in the election. In a different type of inquiry these might be considered to be the most important aspects of the election, but for our present purposes we accept them as being among the *data* of the problem.

The single vote. In this each elector has the right to cast a single vote and the candidate who receives the greatest number of votes is chosen.

As a particular instance let us take it that the three candidates a_1, a_2 and a_3 are up for election and that the scales of the electors

F

are as in Fig. 70. On the single vote the candidate a_1 would receive 25 votes, the candidate a_2, 20 votes, and the candidate a_3, 15 votes. Thus a_1 would be elected. We see, however, either directly from the diagram or from the matrix, that in a direct vote against them, a_1 would be defeated by both a_2 and a_3. When the electors' preference curves are single-peaked, therefore, the single vote need not return the majority candidate.

The effect of the single vote is to suppress evidence of all preferences felt by the voter except his first preference for a single candidate; apart from that he must place all candidates on the same level. Thus a preference schedule of the type shown on the

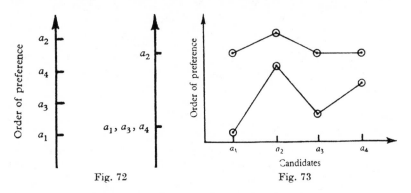

Fig. 72   Fig. 73

left-hand side of Fig. 72 would be treated as if it were equivalent to the schedule shown on the right-hand side of the same figure; or the curve in Fig. 73 which is at a different level at each of the points a_1, a_2, a_3 and a_4, would be treated as if it were identical with the other preference curve shown, which is higher at a_2 and at the same level at each of the other values.*

It could be shown that if the voters' preference curves were in fact of this shape, being higher at one point and at the same level at all others, the single vote would secure the election of the majority candidate. But this restriction on the shape of the preference curves is one of extreme rigour; and this and other shapes of curves which would entail the election of the majority candidate under the single vote, can rarely occur in practice.

---

* If the voter is indifferent as between two or more candidates, each of whom he prefers to any of the others, the single vote falsifies his schedule even in regard to his expression of a first preference.

Double election. In this the single vote is employed to select the final two candidates in the contest; and the single vote is again used to pick out the winner of this pair. If the voters' preference curves are single-peaked, the majority candidate may be thrown out at the first round. Double election would not necessarily lead to the return of the majority candidate, and, in terms of our criterion, this method of election would be judged to be unsatisfactory.

Exhaustive voting. The weaknesses of the single vote (and, by implication, of double election) are very plain; and one of the attempts to improve on it has been by the adoption of the method of exhaustive voting. Exhaustive voting has the practical weakness that it must be carried out in a number of stages, and because of this it is unsuitable for parliamentary or municipal elections, but it is frequently employed in the election of candidates to posts.

Exhaustive voting is a process of elimination. If there are, say, six candidates for a post, each member of the committee to make the appointment is given 5 votes, one less than the number of candidates, and at the first round of voting that candidate is eliminated who receives the lowest number of votes. At the second round each voter is given 4 votes and another candidate eliminated; and so on, until only a single candidate has been left undefeated.

When a particular committee is using exhaustive voting in the selection of a candidate, let p of the electors rank the candidates in the same order of preference, q of the electors rank the candidates in the same order of preference, though a different order from that of the p electors, and similarly for r, s, and t of the electors. The number of electors, n, will be equal to $(p+q+r+s+t)$ and we suppose their preference curves to be single-peaked as in Fig. 74.

Let us consider an elector whose peak does not occur at either end of the range. His preference curve is continually down-sloping as we move from its peak either to the left or to the right. It follows that the lowest point on his entire preference curve must be either at the left-hand extremity of the curve or at the right-hand extremity; that is, in the diagram must be at either a_1 or a_5. The same is true of each elector whose peak occurs at either extremity of the range: for one whose peak occurs at the left-hand extremity, the lowest point on his curve will be at the right-hand extremity of the range; and for one whose peak occurs at the right-hand extremity, the lowest point will be at the left-hand extremity. It must be true of every voter, therefore, that his least-preferred choice corresponds to a candidate at one or other of the extremities of the range. Now when exhaustive voting is used, an elector refrains from giving a vote to the candidate who stands lowest on his scale of preferences. It follows that every elector will refrain from voting either for the candidate at the left-hand or for the candidate at the right-hand extremity of the range; and one of these candidates will be bound to be eliminated at the first round of voting.

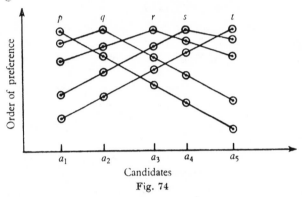

Fig. 74

Since there are five candidates, each of the n electors will be given 4 votes and in all $4n$ votes will be cast. None of the candidates a_2, a_3 or a_4 stands lowest on the scale of preferences of any elector, and each of these candidates will be supported by a vote from every elector. Thus the candidates a_2, a_3 and a_4 will receive n votes each. This uses up $3n$ votes. The remainder of the votes cast, namely, n votes, will be divided between the candidates a_1 and a_5 at the extremities of the range. These n votes, one from each elector, are to be divided between the two candidates; or fewer than this number of votes if some electors are indifferent as between the candidates at the two extremities of the range and refrain from voting. It is clear that the candidate who is eliminated at this round will be that one of the two candidates who stands lower than the other on a relative majority of the electors' scales. The candidate a_1 will be eliminated, or will remain in the contest, according as he stands lower or higher on a relative majority of the electors' scales than does a_5; that is, according as a_1 would be defeated by, or would defeat, a_5. when placed against him in a direct vote.

In visual terms, the effect of the first round of voting is to chop off one or other of the ends of the range; and the end chopped off will be the end which would be defeated by a simple majority in a straight vote against the other. Let us suppose that in this particular case the end which is chopped off is a_1. At the second round of voting again one of the ends will be chopped off; either the candidate a_2 or the candidate a_5 will be deleted according as a_2 would be defeated by, or would defeat, a_5, when placed against him in a direct vote. So the process will continue, one extremity of the range always being deleted until only a single candidate remains and he will be the victor in the contest.

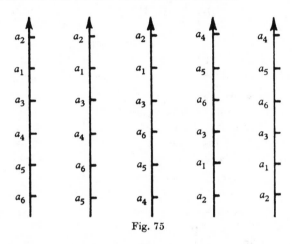

Fig. 75

It follows that it will be the majority candidate who is elected, because the majority candidate can never be eliminated unless he should come to occupy one extremity of the range. And if he does occupy an extremity, in so far as he would get a majority over the candidate at the other extremity, he will be bound to defeat him. That is, the majority candidate can never be eliminated. Hence when exhaustive voting is used, and granted the existence of single-peaked curves, the majority candidate will be selected.

On the other hand, when no ordering of the candidates exists which would render all the preference curves of the voters single-peaked, exhaustive voting may select some candidate other than the majority candidate. As an instance, in Fig. 75 the candidate who disappears at the first vote will be a_2; standing at the foot of two schedules he will get only 3 votes, while every other candidate gets at least 4 votes. But a_2 is the first preference of three electors; and, had the test of being able to get a simple majority against any other candidate been applied, he would have been chosen.

The single transferable vote (proportional representation). The system of proportional representation which is generally held to be the most satisfactory is the single transferable vote, suggested by Thomas Hare and others. When, as we suppose in this chapter, only a single place is to be filled, this method of election is usually known as the *alternative vote*, but this is only a change of name.

In this type of election the voter marks on his ballot paper the order of preference in which he places the different candidates. At the first stage in the count of the votes, only the first preferences expressed by electors are taken into consideration; and at this stage one candidate, or a number of candidates if there are several places to fill, may obtain the necessary quota of votes—we explain presently how the quota is calculated—and be elected. If the quota is, say, 30, and a single candidate obtains a quota, getting, say, 37 first-preference votes, he will be elected, and the ballot papers of seven of his supporters will then be taken and their second-preference votes distributed among the other candidates. If one or more of them are now able to secure a quota, they too will be elected. If it happens that no candidate obtains the necessary quota, the candidate holding the lowest number of votes is eliminated from the contest, and the next preferences marked on the ballot papers by which he has been supported are distributed among the remaining candidates in accordance with the next preferences marked on the papers. The process of election, or elimination, followed by a redistribution of votes of lower preferences, goes on until the necessary number of candidates have obtained the quota and all of the available places have been filled.

The 'quota' used in the system—usually referred to as a Droop quota after the name of its inventor—is the lowest number of votes which a person is required to obtain in order to secure election.* When a single place is to be filled, if a candidate should hold half the total number of votes *plus* one, then he is bound to have a greater number of votes than any other candidate. For this

* If some voters show only the order of preference in which they place certain of the candidates and not others, the quota can vary at different stages in the count.

reason, when the total number of voters is n, and a single place is to be filled, the quota is taken to be the next integer above $\frac{1}{2}n$. If two places are to be filled and one candidate holds at least a third of the total votes *plus* one, then it will be impossible that more than one other candidate should hold as many votes as this. When there are two places and the number of voters is n, the quota chosen is the next integer above $\frac{1}{3}n$. And in general with n electors and r places to be filled, the quota will be the next integer above $n/(r+1)$. This brief description of the single transferable vote will become more intelligible when we give an example of its working.

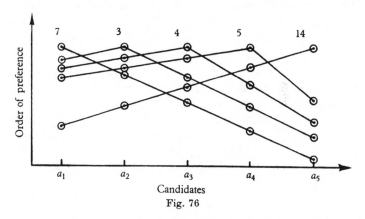

Fig. 76

Let us suppose that in a particular election the voters' preference curves are single-peaked as in Fig. 76. In all there are 33 electors and if there is one place to fill, the quota is the next integer above $\frac{33}{2}$, that is, 17.

At the first count no candidate has a quota and a_2, the candidate with the lowest number of first-preference votes, will be eliminated. His votes go to a_1, since electors who have a_2 as their first preference have a_1 as their second preference. And the voting now stands:

Candidate	a_1	a_3	a_4	a_5
No. of votes	10	4	5	14

In the absence of a quota for any candidate, a_3 will be eliminated. Electors with a_3 as their first choice have a_1 higher on their scales of preferences than any of the remaining candidates and the voting now stands:

Candidate	a_1	a_4	a_5
No. of votes	14	5	14

Still no candidate can obtain a quota and a_4 will be eliminated. As a result 5 votes will be transferred to a_1 who now has a quota and is elected. The majority candidate, however, is a_4.

Thus the voters' preference curves may be single-peaked without the single transferable vote securing the election of the majority candidate.* The single transferable vote has a further drawback which should be emphasized; using it, it is impossible for a voter to show indifference in choice between any of the candidates. If we were to employ some matrix system in voting, this could be done without difficulty.

Comparison between the different methods of election. We have tested these various methods of election by finding whether or not they necessarily pick out the majority candidate when there is one. We might test them also according to whether or not they pick out the candidate with the highest Borda count. If this were done it would be found that none of the methods concerned need select the candidate with the highest Borda count.

So far as the test that we have applied is concerned—namely, conformity to the Condorcet criterion—exhaustive voting is more satisfactory as a method of election than any of the others; it returns the majority candidate when the voters' preference curves are single-peaked.

From the practical side, however, exhaustive voting is subject to some disadvantages from which the other methods are free. If the number of electors is considerable or the electors situated in different places, it would be quite unfeasible to carry out the process of election in stages, eliminating one candidate at a time. Of course in any election we might require the voters to show their complete preferences as between the candidates by marking their first, second and later choices, and from this record deduce what the result of exhaustive voting would be. But if we possessed such a complete record of voters' attitudes, it would be still easier to pick out the majority candidate using the matrix method.

Elections in practice. We would be careful to insist on the limitations of the present investigation in its applicability to practice. Certainly if a single candidate is to be elected in a constituency, and it is legitimate to waive all considerations of party structure or effects on the cabinet system—as it would be when, say, an education committee was electing a headmaster to a school

* If two places were to be filled the candidates selected would be a_1 and a_5.

or a board of directors appointing a manager—then the use of a matrix method which employs either the majority criterion or the Borda count would be highly rational. But when considerations of party structure are relevant or other considerations come in from which we have abstracted in our treatment, a wider body of theory would be needed than that which we give.

If either the Condorcet or the Borda criterion were to be used in parliamentary or municipal elections, it would definitely have an effect on party structure leading to certain dynamic changes; after it had been in use for some time the parties that would come into existence would be different from those that would have existed had, say, the single vote continued to be employed. We can deduce the general nature of these changes. Both the Condorcet and the Borda criteria are an attempt to pick out the candidate who stands highest on the average on the schedules of the electors and each tends to act against candidates who have a low ranking in the estimate of a substantial fraction of the voters; they tend to eliminate candidates who are viewed as extremists of one kind or another. If either of these criteria were used, parties of the extremities would tend to wither and disappear, while parties of the centre would prosper.

CHAPTER XI

PROPORTIONAL REPRESENTATION

Statics. A scheme of proportional representation attempts to secure an assembly whose membership will, so far as possible, be proportionate to the volume of the different shades of political opinion held throughout the country; the microcosm is to be a true reflexion of the macrocosm. We will discuss the statics of P.R. and in the sequel allude to certain dynamic problems which arise.

As an instance of the statical problem we may suppose that two parties each run several candidates in an election and one party gets 40 % of the top places on the voters' schedules, the other 60 %; the one gets 80 % of the second places and the other 20 %, and so on for the third, fourth, ... places on the voters' schedules. The problem is: In what proportion ought the seats to be divided between the two parties and which candidates ought to get the seats for each party? The number of parties running candidates may, of course, be higher than this and the proportion of top places, second places, ... got by each may vary from zero to 100 %.

When we were concerned with the election of a single member to represent a constituency, the problem was to find the candidate who stood highest on the average on the preference scales of the voters—and this permitted of several answers being given. In dealing with the statics of P.R. we have the same sort of difficulty in a more acute form; and this is enough to show that no answer that is given could be completely satisfactory. A little further on we will illustrate the nature of the difficulties that any scheme of P.R. must encounter.

The multi-member constituency is a necessary assumption. It seems quite certain that the solution to the problem of P.R. cannot be sought on the basis of single-member constituencies; because if single-member constituencies were used, whatever the method of election was, a country with 600 members of parliament might return the members of a single party, even though the supporters of that party numbered only 600 more than those of some other; and there would not be proportional representation. For instance, that state of affairs could arise even with the use of the alternative vote in single-member constituencies. We conclude that for any satisfactory scheme of P.R. to be achieved, multi-member constituencies must be employed.

On the other hand, if the constituency became very large, returning, say, 50 members, it would give the voter insufficient opportunity of becoming acquainted with the attitudes and personalities of the candidates who stood. For the purpose of our discussion we will assume that some definite size of multi-member constituency has been chosen, which bears in mind this aspect. Our problem is to find, for such a given constituency, the best method of securing proportional representation.

Two desiderata in any scheme of P.R. It can be said quite definitely—if we accept the attitude of the present book—that a scheme of P.R. will only be satisfactory if it satisfies two requirements: it must be a mathematical scheme, stating a unitary principle, and not merely an arithmetical rule of thumb; and in the second place it must take into account the entire preference schedule of each voter.

A trial scheme in the case of single-peaked curves. Let us suppose that in a multi-member constituency there are n voters and a number of candidates of whom r are to be elected; and let us suppose that a certain ordering of the candidates on the horizontal axis can be found such that the preference scales of all voters become single-peaked.

Now if in a particular case three candidates were to be elected, each of the three midmost candidates—in the neighbourhood of $O_{med.}$—could get a majority against any of the others. But no one would be likely to expect these candidates, neighbours to one another, to provide a microcosm of the group as a whole. In the party problem, for instance, all three might be Liberals and gain very few first-preference votes, the bulk of which go to Labour and Conservative candidates at the extremities of the range. It seems clear that the solution to the general problem does not lie in a choice of the midmost candidates.

Having seen this we might attempt a solution along the following lines. Taking it that three candidates are to be elected and the preference curves of all voters are single-peaked, let us divide the voters into three groups, so far as possible of equal size, the first group containing the third of the voters whose optima are the first to occur as we move from left to right along the horizontal axis, the second group those voters whose optima occur next, and so for the third. And let us select the majority candidate for each of the groups so chosen. Then it might be thought that the three candidates chosen in this way would provide a microcosm that would suitably reflect the opinions held by the entire body of voters.

If the total number of electors were not exactly divisible by 3, the middle group might be slightly reduced in size. For example, if the number of electors is 71, the middle group might consist of 23 voters and each of the others of 24 voters, for there is some case for giving less weight to the end-groups which are less representative of opinion in the electorate as a whole, and requiring a group to contain more voters the further removed it is from $O_{med.}$.

The circumstance that we envisage, that all of the members' preference curves are single-peaked, would rarely be realized in the practical problems where a scheme of P.R. is intended to be used: but it is simple enough to permit some insight into the data of the particular case; and the attempt to find a satisfactory scheme of P.R. may well begin at some such low level of generality.

As an example of how this system of P.R. would work, we take the group of schedules shown in Fig. 77. There are 38 voters and three candidates are to be elected. We would divide up the voters into three groups, one containing the 13 voters, $8A$, $4B$ and $1C$, the middle group containing the 12 voters, $4C$, $6D$ and $2E$, and the third group containing the 13 voters $5E$ and $8F$. The scheme of P.R. which we have outlined would select the majority candidates for these three groups, a_1, a_4 and a_6, respectively.

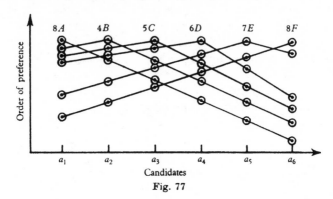

Fig. 77

Matrix for Fig. 77

		(against)						Borda
		a_1	a_2	a_3	a_4	a_5	a_6	count
	a_1	0	(8, 30)	(12, 26)	(17, 21)	(23, 15)	(23, 15)	83
	a_2	(30, 8)	0	(12, 26)	(17, 21)	(23, 15)	(23, 15)	105
(for)	a_3	(26, 12)	(26, 12)	0	(17, 21)	(23, 15)	(23, 15)	115
	a_4	(21, 17)	(21, 17)	(21, 17)	0	(23, 15)	(23, 15)	109
	a_5	(15, 23)	(15, 23)	(15, 23)	(15, 23)	0	(30, 8)	90
	a_6	(15, 23)	(15, 23)	(15, 23)	(15, 23)	(8, 30)	0	68

Fig. 78

The matrix (Fig. 78) shows the first weakness of the scheme. The nearer a candidate lies to the end of the distribution of single-peaked curves, the lower will be his Borda count. The candidates a_1 and a_6, who would be selected on the above scheme, have lower Borda scores than. any of the other candidates. That is, by one of the tests of the suitability of a candidate, their claims are judged to be weak.

In fact a dilemma of a still more acute kind is involved, which we may display by a further example. Let us suppose that in a constituency where there are 99 voters, Liberals, Conservatives and

Labour have each put forward three candidates for the three seats available; that each of these parties has secured 33 first-preference votes; and that when the Labour candidates are placed at the left of the horizontal axis, the Liberals in the middle and the Conservatives at the right, the voters' preferences can be represented by single-peaked curves. Then on this scheme of P.R., if the distribution is as in Fig. 79, the seats will go to the Labour candidate a_2, the Liberal candidate a_5 and the Conservative candidate a_8, who, in terms of the voters' optima, correspond to O_{17}, O_{50}, O_{83} respectively. Yet another Labour candidate a_3, who in the diagram corresponds to O_{33}, if placed in a straight vote against him would be able to get at least 67 votes against a_2; and another Conservative a_7, who corresponds to O_{67}, would get at least 67 votes against a_8.

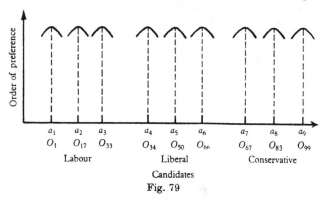

Fig. 79

We might put the dilemma thus: with no more data than that given, a_2 corresponds to Liberal opinion better than a_3 and a_8 corresponds better to Conservative opinion than a_7; but a_3 corresponds to the opinion of the whole group better than a_2, and a_7 better than a_8. Ought we to choose in accordance with the opinion of party voters or the opinion of the whole mass of the voters? This is a difficult question and we ourselves will not attempt an answer; but it would have to be answered by any scheme that was to be theoretically satisfactory.

A further objection which might be made to this scheme is that it gives no particular weight to first-preference votes; and while, to take the diagram we have drawn, a_2 and a_3 must receive at least 17 first-preference votes between them, *either a_2 or a_3* might receive no more than one first-preference vote.

The scheme of P.R. which we have outlined is too primitive mathematically to be satisfactory—it depends only on the positions of the peaks of the curves concerned and does not take into account the entire constellation of the curves. In this respect it contravenes one of the requirements which we had considered necessary in a solution. Our purpose in considering it, indeed, has been to illustrate the difficulties of getting any satisfactory scheme of P.R. of a mathematical nature, even in the simplest of cases.

When the preference curves concerned may be of unspecified shapes, the difficulties of the problem will be considerably increased; and they will be further enhanced when the choices of the electors are complementary in their nature. In its general form the statical problem of P.R. is one of tremendous complexity.

The orthodox system of P.R. has some minor faults under statical conditions. In Great Britain and the United States the commonly advocated system of P.R. is the single transferable vote, as popularized by Thomas Hare, which we have described in the preceding chapter. With regard to it the essential question is: Does it secure a microcosm of representatives that will be a just reflexion of the macrocosm of the electors? But we cannot give any proper answer to this question, since we ourselves have been unable to arrive at a scheme which we regard as satisfactory and which might afford some criterion for the satisfactoriness of other methods.

Certainly Hare's scheme violates the two *desiderata* which we have set out above. It is not a mathematical scheme but is instead a practical directive for counting votes and electing candidates. And in making elections it does not take into account the entire schedules of all of the voters. This, however, is a less serious criticism in so far as the two requirements mentioned would be exceedingly difficult to fulfil.

The chief merit of the scheme seems to us to lie in the Droop quota which specifies, with a fair amount of justice, the number of votes required for election. Yet even this is not infallible. For example, a constituency may be choosing three representatives and a candidate may get just over a quarter of the first-preference votes and be elected. But he may have been the last preference of almost three-quarters of the voters. As another possibility, a party may run a number of candidates all of whom receive about the same number of first-preference votes and none of whom obtains a quota. Then if the electors supporting these candidates have given their second-preference votes to members of other parties, the party concerned may fail to return any representative, even though it has a high proportion of first-preference votes. This second case is relatively unimportant, but the first possibility offers scope for an organized minority to pervert the use of the system and is a real danger. The Droop quota has great merit without infallibly procuring justice.

At another part of the single transferable vote there is a certain amount of heterogeneity. The count takes place in successive stages. At the first stage each candidate will hold only first-preference votes. At the second stage in the count, one candidate may hold only first-preference votes while others hold first- and second-preference votes, or all may hold first- and second-preference votes. At the third stage one candidate may hold only first-preference votes while others hold first-, second- and third-preference votes. There is a certain arbitrariness in the possibility of attributing second-, third- and lower-preference votes to some candidates and not to others, and in giving the same weight to votes of different kinds.

From the practical point of view a disadvantage of the system is that it is a compound of minor complexities and is difficult to remember. A scheme that arose out of some unitary principle would be easier to keep in mind.

In spite of these drawbacks the scheme has merits, and this is borne in on one by the construction of imaginary examples in which Hare's system very often chooses a man whose claims, one would judge, are strong. And it is not difficult to see why many people, *regarding it purely as a statical system*, should hold the single transferable vote in esteem.

The overwhelming objections to the orthodox system of P.R. in electing a parliament lie in its dynamic effects. A solution to the statical problem would show how to choose the group of representatives who best reflect the political opinions held throughout a country or a constituency. Yet even though this could be got, the main political difficulties connected with P.R. would still remain, for they are of a quite different order; they are connected with the dynamic changes which are set in motion when P.R. is used to replace, say, the single vote.

The single vote employed in parliamentary elections in most cases induces the elector to cast his vote in favour of one or other of the two parties he thinks most likely to win, and as between which he considers the real contest to lie. A vote for any other party will usually be regarded as a vote wasted—or at any rate cast only in righteous protest and without influence on the decision that is being fought out. In consequence, when arbitration is by the single vote, third parties tend to wilt and die. Thus the single vote may distort the election result, giving rise perhaps to a majority of seats being held by the party which has only a minority of votes in the country—and even before this causing people to vote for a party which does not represent their true views—but it does have the advantage of strengthening a two-party system in parliament with the party in the majority able to form a cabinet drawn entirely from its own members, and so makes for strong and stable government.

P.R., on the other hand, is expressly designed to give representation to all shades of opinion and tends to multiply the number of parties in the house. It makes it difficult to form a cabinet which can command a parliamentary majority and so makes for weak government. In Great Britain it has been the belief that this is so, which certainly seems to me to be correct, which has prevented the introduction of P.R.*

Among subscribers to the view that for good government there must be only a small number of parties in parliament are the advocates of P.R. themselves, for example, the Proportional Representation Society in Great Britain; but they hold that the single transferable vote does not tend to increase the number of parties in the house. Yet to hold that it is possible both to secure proportional representation and to do so without increasing the number of parties in parliament, would seem to me to be little short of a contradiction in terms. And, one would judge, the longer the length of time allowed to elapse under any system of P.R., the greater would the increase in the number of parties tend to be.

A possible justification of P.R. would be to hold that what is wanted in the modern world is not 'strong' government but rather 'weak' government and a respite from the present turmoil of government activity, not only in one country but throughout the whole world. Accepting this view, P.R. might have much to contribute to civilization by way of cutting down government activity. The difficulty about this solution, of course, is that the

* Cf. A. V. Dicey, *The Law of the Constitution* (8th ed.), pp. lxvi–lxxv.

[82]

first countries to put the proposal into effect might become victims to the aggression of their strong neighbours, who themselves felt no inclination to adopt a system of P.R. In any case it is not on these grounds that proportionalists base their case.*

That there is scope for the single transferable vote, though not in national elections. If we take it that for one reason or another strong government, with its presupposition of a small number of political parties, is a requirement, there seems to be no case at all for the single transferable vote in national elections. But in other circumstances the dynamic effects we have referred to (changes in the party system and in cabinet government) may not arise; one has in mind, for example, the election of subcommittees and local-government elections, in so far as party considerations there are held to be unimportant. And *in such circumstances* the use of the single transferable vote can be appropriate and helpful while the single vote is quite inappropriate.

We would summarize our own opinion on the matter as being that the single vote has the most grave formal weaknesses, and yet has an invaluable part to play in national elections by strengthening the tendency to a two-party system and the type of cabinet government that goes with it; and that the scope of the single transferable vote is narrower than many of its advocates believe.

A Royal Commission. At the present time there is some demand in Great Britain for the appointment of a Royal Commission on Methods of Election, and certainly such a commission would go into proportional representation and other problems more deeply than any individual theorist could do. It would make use of the wealth of evidence that waits to be investigated and its findings would have the publicity, both at home and abroad, which is so desirable in this problem.

At the same time the statical problem, as we have shown, is essentially a mathematical problem, and as such is not one which a Royal Commission is at all qualified to investigate. It is one for

---

* Other dynamic changes induced by P.R. relate to the heightening or lessening of the political interest of the voter, alterations in the types of persons who stand for parliament, increased or lesser control by the electorate over the course of government. These and other facets of P.R. are treated in two works of outstanding merit, *Proportional Representation* (1926), by C. G. Hoag and G. H. Hallett, who give their unqualified support to P.R., and *Democracy or Anarchy?* (1942), by L. R. Hermens, who is invincibly hostile to it. Hermens's is a book which might well be made compulsory reading for politicians.

G

the mathematicians; and early in its proceedings any Royal Commission which might be appointed should call for examination of it both by independent mathematicians and by some of the government mathematical laboratories which already exist in this country.

CHAPTER XII

THE DECISIONS OF A COMMITTEE USING A SPECIAL MAJORITY

1. When the members' preference curves are single-peaked

The limits of the size of majority. Frequently it is provided by the rules of a society that any amendment to the rules must be adopted by a two-thirds majority of the members voting; or the majority required may be one of three-fourths, four-fifths, etc. The same requirement of a majority higher than a simple majority is made in various branches of company law, and sometimes arises in regard to proposed amendments to the constitution of a country.

We assume that in the committee there are n members; and that an ordering on the horizontal axis can be found for the points to represent all the motions, such that the preference curve of each member becomes single-peaked.

The majority stipulated by the committee procedure may be of any definite size whatever, ranging from a simple majority to a unanimous decision. We will denote the majority in use by the ratio $M:n$, where the limits of this ratio are given by $1 \geqslant M/n > \frac{1}{2}$.

If n is odd and equal, say, to $2N + 1$, where N is integral, at the lower limit $M > \frac{1}{2}n > N + \frac{1}{2}$, which gives $M = N + 1 = \frac{1}{2}(n+1)$. Similarly, if n is even, we get at the lower limit $M = \frac{1}{2}n + 1$. Thus we can specify the limits of size of the special majority either as $1 \geqslant M/n > \frac{1}{2}$ for n odd or even, or as $1 \geqslant M/n \geqslant (n+1)/2n$ for n odd and $1 \geqslant M/n \geqslant (\frac{1}{2}n + 1)/n$ for n even. We will use the single inequality.

A series of lemmas. These will deal with the number of votes that particular motions get when put against others lying in certain ranges.

Lemma 1. *If the point h put in a vote against the point k is such that $h < k$, then all of the members with optima at or below h will* *necessarily vote for h, and all of the members with optima at or above k will necessarily vote for k. Each of the other members, i.e. those with optima lying between h and k, will vote for that one of the two values which stands higher on his scale of preferences.*

This follows because the curve of preferences of any member whose optimum is at or below h will fall in moving from the point h on the horizontal axis to the point k (see Fig. 80); he will therefore vote for h against k. Similarly, a member whose optimum is at or above k will vote for k against h.

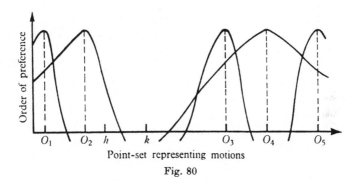

Fig. 80

Lemma 2. Apart from the cases in which a number of optima are coincident at $O_{med.}$, no value of the variable will exist that can obtain more than a bare majority against all counter-proposals.

We have shown that no value of the variable can get even a bare majority against $O_{med.}$; hence if any value exists that is able to get more than a bare majority against all counter-proposals, it must be $O_{med.}$ itself. But it follows from Lemma 1 that, unless there should be a number of optima coincident at that point, $O_{med.}$ itself will get no more than a bare majority against the two neighbouring optima, when n is odd, or against any value intermediate to these optima; and that when n is even $O_{med.}$ will get only a bare majority, through the chairman's deciding vote, against the other midmost optimum or against any point lying between $O_{med.}$ and the other midmost optimum. Hence the lemma is true.

Lemma 3. Given $h < O_{med.}$, then

(a) of the points in the entire range none can obtain a greater number of the votes against h than the point next in order above it, and this point can always get at least a simple majority against h;

(*b*) *of the points below h none can obtain more votes against it than the point next in order below it; but h can always get at least a simple majority against this lower point.*

Given $h > O_{\text{med.}}$, then

(*c*) *of the points in the entire range none can obtain a greater number of votes against h than the point next in order below it, and this point can always get at least a simple majority against h;*

(*d*) *of the points above h none can obtain more votes against it than the point next in order above it; but h can always get at least a simple majority against this higher point.*

Proof follows as a simple application of Lemma 1.

Of the two following, Lemma 4 specifies the conditions under which one motion will be able to defeat a certain range of the other motions by the stipulated majority $M:n$; and Lemma 5 specifies the set of motions which can never be defeated by an $M:n$ majority by any other motion whatever.

Lemma 4. (*a*) *If* $h \leqslant O_{n-M+1}$, *h will be able to defeat any lower value by a majority of at least* $M:n$, *where* $1 \geqslant M/n > \frac{1}{2}$;

(*b*) *if* $h \geqslant O_M$, *h will be able to defeat any higher value by a majority of at least* $M:n$.

In proof we see that if $h < O_{n-M+1}$, there must be at least M optima above h; and if $h = O_{n-M+1}$ there will again be at least M optima either at or above h.

In both cases the point h will secure at least M votes against the point next in order below it. *A fortiori* [Lemma 3 (*b*)] h will secure at least M votes against every other point below it. Hence part (*a*) of the lemma is true.

By symmetry, part (*b*) is true.

Lemma 5. *In the entire range of the variable, no value can exist that is able to defeat a value lying within, or at the ends of the range* $O_{n-M+1}O_M$, *by a majority as high as* $M:n$, *where* $1 \geqslant M/n > \frac{1}{2}$.

If h be any point in the range $O_{n-M+1}O_M$, there are fewer than M optima above it and fewer than M optima below it. For example, there are $n - (n - M + 1) = (M - 1)$ optima above the extreme left-hand point O_{n-M+1} of the range. Hence if the curves of preference are drawn to pass through h as a common point on the horizontal axis, fewer than M curves will rise either to the right or to the left of h. No point on the axis, therefore, can get as high a majority as $M:n$ in a vote against h.

Statement of the geometrical problem and a theorem. Let h be the value of the variable against which an $M:n$ majority must be obtained, where $1 \geqslant M/n > \frac{1}{2}$.

Case 1. Given $O_{n-M+1} \leqslant h \leqslant O_M$.

From Lemma 5, since h lies within or at the extremities of the range $O_{n-M+1}O_M$, no value of the variable exists that can defeat h by the necessary majority.

Case 2. Given $h < O_{n-M+1}$ or $h > O_M$.

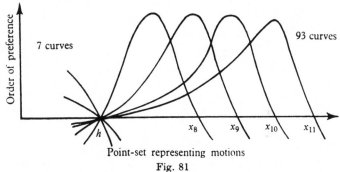

Point-set representing motions

Fig. 81

If h lies outside the range $O_{n-M+1}O_M$, when the preference curves of the members are drawn through h as a common point on the horizontal axis, let the left-hand intersections of the curves with the axis be named $x_1', x_2', \ldots, x_n'$, being numbered in the order in which they occur, moving from left to right; and let the right-hand points of intersection of the curves with the horizontal axis be named $x_1, x_2, \ldots, x_n$, the numbering again being in the order in which they occur.

The preference curves are single-peaked and each has h as a point of intersection with the axis. There will be n points x and n points x'; and of the $2n$ points x or x', n will be coincident at h.

If $h < O_{n-M+1}$, at least M of the curves drawn through h will pass upwards from h moving to the right; and a range of values lying above h will be able to defeat h by a majority of at least $M:n$.

For example, if we are dealing with a group of 100 members in a committee whose majority requirement is 90 %, let us suppose that the optima of 7 members lie below h and of 93 members lie above h. Then 7 curves will pass upwards from h to the left and 93 will pass upwards from h to the right (Fig. 81). The points $x_1, x_2, \ldots, x_7$ will coincide at h and the points $x_8', x_9', \ldots, x_{100}'$ will also coincide at h. All points within the segment hx_8 (the end points of the segment being excluded) will lie under 93 curves, all points in the segment hx_9 (the end points excluded) will lie under at least 92 curves, ..., all points within the segment hx_{11} (the end points excluded) will lie under at least 90 curves. Hence, the end points being excluded, all points within the segment hx_{11} (that is, within the segment hx_{n-M+1}) will be able to obtain at least a 90 % majority over the value h.

The extreme point of this segment is at the same preference level on one curve as the point h. Hence against h, x_{11} can obtain a majority of $89:99 < 90:100$, as can be tested by arithmetic and as

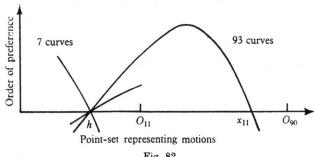

Fig. 82

follows from the inequality $(M-1)/(n-1) < M/n$, where $M < n$. That is, x_{11} cannot defeat h by the necessary size of majority.

The general rule, indeed, is readily seen to be that, given $h < O_{n-M+1}$, all points in the range hx_{n-M+1} (the end points excluded) can obtain the necessary majority $M:n$ in a vote against h.

Similarly, for $h > O_M$, all points in the range $x'_M h$ can obtain a majority $M:n$ against h.

Recurring to the numerical example, it is clear that the point x_{11} must lie above the position of the 11th optimum O_{11}, since, moving along the horizontal axis from left to right, we must have passed at least 11 optima before we encounter the 11th intersection of the right-hand slope of a curve with the axis. That is $x_{11} > O_{11}$. The point x_{11} may lie in any part of the horizontal axis to the right of O_{11}.

Two possibilities must be distinguished. x_{11} may occur inside the range $O_{11}O_{90}$. In this case (Fig. 82) all points within the segment hx_{11} (the end points being excluded) can defeat h by a majority of

[88]

90 %; and of such points none within the segment $O_{11}x_{11}$ can itself be defeated by a 90 % majority by any other value in the entire range of the variable. The limiting value of x_{11} for which this is true occurs when x_{11} is equal to the point lying next above O_{90}, or, as we can say, when x_{11} is equal to the value '$O_{90}+$'. That is, this class of cases holds good for $x_{11} \leqslant O_{90}+$.

The other possibility is that $x_{11} > O_{90}+$. Points within or at the ends of the range $O_{11}O_{90}$ (Fig. 83) would then be able to defeat h by a 90 % majority and could not themselves be defeated by any other value by a majority of this size (Lemma 5). Points lying within either of the ranges hO_{11} (except the point h) and within

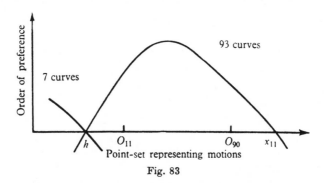

Fig. 83

$O_{90}x_{11}$ (except the point x_{11}) would be able to defeat h by a 90 % majority; but every point lying within either of these ranges, except the points O_{11} and O_{90} respectively, could itself be defeated by a 90 % majority by one or more other values of the variable.

The lemmas and the preceding reasoning culminate in the following theorem. It specifies the set of motions, if any, which is able to get an $M:n$ majority against any given motion; and specifies which of these motions can themselves be defeated by an $M:n$ majority by others, and which cannot be so defeated.

THEOREM. *Given that against the value h a majority of $M:n$ is required, where $1 \geqslant M/n > \frac{1}{2}$. Then*

(a) *if $O_{n-M+1} \leqslant h \leqslant O_M$, no value exists that can defeat h;*

(b) *if $h < O_{n-M+1}$, the values within the range hx_{n-M+1} (the end points being excluded) can defeat h by the necessary majority. Of the values within this range, if $x_{n-M+1} \leqslant O_M+$, those within the segment $O_{n-M+1}x_{n-M+1}$ cannot themselves be defeated by an $M:n$ majority by* *any other point; and if $x_{n-M+1} > O_M +$, points within or at the ends of the segment $O_{n-M+1} O_M$ cannot themselves be defeated by an $M:n$ majority by any other point;*

(c) and (d) if $h > O_M$ similar conclusions can be stated in terms of O_M, 'O_M^-' (i.e. the point next in order below O_M) and x_M'.

The types of committee procedures (a) and (b) and some examples. We have used the symbol h to denote the motion against which a special majority must be obtained; and, if desired h can be taken to be 'the existing state of affairs', a_0. The geometry will then apply, provided an ordering of the points $a_1, a_2, ..., a_n$ and a_0 can be found on the horizontal axis, such that the members preference curves become single-peaked. In other instances, h, it desired, can be taken to be one of the motions put forward in the meeting.

We proceed to investigate the main types of committee procedure which employ a special majority.

In the usual practice, when the majority stipulated is one of say, two-thirds, any amendment to the original motion could displace that motion on a simple majority; and further amendments put against the original motion or substantive motion, whichever had been carried, would also require only a simple majority. But when the original motion or substantive motion which has sur vived these tests on a simple majority is put against the existing rule which it is intended to replace, it requires to obtain the two-thirds majority that had been stipulated.

We may formulate this procedure as follows:

Procedure (a). Test (i). The motions are to be put forward suc cessively and a simple majority used. The first pair of motion moved, are to meet in a vote, then the survivor of this vote is to be put against the motion which is next put forward, and so on so that if m motions are put forward, in all $(m-1)$ vo es will be held.*

Test (ii). The motion selected by test (i) is to be placed against a_0, being required to get a majority of at least $M:n$ in order to become the decision of the committee.

We can state the consequences of this procedure.

If $O_{n-M+1} \leqslant a_0 \leqslant O_M$, we know immediately that the decision of the committee will be unchanged and will be a_0.

---

* The remarks of chapter VIII in regard to the possible incompleteness of the members' schedules will again apply.

If, however, $a_0 < O_{n-M+1}$ or $a_0 > O_M$, we must go through both tests.

Test (i) is bound to give $O_{\text{med.}}$.

To get the result of test (ii), draw the members' preference curves with a_0 as a common point on the horizontal axis. Suppose $a_0 < O_{n-M+1}$; then, provided that $O_{\text{med.}}$ lies within the segment $a_0 x_{n-M+1}$, the point x_{n-M+1} being excluded, it will defeat a_0 by the necessary majority. Or, if $a_0 > O_M$, provided $O_{\text{med.}}$ lies within the segment $x'_M a_0$, the point x'_M being excluded, it will defeat a_0 by the necessary majority. Only if $O_{\text{med.}}$ lies within these limits will it pass test (ii).

EXAMPLE 1. A committee of five members that follows procedure (a), requires at test (ii) that the value selected by test (i)

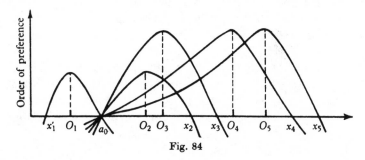

Fig. 84

should be able to get a $4:5$ majority against a_0. It is given that the members' preference curves are shown in Fig. 84, with a_0 as a common point on the horizontal axis. What is the outcome of the voting?

$M = 4$, $n - M + 1 = 2$, and a_0 lies outside the range $O_2 O_4$. We therefore go through the two tests.

In test (i), O_3 is selected.

In test (ii), O_3, since it lies within the segment $a_0 x_2$, can defeat a_0 by a $4:5$ majority, and becomes the decision of the committee.

If procedure (a) is in use, we can get the result by the same technique as in chapter IV, pp. 21–4, where we count the number of curves under which a motion lies. Indeed for procedure (a) that method is more general, in so far as the members' preference curves are assumed to be single-peaked in relation to only the motions $a_1, a_2, ..., a_m$, whereas in the present chapter they are assumed to be single-peaked in relation to $a_1, a_2, ..., a_m$ and a_0.

EXAMPLE 2. The same data as in the previous example. Find the decision of the committee, using the method of chapter IV.

The motion corresponding to O_3 will be selected at test (i). Each member's curve intersects the horizontal axis at a_0, and O_3 lies under four curves. O_3 will therefore get a majority of $4:5$ against a_0 at test (ii) and will become the committee's decision.

EXAMPLE 3. Given the group of preference curves of Fig. 17, p. 21, what is the outcome of the voting when the committee uses procedure (a) and requires a majority of $4:5$?

O_3 passes test (i) and, lying under three curves, is rejected at test (ii). The committee's decision is a_0.

The curves in question are single-peaked in relation to a_1, a_2, ..., a_m but not in relation to a_1, a_2, ..., a_m and a_0. The geometry of the present chapter would therefore not apply.

Other procedures with a special majority, however, may necessitate the use of the geometry which we have just given. This is true of the following:

Procedure (b). Test (i). All of the motions are to be put forward before the voting begins, and one after another the motions made are to be selected by the chairman, or in some other arbitrary fashion, and put against the existing motion a_0, until one is found which can obtain an $M:n$ majority against it.

Test (ii). The first motion, if any, which can obtain an $M:n$ majority against a_0 is to stand until it is itself defeated by an $M:n$ majority by one of the other motions which had been made.

Test (iii), etc. Similarly, the next motion, if any, that is selected will stand until it is defeated by an $M:n$ majority by one of the other motions which had been made, and so on. The motion that survives the whole process is to be the decision of the committee.

The interesting feature about this procedure is that the final outcome will in some circumstances depend on the order in which the motions are brought against a_0.

Given $O_{n-M+1} \leqslant a_0 \leqslant O_M$, a_0 will remain the decision of the committee.

Given $a_0 < O_{n-M+1}$, draw the members' curves with a_0 as a common point on the horizontal axis. Then if the first value to defeat a_0 lies within the range $O_{n-M+1} x_{n-M+1}$ (the point x_{n-M+1} excluded), or, if this range is smaller, lies within $O_{n-M+1} O_M$, this will be the decision of the committee. If the first value to defeat a_0 is, say, the point k, where $a_0 < k < O_{n-M+1}$, we must draw the members' curves with k as a common point on the horizontal axis and continue the search for an equilibrium position. Similarly if $x_{n-M+1} > O_M$, and the first point to defeat a_0 is, say, i, where $O_M < i < x_{n-M+1}$, we must draw the members' curves with i as a common point on the horizontal axis and continue the search for a solution.

Given $a_0 > O_M$, the same considerations apply.

EXAMPLE 4. If the committee for which preference curves are drawn in Fig. 84 follows procedure (b), what will be the outcome of the voting?

Points within the range $a_0 x_2$, the end-points excluded, can defeat a_0 by the necessary majority; but points within $a_0 O_2$, the point O_2 excluded, can themselves be defeated by other values. If a_0 should

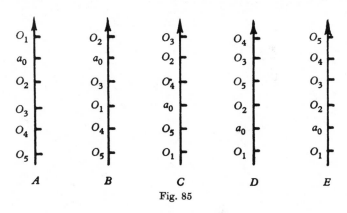

Fig. 85

first be defeated by a point within $O_2 x_2$, the point x_2 excluded, this point would remain the decision of the committee. But if the first defeat of a_0 comes from a point k, say, where $a_0 < k < O_2$, we would require to draw new curves having k as a common point on the horizontal axis, and continue the search until we had reached a value that could not itself be defeated by a 4:5 majority by any other value. It can be seen that however many steps there are in reaching it, the solution when found must lie within the range $O_2 x_2$. Each additional step in the process of reaching it narrows the range of values beyond O_2 within which a possible solution can lie. Values nearer to O_2, therefore, have a greater chance of being selected than those nearer to x_2.

EXAMPLE 5. The preference schedules of the members of a committee are as shown in Fig. 85 and the committee uses a 4:5

[93]

majority. What decision will be reached on procedure (a) and what decision on procedure (b)?

Procedure (a). Fig. 86 shows the preference curves of the members drawn with a_0 as a common point on the horizontal axis. The curves are only to be taken as real at the points O_1, O_2, ..., O_5 and a_0.

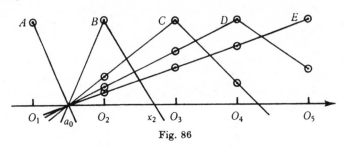

Fig. 86

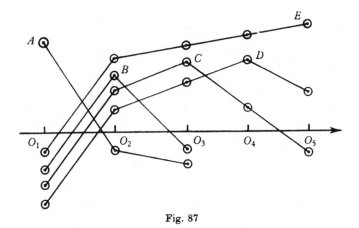

Fig. 87

$M = 4$, $n - M + 1 = 2$ and a_0 lies outside the range O_2O_4. The point x_2 lies between O_2 and O_3, so that of the significant points in the diagram only O_2 can defeat a_0 by a $4:5$ majority.

At test (i) O_3 is selected.

At test (ii) O_3 will fail to get a $4:5$ majority against a_0, and a_0 will remain the decision of the committee.

Alternatively, Fig. 87, as was suggested in chapter IV, plots the values ranked by the members higher than a_0 above the horizontal axis.

At test (i) O_3 will be selected.

At test (ii) O_3, lying under three curves, will get a $3:5$ majority against a_0, and a_0 will remain the decision of the committee.

Procedure (b). From Fig. 86 the only value which can pass test (i) is O_2, lying as it does in the range a_0x_2. No value can get a $4:5$ majority against any point in the range O_2O_4, and O_2 becomes the decision of the committee.

Alternatively, from Fig. 87 we can see that O_2 is the only value which is able to get a $4:5$ majority against a_0, since it is the only significant point lying under four curves. Before we can prove that O_2 cannot itself be defeated by a $4:5$ majority by any other value put forward, we must either carry out a number of empirical tests or use Lemma 5 of this chapter. Where, as here, the number of motions put forward is small, the empirical test can easily be made; but where the number of motions becomes large or infinite, the theoretical solution becomes necessary, and the methods of chapter IV do not suffice.

EXAMPLE 6. Examine Lemma 5 at the lower limiting value of M, for n odd or even.

When n is odd, the range $O_{n-M+1}O_M$ can be reduced to a single point. This occurs when

$$n - M + 1 = M,$$
$$M = \tfrac{1}{2}(n + 1).$$

If $n = 101$, say, $M = 51$. The range $O_{n-M+1}O_M$ reduces to the single point O_{51}; and no value in the range, i.e. at the point O_{51}, can be defeated by a majority of $51:101$ by any other point in the entire range.

When n is even, the range $O_{n-M+1}O_M$ does not contract to a point, since this would require $n - M + 1 = M$ and $n + 1 = 2M$, which is impossible for n even.

The minimum extent of the range, given by $M = \tfrac{1}{2}n + 1$, would be $O_{\frac{1}{2}n}O_{\frac{1}{2}n+1}$. For example, if $n = 100$, this range becomes $O_{50}O_{51}$; and no point in this range can be defeated by a majority of $51:100$ by any outside point.

Some conclusions in regard to procedures (a) and (b). It is obvious that the lower the size of special majority required, the greater will be the chance of a_0 being displaced and a new decision brought into force.

As is borne out by the examples and as may be deduced on

common-sense grounds, the chance of a_0 being displaced by a new decision is greater with procedure (b) than with procedure (a).

When procedure (a) alters the already-existing decision, it replaces it by a definite and specifiable motion. When procedure (b) alters the already-existing decision, it does so in favour of another motion which, beyond the fact that it must lie in a particular range, is indeterminate; and certain values within this range have a greater chance of adoption than others.

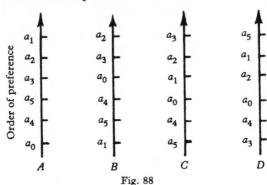

Fig. 88

Matrix for Fig. 88

(against)

(for)		a_1	a_2	a_3	a_4	a_5	a_0
	a_1	0	(2, 2)	(2, 2)	(3, 1)	(2, 2)	(3, 1)
	a_2	(2, 2)	0	(3, 1)	(4, 0)	(3, 1)	(4, 0)
	a_3	(2, 2)	(1, 3)	0	(3, 1)	(3, 1)	(3, 1)
	a_4	(1, 3)	(0, 4)	(1, 3)	0	(2, 2)	(1, 3)
	a_5	(2, 2)	(1, 3)	(1, 3)	(2, 2)	0	(2, 2)
	a_0	(1, 3)	(0, 4)	(1, 3)	(3, 1)	(2, 2)	0

Fig. 89

2. When the members' preference curves are subject to no restriction

Some examples. When the members' preference curves are subject to no restriction, the matrix theory applies.

EXAMPLE 7. Given the group of schedules of Fig. 88. C is to be taken as chairman and the size of special majority in use is $3:4$. What decisions are arrived at by procedures (a) and (b) respectively?

Procedure (a). From the matrix we see that a_2 can get a majority over each of the other values and can defeat a_1 with

[96]

the aid of the chairman's casting vote. Test (i) therefore will pick out a_2.

At test (ii), a_2 will be able to get the necessary $3:4$ majority against a_0 and will become the decision of the committee.

Procedure (b). At test (i) a_1, a_2 and a_3 could each get the stipulated majority against a_0. But if a_3 were to pass this test, it would be defeated at test (ii) by a_2 which could get a $3:4$ majority against it, and a_2 would become the decision adopted. Whichever of the motions a_1 or a_2 were first put to the vote in test (i) would pass this test and would be undefeated in test (ii).

a_1	a_1	a_1	a_3	a_3	a_4	a_4	a_4	a_5
a_0	a_5	a_3	a_2	a_2	a_1	a_5	a_5	a_1
a_2	a_4	a_2	a_0	a_1	a_2	a_2	a_2	a_2
a_3	a_3	a_4	a_1	a_4	a_4	a_0	a_1	a_0
a_4	a_2	a_0	a_5	a_0	a_5	a_0	a_1	a_4
a_5	a_0	a_5	a_4	a_5	a_3	a_3	a_3	a_3
A	B	C	D	E	F	G	H	I

Fig. 90

Matrix for Fig. 90

(against)

(for)		a_1	a_2	a_3	a_4	a_5	a_0
	a_1	0	(5, 4)	(7, 2)	(6, 3)	(6, 3)	(7, 2)
	a_2	(4, 5)	0	(5, 4)	(5, 4)	(5, 4)	(8, 1)
	a_3	(2, 7)	(4, 5)	0	(4, 5)	(4, 5)	(4, 5)
	a_4	(3, 6)	(4, 5)	(5, 4)	0	(6, 3)	(6, 3)
	a_5	(3, 6)	(4, 5)	(5, 4)	(3, 6)	0	(4, 5)
	a_0	(2, 7)	(1, 8)	(5, 4)	(3, 6)	(5, 4)	0

Fig. 91

The decision will be either a_1 or a_2. Since there is only one route by which a_1 can become the committee's decision, viz. by being put against a_0 before a_2 or a_3 has been put, and there are two routes by which a_2 can become the decision, viz. by a_2 or a_3 being put to test (i) before a_1 has been, the chance of a_2 being the decision is twice that of a_1.

EXAMPLE 8. Given the schedules of Fig. 90 for which the matrix is attached. What is the result on procedure (a) and on procedure (b), when the special majority required is two-thirds?

Procedure (a). From the matrix, a_1 is the only motion that can pass test (i), and at test (ii) it becomes the decision of the committee.

Procedure (b). Each of the motions a_1, a_2 and a_4 would be able to pass test (i); but at test (ii) a_4 would be displaced by a_1 which can get a two-thirds majority against it. The committee's decision will be a_1 or a_2, with a_1 having twice the chance of a_2.

EXAMPLE 9. As in Example 8, but with a special majority of $8:9$.

Procedure (a). The motion a_1 would pass test (i) and be rejected in favour of a_0 at test (ii).

Procedure (b). The motion a_2 would be selected at test (i) and would pass test (ii).

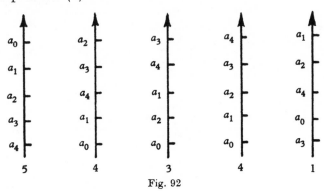

Fig. 92

Matrix for Fig. 92

		a_1	a_2	a_3	a_4	a_0
				(against)		
(for)	a_1	0	(9, 8)	(6, 11)	(6, 11)	(12, 5)
	a_2	(8, 9)	0	(10, 7)	(10, 7)	(12, 5)
	a_3	(11, 6)	(7, 10)	0	(12, 5)	(11, 6)
	a_4	(11, 6)	(7, 10)	(5, 12)	0	(12, 5)
	a_0	(5, 12)	(5, 12)	(6, 11)	(5, 12)	0

Fig. 93

EXAMPLE 10. Given the group of schedules of Fig. 92. What decisions are arrived at by procedures (a) and (b) respectively, when a two-thirds majority is required?

Procedure (a). There is no majority motion. Suppose that at test (i) the motions are put forward in the order a_1, a_2, a_3, a_4, then from the matrix a_3 will pass test (i); and at test (ii) will be rejected in favour of a_0, since a two-thirds majority requires at least 12 out of 17 votes.

Assuming the motions to be put forward in the order a_1, a_3, a_4, a_2, test (i) accepts a_2 and this motion is adopted at test (ii).

It can be shown that, provided the motions enter test (i) in a

[98]

suitable order, any of the motions may be adopted by the committee, except a_3 which must be rejected at test (ii).

Thus in a case like this where there is no majority motion, we cannot say that procedure (a) will alter the already-existing decision, if at all, by a particular motion, though this had been true for single-peaked curves (see p. 96).

Procedure (b). Whichever of the motions a_1, a_2, a_4, is first to be put against a_0 will be adopted at test (i) and cannot be dislodged at any subsequent step.

CHAPTER XIII

THE ELASTICITY OF COMMITTEE DECISIONS WITH AN ALTERING SIZE OF MAJORITY*

1. When the members' preference curves are single-peaked

Introductory notions. The procedure of a committee when it is reaching a decision may require a simple or a special majority. The larger the size of majority needed to arrive at a new decision on a topic, the smaller will be the likelihood of the committee reaching a decision that alters the existing state of affairs. If a club subscription is £1 and is fixed by the annual general meeting of the members, the chance of the subscription being raised or lowered will be less great if a two-thirds majority is needed to make the change, than if only a simple majority is needed; and if a unanimous decision is needed the chance of the subscription being altered becomes still less. Similarly, if a number of countries are in committee, in say, a United Nations Assembly, the greater the size of majority needed, the smaller will be the number of alterations made in the existing state of affairs, whatever that may be, and the smaller the number of new decisions taken.

This makes it desirable to investigate the degree to which, with an increase in the size of majority needed in a committee, the existing state of affairs becomes less liable to change. The problem resembles that in which the price of a good alters and the demand for it changes to a greater or smaller extent. This feature is dealt with in Economics using the concept of elasticity; and it will be

* The reader who is unacquainted with Economics should omit this chapter.

shown that the same concept of elasticity can be employed in the case of the committee.

The assumptions. We suppose that we have a committee of n members, one of whom, the chairman, in the event of a tie has the right to a deciding vote. The motions before the committee, including the motion already in existence and by which the state of affairs is at present regulated, are taken to be $a_1, a_2, ..., a_m$; and we assume that an ordering for the points on the horizontal axis to represent the motions can be found, such that the preference curve of each member becomes single-peaked.

We inquire whether any one of the motions, if it is the already-existing motion, will be superseded by another. In doing this we assume that each of the others of the motions $a_1, a_2, ..., a_m$ can be brought against the existing motion, as in procedure (b) of the preceding chapter (p. 92).

The size of majority used by the committee will be taken to be $M:n$, where M is a parameter defined by the limits $1 \geqslant M/n > \frac{1}{2}$. Whichever motion is in force at present is to be taken as liable to change, if any of the other motions is able to obtain an $M:n$ majority over it, when the two meet in a vote.

First we will assume that the motions before the committee can be represented by a measurable variable, each point on the horizontal axis standing for a particular size of numerical quantity put forward in a motion, as, for example, a wage rate of £4, £5, £6, etc.

Number of members finite. The problem is to investigate the tendency to increased stability of a motion already in force, when there is an increase in the size of majority that any other motion must get in order to supersede it. As an illustrative instance we take a committee of seven members, the optima of whose preference curves occur at the values $O_1, ..., O_7$, as shown in the upper part of Fig. 94.

The median optimum is O_4 and O_4 can get a $4:7$ majority against any other value of the variable. If O_4 is the existing size of the variable and if the majority stipulated by the committee is $4:7$, O_4 will persist as the committee decision, and no other value would be able to do so.

Next from Lemma 5 of the preceding chapter, no value is able to secure a $5:7$ majority against any point in the range O_3O_5, the end-points included. If, in order to be adopted, a new value had to be able to obtain a $5:7$ majority against the existing value, any existing value that lay in the range O_3O_5 would persist as the committee decision.

If the size of majority required is 6:7, any existing value lying in the range O_2O_6, the end-points included, would continue to be the value adopted by the committee. And if the size of majority required is 7:7, any value in the range O_1O_7, the end-points included, that already existed, would continue in existence; but if the existing value of the variable lay outside this range it would be altered by the committee.

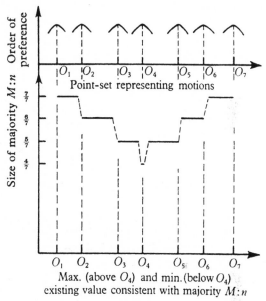

Fig. 94

From the data of the problem shown in the upper part of Fig. 94 we can construct the diagram shown in the lower part of Fig. 94 in which the entire position is set out. In this, along the vertical axis the size of majority is shown and along the horizontal axis the maximum or minimum value of the variable that, if it already existed, would be immune from change, in so far as no value proposed against it would be able to get a majority of the requisite size. If the size of majority needed is 4:7, only the value O_4 is immune from change. If the majority needed is 5:7, any value in the range O_3O_5, the end-points included, is immune from change, and so on. The lower diagram is easily constructed from the upper.

Number of members infinite. When the number of members in the committee is small, as in the above case, the size of majority in use can only alter by finite steps at a time, as from $4:7$ to $5:7$. The only real points on the curve are those corresponding to the points on the vertical axis $4/7$, $5/7$, $6/7$ and $7/7$; and the curve is discontinuous, being imaginary except at these values on the vertical axis.

If we were to attempt to introduce any measure of elasticity here, it would require to be a measure of 'arc elasticity'; but in Economics arc elasticity has proved difficult to work with and has

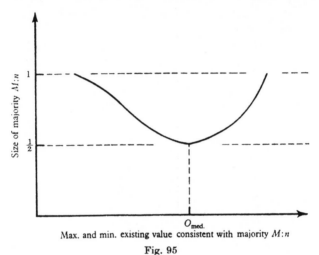

Max. and min. existing value consistent with majority $M:n$

Fig. 95

been very little used. For the case, therefore, in which the number of members is small, it would probably be desirable simply to leave the results in the form of a diagram without attempting to calculate any measure of elasticity.

When, however, we suppose the number of members in the committee to increase progressively, we add progressively to the number of values on the vertical axis at which the curve becomes real. If we also take it that these new members have a variety of different optima, the horizontal steps on the curve become shorter; and if the number of members and the number of optima become sufficiently great, the curve will tend to become smooth. In these circumstances we can employ a measure of 'point elasticity' similar to the one which has proved of use in Economics.

[102]

In the limit, when the number of members in the committee can be taken to be infinitely great, the type of curve shown in the lower part of Fig. 94 becomes a continuous smooth curve. In Fig. 95 a curve of this kind shows the minimum size of variable below $O_{med.}$, and the maximum size of variable above $O_{med.}$, consistent with a majority requirement $M:n$.

To show the meaning of this type of curve, in Fig. 96 we suppose that the same motions are before two different committees; and we suppose that the number of members in each committee and the number of their optima are sufficiently large to be regarded as infinite. The members' preference schedules in the case of one committee are different from those of the other, so that the curve

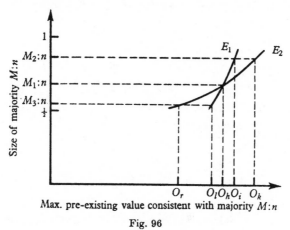

Fig. 96

derived for the one committee is E_1, for the other E_2. Only a portion of each curve above $O_{med.}$ is drawn. The two curves have a single point in common, corresponding to the size of majority $M_1:n$. For each curve a size of majority $M_1:n$ would leave the pre-existing values between some lower limit and O_h (including that at O_h) immune from change.

The curve E_2 is flatter and the curve E_1 more vertical. The significance of this is that if the majority requirement were to be raised above $M_1:n$, the range of values which, if they existed, would become immune from change would be more extensive for the curve E_2 than for E_1. For example, an increase in the majority requirement to $M_2:n$ would give immunity from change to an added range O_hO_k (including the value O_k) for the curve E_2, and would give immunity to the smaller range $O_h O_i$ (including the value O_i) for the curve E_1. The curve E_2 is said to be more elastic than E_1 with a changing size of majority, and the curve E_1 to be more rigid.

Going in the reverse direction, a reduction in the majority requirement from $M_1:n$ to $M_3:n$, in the case of the curve E_2, would leave open to change the greater range of existing values $O_r O_h$ (excluding the value O_r), and in the case of E_1 would leave open to change the smaller range of existing values $O_l O_h$ (excluding the value O_l).

The coefficient of elasticity when the variable is measurable. As in Economics we can calculate the numerical measure for the elasticity of such a curve at every point on it. We can define the elasticity (e) of the decision with a changing size of majority as being equal to, on the left-hand branch of the curve,

$$\frac{-dx/x}{\dfrac{d(M/n)}{M/n}} = \frac{-dx/x}{dM/M}$$

(since n is a constant), where x is the lowest value of the variable consistent with the majority $M:n$; and on the right-hand branch of the curve we define the elasticity of the decision with a changing size of majority to be equal to

$$\frac{+dx/x}{dM/M}$$

The meaning of this coefficient. For values at or above $O_{\text{med.}}$, $e = 1$ corresponds to circumstances in which an increase by 1% in the size of the majority required gives rise to immunity from change to values equal to an additional 1% of the maximum size of the variable already immune. Other sizes of e, and the case for values at or below $O_{\text{med.}}$, can be similarly interpreted, with, of course, the same qualifications in regard to 'point elasticity' as in Economics.

Pursuing the example of Economics we may, if we choose, refer to a curve or a portion of a curve that has an elasticity greater than 1 at every point on it as being elastic, and a portion of a curve for which at every point elasticity is less than 1 as being rigid. This step takes one value of the coefficient, namely unity, as the critical case and separates out the possible curves into one or other of two classes by reference to unity as the dividing value.

When we put $e = 1$ in the above equations and integrate, taking the *minus* sign we get

$Mx/n = K_1$, where n is a constant and K_1 an arbitrary constant; and taking the *plus* sign we get

$M/n = K_2 x$, where K_2 is an arbitrary constant.

These two equations represent respectively a family of rectangular hyperbolas and a family of straight lines; and by superimposing the two sets of curves on the diagram, after the manner of Marshall,* it could be seen at a glance whether the elasticity at any point on a given curve was greater than or less than unity. But whereas in Economics, because of the different behaviour of total

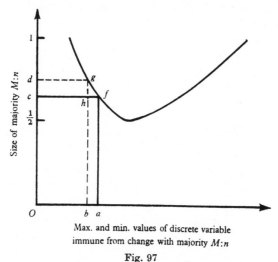

Max. and min. values of discrete variable
immune from change with majority $M:n$

Fig. 97

producers' receipts according as e is greater or less than unity, there is the best of practical reasons for selecting $e = 1$ as the critical case, in the theory of committee decisions there is no reason of a practical kind for making such a distinction and giving special importance to this particular value of e.

A non-measurable variable. When the variable representing the motions on the horizontal axis is discrete, with a committee consisting of a small number of persons, each with a single-peaked preference curve, exactly the same treatment applies as for the case in which the variable is measurable. Thus Fig. 94 above applies in either case.

When the variable representing the motions is discrete and the number of members in the committee can be regarded as infinite,

---

* Alfred Marshall, *Principles of Economics*, 8th ed., pp. 839-40.

each having a single-peaked preference curve, the geometrical equivalent of the preceding equations would still apply. Thus for the curve of Fig. 97 the elasticity of the committee's decision with a changing size of majority on the left-hand branch of the curve would be defined as

$$\lim_{cd \to 0} -\frac{ba/Oa}{cd/Oc},$$

and on the right-hand branch of the curve a corresponding fraction with the *plus* instead of the *minus* sign.

But when we are dealing with a discrete variable, only the relative position of points on the horizontal axis has significance, not the absolute position. There is no single numerical measure attaching to the length Oa or ba. The ratio in the numerator is without definite numerical meaning and no numerical significance would attach to the coefficient e.

2. When the members' preference curves are subject to no restriction

Two examples. The same system of ideas applies and the elasticity of the committee's decision with a changing size of majority can be shown by reference to the matrix.

EXAMPLE 1. Given the group of schedules of Fig. 98, we can write down from the accompanying matrix, the maximum size of majority against each motion.

The maximum number of votes against a_1 is $5:5$ when a_1 is placed against a_3. If a_1 were the existing value, even though a unanimous verdict were required against it, a_1 would still be defeated.

The maximum number of votes against a_2 is $3:5$. Provided that a $4:5$ majority is needed before any motion can defeat an existing value, a_2, if it were the existing value, would remain undefeated. And we can deal similarly with the other values.

The information can be summarized thus:

Motion	Maximum size of majority against the motion	Minimum size of majority which would leave the motion undefeated
a_1	$5:5$	—
a_2	$3:5$	$4:5$
a_3	$4:5$	$5:5$
a_4	$2:5$	$3:5$

Fig. 100 is the diagram constructed from the table. a_4 would remain unchanged when the majority needed against it was 3:5 or higher, a_2 and a_3 when the majorities needed were 4:5 and 5:5

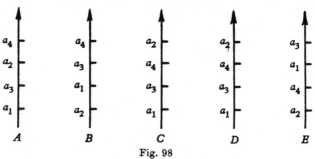

Fig. 98

Matrix for Fig. 98

		(against)		
	a_1	a_2	a_3	a_4
a_1	0	(2, 3)	(0, 5)	(1, 4)
a_2	(3, 2)	0	(3, 2)	(2, 3)
a_3	(5, 0)	(2, 3)	0	(1, 4)
a_4	(4, 1)	(3, 2)	(4, 1)	0

(for)

Fig. 99

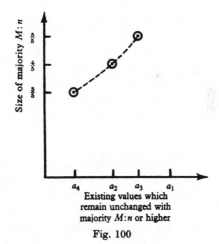

Fig. 100

respectively. a_1 is shown on the horizontal axis of Fig. 100, but there is no corresponding point on the curve, since the maximum size of majority that could be stipulated would still leave it open to defeat.

EXAMPLE 2. Given the group of schedules of Fig. 90, p. 97, and the corresponding matrix, construct the curve showing the elasticity of the committee's decision with a changing size of majority.

From the matrix we get the following table and Fig. 101:

Motion	Maximum size of majority against the motion	Minimum size of majority which would leave the motion undefeated
a_1	4:9 (minority)	5:9
a_2	5:9	6:9
a_3	7:9	8:9
a_4	6:9	7:9
a_5	6:9	7:9
a_0	8:9	9:9

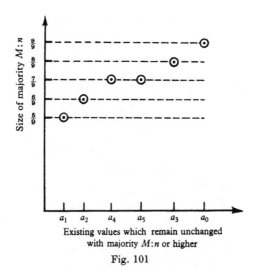

Existing values which remain unchanged
with majority $M:n$ or higher

Fig. 101

It will be observed that, when the members' preference curves are single-peaked, the curve showing elasticity of the committee's decision with a changing size of majority is U-shaped. When the members' preference curves are not single-peaked the diagram is best indicated as a series of points rising from left to right.

CHAPTER XIV

THE ELASTICITY OF COMMITTEE DECISIONS WITH ALTERATIONS IN THE MEMBERS' PREFERENCE SCHEDULES*

1. When the members' preference curves are single-peaked†

The problem stated. To illustrate the type of problem that we wish to consider, we may take the example of a cartel in which price-fixing is done once a year by a committee which uses a simple majority. Let us suppose that at a meeting of this committee, the basic phenomena (the demand for its product and its cost position) leave the position of each firm identical with what it had been at the last annual meeting. The preference schedule of each firm in regard to price will be identical with its preference schedule of the previous year. Unless some new source of change is introduced, the same price as before will be selected. One or more of the firms, we may suppose, are pondering the chance of being able to influence the decision of the cartel by inducing others, through enticement or threat, to alter their voting behaviour at the next meeting of the committee. The enticement may be the offer of some trading or business advantage, or the threat may be to leave the cartel and enter into competition with the remaining members. We wish to examine and, if possible, to measure the effect on the committee's decision when some of the members alter their voting.

Number of members odd. In the example of the cartel let us suppose that there are seven firms, A, B, ..., G, voting on price, each with a single-peaked scale of preferences. When each voted in accordance with its scale of preferences the decision accepted would be O_4, corresponding to the median optimum (see upper part of Fig. 102). Now if a firm whose optimum is above O_4 is considering the extent of the change in the committee's decision which it can secure by inducing a voting alteration on the part of one or more other firms, it is clear that it must bring about this alteration on the part of a firm whose optimum is at or below O_4; because,

---

* The reader who is unacquainted with Economics should omit this chapter.

† The theory holds whether the committee follows the ordinary procedure (α) or either of the other procedures (β) or (γ) defined on pp. 21–4 above.

even though the firms E, F, G should alter their voting behaviour, voting as they would have done had their optima been further to the right of O_4, nevertheless, the decision accepted by the committee would still remain O_4. The requirement to secure a rise in the price fixed by the committee, is that one or more of the firms A, B, C, D should alter their manner of voting: to raise the decision of the committee above O_4, they will have to vote as if their optima lay above O_4.

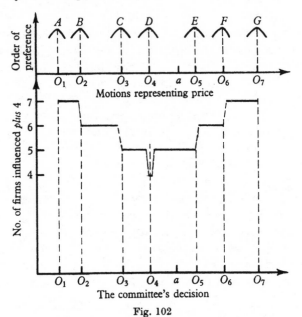

Fig. 102

If, however, any one of these four firms could be induced to vote as if its optimum lay in the range between O_4 and O_5, for example, to vote as if its optimum were at the point a shown in Fig. 102, then the point a would become the decision of the committee. Even though one of the firms A, B, C, D should vote as if its optimum were higher than O_5, no higher price would be adopted by the committee than if it had voted as if its optimum were at O_5, because O_5 would still be the median optimum.

Thus a firm whose optimum lies at or above O_5 can alter the decision of the committee to the point a, where $O_4 < a \leqslant O_5$, by inducing one firm whose optimum lies below O_5 to vote as if it had an optimum at a.

To bring into existence a decision higher than O_5, it is sufficient if two of the firms whose optima lie at or below O_5 are induced to vote as if their optima lay at some point between O_5 and O_6. By getting two of the firms A, B, C, D, E to vote as if they had common optima at the point b, say, where $O_5 < b \leqslant O_6$, the committee's decision can be altered from O_4 to b.

Similarly, the committee's decision can be brought to the point c, where $O_6 < c \leqslant O_7$, if three of the firms with optima below O_7 can be brought to vote as if they had common optima at c.

If a firm with optimum below O_4 wishes to move the committee decision from O_4 to some lower point, corresponding conclusions will apply.

The effect produced on the committee decision by influencing the voting behaviour of 1, 2, 3 firms, so that they vote as if they had common optima, is represented in the lower part of Fig. 102. In it, along the horizontal axis, the decision of the committee is shown, and along the vertical axis 4 *plus* the number of firms whose voting behaviour must be altered in order to produce the result shown on the horizontal axis. This diagram is a summary of the entire position. It is to be read in conjunction with our finding that if the decision of the committee is to be raised to the point h, say, where $h > O_{\frac{1}{2}(n+1)}$, the members whose voting behaviour must be influenced will be those with optima below h; or, if the decision is to be altered to a point k, where $k < O_{\frac{1}{2}(n+1)}$, the members influenced must have optima above k.

In drawing the diagram our supposition is that the members influenced to alter their voting behaviour vote as if they all have their optima at a common point. In practice this might not be so, and the members may be influenced so that they vote as if their optima were displaced and located at different points on the horizontal axis. The effect which this produces in altering the decision of the committee could then be got by comparing the median optimum among the final curves with the original position of the median optimum.

Number of members even. Let us suppose that there are six members in the committee, with optima situated as in the upper part of Fig. 103; and let B be the chairman. The decision of the committee, if the members voted in accordance with the preference curves shown, would be O_3.

The members A and B can bring the decision of the committee to any point between O_2 and O_3 (the point O_2 included), provided they can induce one of the other members to vote as if his optimum lay at this point.

A can bring the committee's decision to any point between O_1 and O_2 (the point O_1 included), provided he can induce B, the chairman, and any one of the other members C, D, E, F to vote as

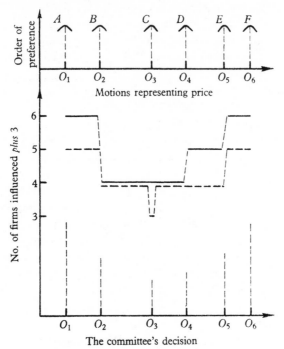

The broken curve applies if B, the chairman, is among the members influenced. The continuous curve applies if B is not among the members influenced.

Fig. 103

if they had their optima at this point; or if he is unable to influence B, provided he can induce any three of the members C, D, E, F to vote as if their optima lay at this point. Influencing two members other than B to vote as if their optima lay at a point between O_1 and O_2 would not be sufficient to make this point the decision of the committee; because there would then be three optima effective to the left of B's optimum O_2, and three effective at or above O_2. With B as chairman this would leave O_2 as the decision.

To raise the committee's decision to a point between O_3 and O_4 (O_4 included), it would be sufficient to induce one of the members A, B or C to vote as if his optimum lay at such a point.

To raise the decision to a point between O_4 and O_5 (O_5 included), it would be sufficient to induce any two of the members A, C or D to vote as if their optima lay there, or to induce B alone to vote as if his optimum lay there.

The decision could be brought to any point between O_5 and O_6 (O_6 included) by inducing either three of the members A, C, D, E to vote as if their optima lay there, or by inducing one of these members and B to vote as if their optima lay there.

The position is set out in the lower part of Fig. 103, where the decision adopted by the committee is shown along the horizontal axis, and along the vertical axis we show 3 *plus* the number of members influenced. To the left of the chairman's optimum, and again to the right of O_4, the curve is double-branched, and the branch which applies depends on whether or not the chairman has been among the members influenced. When the chairman has been influenced it is the curve shown as a broken line which applies.

Two types of case. Sometimes it would be possible to apply the theory to compare the movement as between one recorded decision of the committee and another; or the theory may cover the phenomena in which there is only a single recorded decision. For example, trade union representatives who are deciding on hours of labour or wage rates, may be influenced late in the meeting, after their preference schedules have already been formed, by another speaker; and their preference schedules may be formed anew. The comparison used by our theory now would be, not between one recorded decision and another, but between the decision reached after this speaker has addressed them and the decision which would have been reached had the representatives voted before his speech was made. Similarly, the theory would apply where a member was addressing parliament late in the debate and influencing the preference schedules, as so far formed, of the other members of the house. The comparison would be between the decision reached in a vote after the member's speech has influenced the preference schedules of the members, and the decision which would have been reached in a vote before his speech was made.*

* Like the firms in the cartel, the members of parliament can influence the decision by preaching 'not to the converted but to the unconverted'.

An explanation in common-sense terms. Let us consider further the type of curve that appears in the lower part of Figs. 102 and 103. The properties of such a curve can be better examined from the instance shown in Fig. 104. In it, for simplicity, n is taken as odd.* From O_1 to the point a lying to the right of $O_{\frac{1}{2}(n+1)}$, the curve is comparatively rigid; and to the right of a is comparatively elastic. The significance of this is that if a member of the committee whose optimum is to the left of $O_{\frac{1}{2}(n+1)}$ (being, say, in the neighbourhood of O_1) is able to influence a given number of

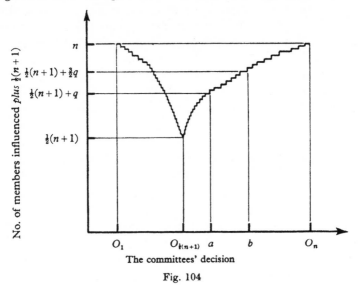

Fig. 104

members with optima to the right of $O_{\frac{1}{2}(n+1)}$, so that they vote as if their optima were lower than this, the decision of the committee would alter comparatively little. The same would be true of a member with optimum to the right of $O_{\frac{1}{2}(n+1)}$ (being, say, in the neighbourhood of O_n) as regards the first members whose voting he managed to influence; in the diagram he would have to influence q members to alter the committee's decision from $O_{\frac{1}{2}(n+1)}$ to a. But after this each increase in the number of members whose voting was influenced would bring a comparatively large change in the decision of the committee; and influencing an additional $\frac{1}{2}q$ members would shift the decision considerably to the right to b.

* This type of curve is, of course, only real for values corresponding to integers on the vertical axis. It is impossible to influence the fraction of a member.

If it were found readily possible to influence q members, the person instigating the change might exert himself strenuously to influence still more of them.

A case which may arise in practice is that in which the bulk of the members have optima lying towards the extremities of the range, and only a few have optima in the region between. The diagram would then tend to be like that shown in Fig. 105. In these circumstances there is a very precarious balance ready to swing violently in favour of whichever side manages to influence

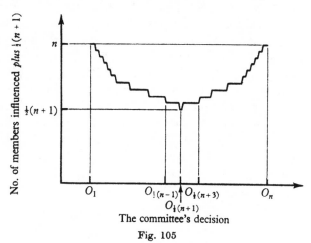

The committee's decision

Fig. 105

the voting of a few members with optima at $O_{\frac{1}{2}(n+1)}$ or beyond it. Mathematically it is of no consequence whether the members influenced are those with optima in the centre of the range or not; but the shift needed in *their* voting behaviour to alter the balance is less than that for other members, and in practice it might mainly be them who were subjected to inducement or threat. They would be in the position too to make the change less obtrusively than other members and they would run less risk of ostracism. Thus the small centre parties in a committee or coalition will sometimes be subject to extreme pressure from the wings; and at the same time they will sometimes hold the key to power. The diagram has possibilities that might have interested Machiavelli.

With the balance thus precarious, it would sometimes be easier for one of the parties of the extremities to bring about a change in his favour by introducing new members; or, less easy than this as

i

a rule, by eliminating some of the existing members. New allies with a community of interests would be more dependable than those whose support had to be won, and they might be cheaper. Strictly speaking, however, this consideration is extraneous to the present treatment in which the number of members is assumed constant.

The coefficient of elasticity. Let us now suppose that the number of members in the committee becomes sufficiently large, with their optima sufficiently evenly distributed, so that the type of curve of the lower part of Fig. 102 can be regarded as smooth, or the two curves of Fig. 103 can be regarded as smooth and coincident. And let us assume that the committee is discussing the size of some measurable variable such as price.

Granted this we can introduce an index of the shape of the curve at each point that will show the proportionate extent to which the committee's decision alters in response to a given increase in the proportion of members influenced. Let us denote the number of members influenced by N and the committee's decision by a. A suitable index to show the effect is

$$e = \pm \frac{da}{dy} \frac{y}{a},$$

where $\qquad y = \frac{1}{2}(n+1) + N$ for n odd $\quad (0 \leqslant N \leqslant \frac{1}{2}(n-1))$,

or $\qquad y = \frac{1}{2}n + N$ for n even $\quad (0 \leqslant N \leqslant \frac{1}{2}n)$;

the *plus* or *minus* sign to apply according as a is increasing or diminishing when N increases.* This is a measure of point elasticity similar to that used in Economics to show the alteration in quantity sold in response to an alteration in price.

If we chose we could take one value of the coefficient, namely, unity, as the critical case, and regard curves with elasticity less than unity as being rigid and those with elasticity greater than unity as being elastic. Cournot, the first economist to investigate the matter, saw that the case in which elasticity is equal to unity has an exact and important meaning when we are dealing with economic phenomena; but when we are dealing with committee decisions the case of unit elasticity does not have the same importance.

* We avoid choosing the coefficient $\pm \dfrac{da}{dN} \dfrac{N}{a}$, since elasticity would then always be equal to zero for $N = 0$ and $da/dN \neq \infty$.

[116]

The general interpretation of the index that we have given will be familiar from Economics. If for a particular point on a curve the measure of elasticity is, say, 2, then a 1% increase in y will give rise to an alteration of 2% in the size of the variable that represents the committee decision. Other values of the coefficient would be similarly interpreted. Also it is clear that, *ceteris paribus*, the greater the elasticity of a curve, the greater will be the inducement to some members of the committee to bring about alterations in the voting of others. The members who will be keenest to alter the voting will be those whose optima lie towards the extremities of the range. This is the practical significance of the coefficient and of the ideas underlying it.*

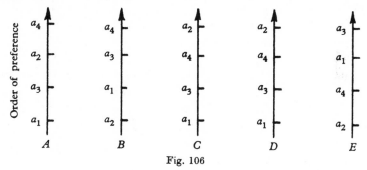

Fig. 106

Matrix for Fig. 106

		(against)			
		a_1	a_2	a_3	a_4
	a_1	0	(2, 3)	(0, 5)	(1, 4)
(for)	a_2	(3, 2)	0	(3, 2)	(2, 3)
	a_3	(5, 0)	(2, 3)	0	(1, 4)
	a_4	(4, 1)	(3, 2)	(4, 1)	0

Fig. 107

2. When the members' preference curves are subject to no restriction

The complexity of the mathematical problem. With the group of schedules of Fig. 106 and the corresponding matrix, the majority motion is a_4.

The problem is to examine the ease or difficulty with which some

---

* When the members' preference curves are single-peaked and the variable representing the motions is discrete, the same considerations will apply as have been set out in the previous chapter, pp. 105-6 above.

motion other than a_4 can be made the majority motion. The member C, for instance, prefers the motion a_2 to any other. This motion can get a majority over a_1 and a_3, but is defeated by a_4. In order to see how the member C might attempt to convert a_2 into the majority motion, we might place a_2 above a_4 on A's schedule of preference; or we might place a_2 at the top of B's scale instead of at the foot, interchanging the places of a_2 and a_4; or we might envisage the circumstances of the change as being that B is induced to place a_2 at the top of his scale, while a_4, a_3, a_1 follow in their present order. Or there might be interchange of places between a_2 and a_4 on E's scale; or a_4 might remain unchanged at third highest position on E's scale and a_2 be placed in a higher position. Or, still seeking to find under what conditions a_2 becomes the majority motion, some other rearrangement of motions on E's scale might be introduced.

Thus even with this simple group of preference schedules, the number of deformations of the scales by which the majority motion might be altered from a_4 to a_2 is quite great. The underlying mathematical problem appears to be one of some complexity; and this conclusion would be reinforced if we were to consider further examples.

The difference between the theory of this case and that in the preceding section of the chapter in which the members' curves were assumed to be single-peaked is that there we needed only to take into account the position on the horizontal scale of a member's optimum valuation, disregarding the remainder of his scale. The necessary and sufficient conditions for the solution of the problem were expressible in terms of optima alone. When the members' preference curves are not single-peaked, it is not sufficient to look to the optimum or highest values on their scales; the majority motion may be altered by inducing changes among the lower values on their scales; and the possible ways of inducing some prescribed change are multiplied. When the preference curves of the members are not single-peaked we are without the assistance of a powerful simplifying factor; and when we are forced to look to the entire preference schedules of some or of all of the members, the theory becomes involved and, at the present stage, would be too difficult to pursue further.

CHAPTER XV

THE CONVERSE PROBLEM: THE GROUP OF SCHEDULES TO CORRESPOND TO A GIVEN VOTING MATRIX

The problem stated, and some propositions. We have seen that given any set of preference schedules it is possible to obtain the corresponding matrix. The converse problem is: Given any matrix is it possible to find a corresponding set of schedules?

Let us suppose that we *have* found a group of schedules which corresponds to a given matrix. Then further groups of schedules could be got from this group by adding any number of schedules to it on which all of the motions concerned are ranked at the same level of preference. In the following discussion we exclude this trivial case from consideration and assume that on no schedule of the group are all the motions ranked at the same level.

It is obvious that the number of voters must be at least equal to the highest number got by adding together the figures on the left and right of any of the cells in the given matrix.

Proposition 1. *While it may not be possible to find a group of schedules for which the total number of voters is equal to the highest of the sums of the figures in any cell, it may be possible to find a group of schedules to correspond to the matrix if the total number of voters is greater than this.*

		(against)		
		a_1	a_2	a_3
	a_1	0	(1, 1)	(1, 1)
(for)	a_2	(1, 1)	0	(1, 1)
	a_3	(1, 1)	(1, 1)	0

Fig. 108

In the matrix of Fig. 108, the sum of the figures in each cell is 2 and the number of voters cannot be less than this. The matrix is symmetrical in a_1, a_2 and a_3, the figures in each of its cells being identical. But with only 2 voters, no arrangement on their schedules of three motions a_1, a_2 and a_3 exists which is symmetrical. Hence the matrix of Fig. 108 cannot arise from a group consisting of only 2 schedules.

The group of schedules of Fig. 109 with the 3 voters A, B and C is consistent with the given matrix.

Proposition 2 (the non-uniqueness theorem). A given voting matrix may be consistent with different groups of schedules.

a_1, a_2	a_2, a_3	a_3, a_1
a_3	a_1	a_2
A	B	C

Fig. 109

		(against)		
		a_1	a_2	a_3
	a_1	0	(14, 3)	(7, 10)
(for)	a_2		0	(6, 11)
	a_3			0

Fig. 110

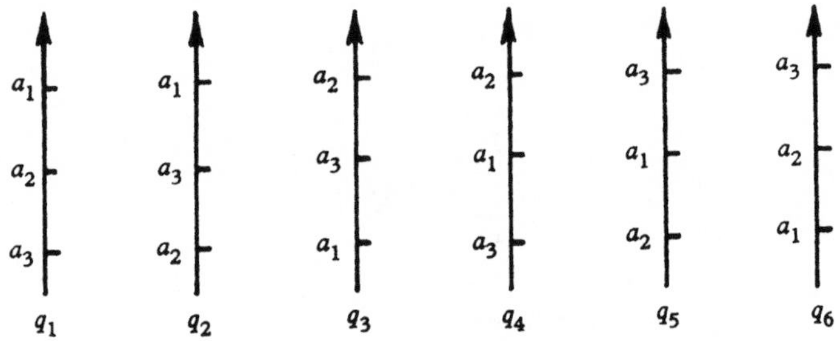

Fig. 111

Matrix for Fig. 111

		(against)		
		a_1	a_2	a_3
	a_1	0	$\left(\dfrac{q_1+q_2+q_5}{q_3+q_4+q_6}\right)$	$\left(\dfrac{q_1+q_2+q_4}{q_3+q_5+q_6}\right)$
(for)	a_2		0	$\left(\dfrac{q_1+q_3+q_4}{q_2+q_5+q_6}\right)$
	a_3			0

Fig. 112

It is enough to show an instance of this. Let us suppose that we are given the matrix of Fig. 110 and try to generate this matrix from the schedules of Fig. 111, in which there are no cases of motions marked at the same level of preference. The numbers of the schedules are taken to be $q_1, q_2, \ldots$, and they give rise to the matrix shown in Fig. 112.

Equating the figures in the two matrices we obtain

$$q_1 + q_2 + q_5 = 14, \tag{1}$$

$$q_3 + q_4 + q_6 = \ \ 3, \tag{2}$$

$$q_1 + q_2 + q_4 = \ \ 7, \tag{3}$$

$$q_3 + q_5 + q_6 = 10, \tag{4}$$

$$q_1 + q_3 + q_4 = \ \ 6, \tag{5}$$

$$q_2 + q_5 + q_6 = 11, \tag{6}$$

Addition of each of the first, second and third pairs of equations gives

$$q_1 + q_2 + q_3 + q_4 + q_5 + q_6 = 17,$$

so that there are really only four independent equations. We will take them to be (1), (2), (3) and (5). There are six unknowns, and solving for q_3, q_4, q_5, q_6 in terms of q_1, q_2 gives

$$q_3 = q_2 - 1,$$
$$q_4 = 7 - q_1 - q_2,$$
$$q_5 = 14 - q_1 - q_2,$$
$$q_6 = q_1 - 3.$$

Taking $q_1 = 3$, $q_2 = 4$ gives

$$q_3 = 3, \quad q_4 = 0, \quad q_5 = 7, \quad q_6 = 0.$$

Taking $q_1 = 4$, $q_2 = 2$ gives

$$q_3 = 1, \quad q_4 = 1, \quad q_5 = 8, \quad q_6 = 1.$$

These solutions provide two different groups of schedules corresponding to the given matrix, and there are others.

When seeking a group of schedules to correspond to a given matrix, the general procedure would be to write down the schedules corresponding to all the possible permutations of the motions on the schedules, including those in which motions are ranked at the same level, and to suppose that there are $q_1, q_2, \ldots$ schedules of each kind. This gives rise to a voting matrix in which $q_1, q_2, \ldots$ appear. Then equating the figures in the two matrices we attempt to solve for the unknowns $q_1, q_2, \ldots$. Since there cannot be either a fractional or a negative number of voters, the solution obtained will only be admissible if the values got are integral and positive (or zero).

[121]

If there are only two motions involved, a_1 and a_2, a determinate and unique group of schedules can always be found. For instance, given the matrix of Fig. 113, let the corresponding group of schedules be those of Fig. 114.

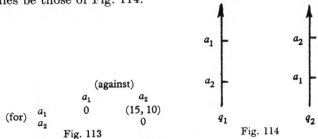

	(against)	
	a_1	a_2
(for) a_1	0	(15, 10)
a_2		0

Fig. 113

Fig. 114

These schedules give the matrix:

	(against)	
	a_1	a_2
(for) a_1	0	(q_1, q_2)
a_2		0

Fig. 115

which yields the solution $q_1 = 15$, $q_2 = 10$.

When there are three motions, let the given matrix be that of Fig. 116. For the schedules of Fig. 117, the voting would be as follows:

	(against)		
	a_1	a_2	a_3
(for) a_1	0	(28, 27)	(26, 0)
a_2		0	(25, 0)
a_3			0

Fig. 116

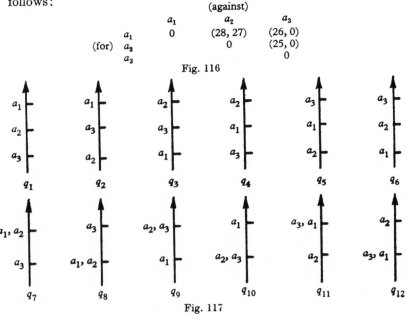

Fig. 117

a_1 against a_2,

$$q_1 + q_2 + q_5 + q_{10} + q_{11} : q_3 + q_4 + q_6 + q_9 + q_{12};$$

a_1 against a_3,

$$q_1 + q_2 + q_4 + q_7 + q_{10} : q_3 + q_5 + q_6 + q_8 + q_9;$$

a_2 against a_3,

$$q_1 + q_3 + q_4 + q_7 + q_{12} : q_2 + q_5 + q_6 + q_8 + q_{11}.$$

Equating these expressions to the appropriate figures in the cells of the matrix gives:*

$$q_1 + q_2 + q_5 + q_{10} + q_{11} = 28, \tag{1}$$

$$q_3 + q_4 + q_6 + q_9 + q_{12} = 27, \tag{2}$$

$$q_1 + q_2 + q_4 + q_7 + q_{10} = 26, \tag{3}$$

$$q_3 + q_5 + q_6 + q_8 + q_9 = 0, \tag{4}$$

$$q_1 + q_3 + q_4 + q_7 + q_{12} = 25, \tag{5}$$

$$q_2 + q_5 + q_6 + q_8 + q_{11} = 0. \tag{6}$$

These equations are consistent whatever the numbers on the right-hand sides may be. There is the further requirement, however, that the value obtained for each unknown must be integral and positive (including zero); and if no solution of this kind exists, there is no group of schedules corresponding to the given matrix.

From equations (4) and (6) above, taken in conjunction with this condition, we get

$$q_2 = q_3 = q_5 = q_6 = q_8 = q_9 = q_{11} = 0.$$

$$q_1 + q_{10} = 28, \tag{i}$$

$$q_4 + q_{12} = 27, \tag{ii}$$

$$q_1 + q_4 + q_7 + q_{10} = 26, \tag{iii}$$

$$q_1 + q_4 + q_7 + q_{12} = 25. \tag{iv}$$

There are now five unknowns and four equations. But if all the unknowns are to be positive, equations (i) and (iii) are incompatible and also equations (ii) and (iv). Hence there is no corresponding group of schedules and the matrix of Fig. 116 could not arise in practice.

The same treatment could be extended to the case of four or more motions, and this establishes our main conclusion:

* If the total number of voters is known, a further equation is added.

Proposition 3. *When there are more than two motions before a committee there may be no group of schedules from which a given matrix could be derived.*

The further step would be to investigate the necessary and sufficient conditions for the existence of a real group of schedules which will correspond to any given matrix, i.e. to establish an Existence Theorem. We ourselves will not attempt this.

EXAMPLE. The schedules of Fig. 118 correspond to single-peaked curves with plateaus on top, when the ordering of the points on the horizontal axis is a_1, a_2, a_3, a_4. Examine whether any values can be found for q_1, ..., q_9 so as to yield the cyclical majorities $a_1a_2a_3a_1$ and $a_1a_3a_4a_1$.

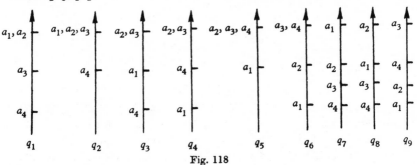

Fig. 118

When the matrix is formed the figures in the cells (a_1, a_2), (a_2, a_3), (a_3, a_1) respectively become

$$(q_7 \qquad\qquad\qquad : q_3+q_4+q_5+q_6+q_8+q_9),$$
$$(q_1+q_7+q_8 \qquad\quad : q_6+q_9),$$
$$(q_3+q_4+q_5+q_6+q_9 : q_1+q_7+q_8).$$

The cyclical majority $a_1a_2a_3a_1$ would require that

$$q_7 \qquad\qquad\qquad > q_3+q_4+q_5+q_6+q_8+q_9, \qquad (1)$$
$$q_1+q_7+q_8 \qquad\quad > q_6+q_9, \qquad\qquad\qquad\qquad (2)$$
$$q_3+q_4+q_5+q_6+q_9 > q_1+q_7+q_8. \qquad\qquad\quad (3)$$

But granted the inequality (1)

$$q_1+q_7+q_8 \geqslant q_7$$
$$> q_3+q_4+q_5+q_6+q_8+q_9$$

which is incompatible with (3).

Hence no values can be found for the unknowns which give rise to the cyclical majority $a_1a_2a_3a_1$.

[124]

Similarly, it can be shown that the attempt to form the cyclical majority $a_1 a_3 a_4 a_1$ gives rise to inequalities which are incompatible. Indeed for a group of curves which are single-peaked with plateaus on top, the transitive property holds (page 31 above) and no cyclical majorities can arise.

CHAPTER XVI

A COMMITTEE USING A SIMPLE MAJORITY: COMPLEMENTARY MOTIONS

The meaning of complementarity. In Economics, if the price that a person is willing to pay for a given quantity of one good depends on the quantity of another good that he expects to possess, the two goods are said to be complementary, in relation to his valuations.

Similarly, in the theory of committees, if a member's ranking of the motions on one topic depends on the arrangement that he expects to be in force in regard to another topic, the motions are said to be complementary in relation to his valuations. For instance, if the proposals put forward on one topic (denoted by a) are a_1, a_2, a_3 and a_4, a member's order of preference in regard to these proposals may depend on which arrangement, say b_1 or b_2, he expects to be in force on another topic. If he expects b_1 to be in force, he would rank the a's in the order, say, $a_2 a_4 a_1 a_3$; while if he expects b_2 to be in force, his ranking would be $a_4 a_3 a_1 a_2$. Or, vice versa, the b arrangement which he would prefer, may depend on the arrangement which he expects to be in force on the topic a.

There is no doubt that, whether in politics or economics, complementary valuation is the rule and independent valuation the exception.

Partial schedules of preference. Let us suppose that the proposals put forward on two topics (or the arrangements envisaged by a person as possibly existing on these topics) are a_1, a_2, a_3, a_4 and b_1, b_2, b_3 respectively. And let us suppose that if the member expects b_1 to be adopted, he ranks the a's in the order $a_1 a_2 a_3 a_4$; if b_2 to be adopted, in the order $a_2 a_3 a_1 a_4$; if b_3 to be adopted, in the order $a_3 a_1 a_2 a_4$. Then his valuations of the a's are as shown in Fig. 119, where the arrangement he expects on the second topic is shown at the foot of the schedule.

Similarly, let the individual's ranking of the b's, according to the a that he expects to be in force, be as shown in Fig. 120.

These two diagrams give the *partial schedules* for the individual concerned. When we are given h values of the type a, and k values of the type b, in all there are $h + k$ partial schedules containing $2hk$ values.

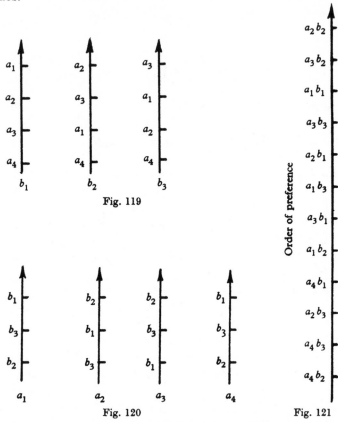

Fig. 119

Fig. 120

Fig. 121

From Fig. 119 we see that the most-preferred value of (a, b) for the member in question is $a_1 b_1$ or $a_2 b_2$ or $a_3 b_3$, the values at the top of these schedules; while from the third schedule of Fig. 120 we see that he places $a_3 b_3$ below $a_3 b_2$. We can deduce, therefore, that his most-preferred value of (a, b) is either $a_1 b_1$ or $a_2 b_2$, or else that these two values stand together at the top of his preferences if he is indifferent between them. We could have got the same information by looking first to Fig. 120 and then to Fig. 119.

The complete schedule of preferences. The partial schedules do not give the member's complete ranking of all of the values (a, b), but this information would be provided by the *complete schedule* of preferences of the individual. For the individual with whom we have been concerned the complete schedule of preferences might be that of Fig. 121. It will be seen that the partial

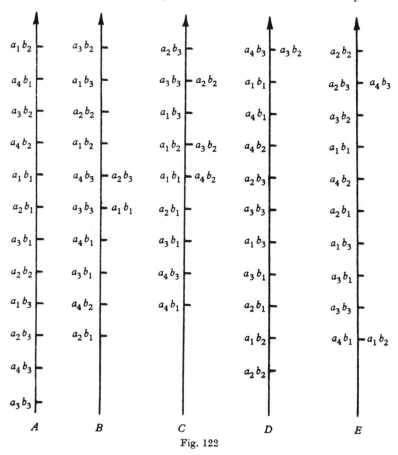

Fig. 122

schedules of Figs. 119 and 120 may be got by giving b the values b_1, b_2, b_3 and a the values a_1, a_2, a_3, a_4 in turn. The complete schedule provides all of the information contained in the partial schedules and other information as well.

Committee voting on a and b alternately: number of motions finite. We will suppose that the committee procedure in use is one in which values of a and b are voted on alternately; using a simple majority, the committee first chooses an arrangement on the topic a, then an arrangement on the topic b. And we will examine what will happen if it then goes on to vote again in regard to the topic a, in regard to the topic b, and so on.

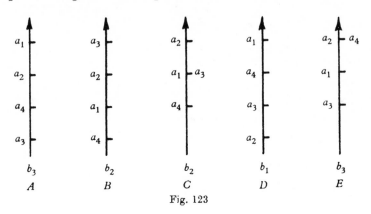

Fig. 123

Matrix for Fig. 123

		(against)			
		a_1	a_2	a_3	a_4
	a_1	0	(2, 3)	(3, 1)	(4, 1)
(for)	a_2	(3, 2)	0	(3, 2)	(3, 1)
	a_3	(1, 3)	(2, 3)	0	(2, 3)
	a_4	(1, 4)	(1, 3)	(3, 2)	0

Fig. 124

Let the committee consist of the five members A, B, C, D, E, with complete preference schedules as shown in Fig. 122. Let us also take it that the member A expects that the arrangement that will be reached in regard to the topic b will be b_3; that B expects b_2; C expects b_2; D expects b_1; and E expects b_3. If so, the schedules in reaching a decision on the topic a become those of Fig. 123. From the corresponding matrix we see that a_2 would be the proposal adopted.

If the members expect the decision a_2 to persist, and the committee proceeds to select a value of b, the scales of the members become those of Fig. 125 and b_2 would be the motion adopted.

Now, having selected b_2, the committee might proceed to vote again on the first topic. This time, if each member took for granted

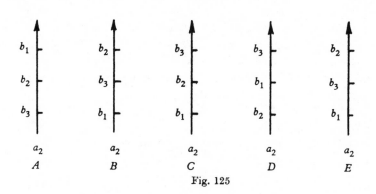

Fig. 125

Matrix for Fig. 125

		(against)		
		b_1	b_2	b_3
	b_1	0	(2, 3)	(1, 4)
(for)	b_2	(3, 2)	0	(3, 2)
	b_3	(4, 1)	(2, 3)	0

Fig. 126

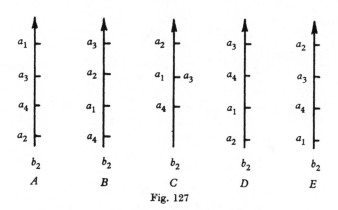

Fig. 127

Matrix for Fig. 127

		(against)			
		a_1	a_2	a_3	a_4
	a_1	0	(2, 3)	(1, 3)	(3, 2)
(for)	a_2	(3, 2)	0	(2, 3)	(3, 2)
	a_3	(3, 1)	(3, 2)	0	(5, 0)
	a_4	(2, 3)	(2, 3)	(0, 5)	0

Fig. 128

that b_2 was to be the proposal adopted on the other topic, their schedules of preference in relation to the a's would be as in Fig. 127; and a_3 would be the decision adopted.

If each member of the committee now expected the arrangement a_3 to be maintained on this topic, their partial schedules in relation to b would be those of Fig. 129; and the decision arrived at by a further vote on the second topic would remain b_2. Thus granted the total schedules and expectations of the members were as stated, the arrangement (a_3, b_2) would be reached at the end of three votes; and once reached it would not be departed from. It would be a position of stable equilibrium. Such positions of stable equilibrium, however, as can be shown by the geometrical treatment, only arise provided the members' preference schedules satisfy certain conditions.

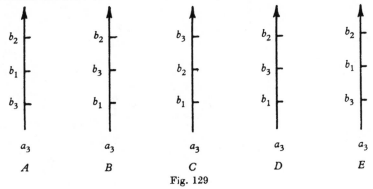

Fig. 129

Matrix for Fig. 129

(against)

		b_1	b_2	b_3
	b_1	0	$(0, 5)$	$(2, 3)$
(for)	b_2	$(5, 0)$	0	$(4, 1)$
	b_3	$(3, 2)$	$(1, 4)$	0

Fig. 130

There may be no majority motion. In the above example a majority motion exists at each stage. When no majority motion exists, we could still deduce the result of the voting at any stage, provided we also knew the order in which the motions were put.

More than two variables. The extension of the treatment to complementary valuation with the number of motions finite and more than two variables will be fairly obvious.

[130]

Number of motions infinite: the geometrical representation of preferences. When there are two variables a and b, each taking an infinite number of values, a member's valuations can be represented by a three-dimensional figure whose third axis shows order of preference. When there are three variables a four-dimensional figure is needed, and so on. Even three-dimensional figures, however, are difficult to work with; and when we are dealing with two variables it may be more convenient to represent a person's orderings of the different choices (a, b) by means of indifference curves. A fairly full treatment has been given elsewhere, and we will only refer briefly to some of the main results.*

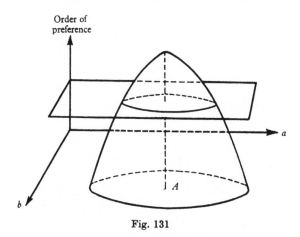

Fig. 131

Let us suppose that a member's valuations in regard to (a, b) are represented by the single-peaked hump of Fig. 131. The point A in the a-b plane, corresponding to the peak of the hump, gives the most preferred value for the member.

A horizontal plane will intersect this hump in a contour line; and the member concerned will be indifferent as between all points on the contour, since they are at the same level of preference. That is, the contour, or its projection on to the base plane, is an indifference curve for the member.

Other contours can be got by varying the height of the horizontal plane which makes the intersection with the hump; and it can be seen that as between any two such contours drawn in the a-b plane

* Cf. Duncan Black and R. A. Newing, *Committee Decisions with Complementary Valuation* (William Hodge and Co., 1951).

(Fig. 132), the individual will prefer any point lying on the inner contour to any point lying on the outer contour. Or, in general, given a hump of this shape, the individual will prefer any point lying inside a contour to any point on the contour; and will prefer any point on the contour to any point lying outside it.

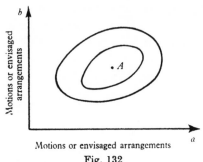

Fig. 132

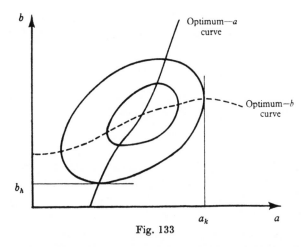

Fig. 133

The curves of optimum-a and optimum-b for the individual. If the value of b is given, say $b = b_h$, the most preferred value of a for the member concerned will be that lying on the innermost contour which he can reach, consistently with $b = b_h$. This will be given by drawing the horizontal through $b = b_h$, finding the in-difference contour which this horizontal just touches, and taking the a-coordinate of the point of contact (cf. Fig. 133). It follows that the locus of points at which tangents to the contours are

[132]

horizontal provides the optimum value of a corresponding to any given value of b. We denote this locus in any diagram by a continuous line, and we refer to it as *the curve of optimum-a* for the member concerned.

In the same way, given any value of a, say $a = a_k$, the optimum value of b for the member will be given by the point of contact of the vertical through $a = a_k$, with one of his indifference contours. As a varies, this point of contact will trace out the *optimum-b curve* for the member, from which we can get his most preferred value of b corresponding to any given a. We denote this curve in the diagrams by a broken curve.

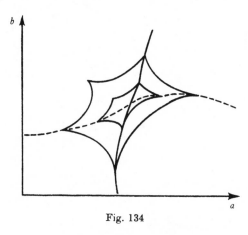

Fig. 134

It is clear that the same line of argument applies even though the indifference contours are of more complicated shapes than those of Fig. 133. In effect the curve of optimum-a is given by joining all points at the extreme south of successive indifference contours, and then, when we pass through the point corresponding to the peak of the hump, continuing this in the curve that joins the points at the extreme north of the successive indifference contours. Similarly the optimum-b curve is given by joining points at the extreme west of the successive contours and continuing this in the curve which joins up points at the extreme east of the contours. For instance, the optimum-a and optimum-b curves respectively for Fig. 134 are as shown.

Committee voting on a and b alternately: the midmost curves of optimum-a and optimum-b. Let us consider a committee of three members, A, B and C; and let us suppose, as before, that the committee chooses values of a and b alternately, using a simple majority. To simplify the statement of the problem, we will suppose that when selecting any value of a, all of the members expect the already-existing value of b to remain in operation; and that when selecting any value of b they expect the existing value of a to remain in operation. Then if the first vote is taken in re-

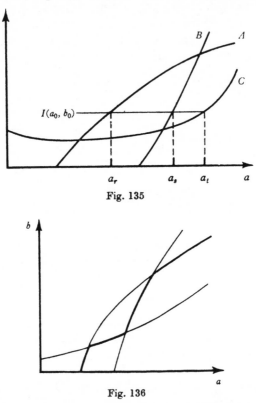

Fig. 135

Fig. 136

lation to a and the initial point from which the system starts is $I(a_0, b_0)$, through I draw a horizontal meeting the curves of optimum-a for the three members, in the points $a = \dot{a}_r, a = a_s, a = a_t$ respectively (see Fig. 135).

Now the further the value of a departs from the value $a = a_r$, the less preferred will it be to the member A; and similarly for a_s in relation to B and a_t in relation to C. In these circumstances the value of a chosen by a simple majority must be the middle one of these three values, namely, a_s. That is, the value of a chosen will be given by the midmost curve, at the height $b = b_0$. Thus in the diagram we need only have drawn that curve which is midmost in relation to the b-axis.

When the curves intersect, the midmost curve will consist of a number of segments of the different curves, as in Fig. 136; and we show this midmost curve as a heavy curve.

Moreover, the same argument holds whatever be the number of members in the committee, provided that when there is an even number of members the chairman's curve is counted twice, since he has a casting vote. Thus in any problem we need only show the midmost curve of optimum-a.

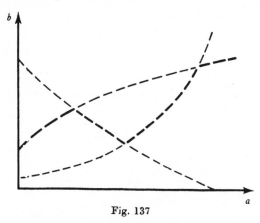

Fig. 137

Similarly, when given any value of a, the value of b that will be selected will be given by that one of the optimum-b curves which is midmost in relation to the a-axis. See the heavy broken curve of Fig. 137.

Committee voting on a and b alternately: the successive decisions arrived at. For a committee of any given size let the two midmost curves of optimum-a and optimum-b, respectively, be as shown in Fig. 138; and let the system start from the point $I(a_0, b_0)$, with the first vote taken on a, then a vote on b, followed by a vote on a, and so on.

The result of the first vote will be given by the point of intersection of the horizontal through I with the midmost curve of optimum-a, the point H in the diagram, because H can get a simple majority against any other point at the same height.

At the next vote all of the members, our assumption is, expect that the value of a will remain a_H. The value of b selected by the voting will be that corresponding to the point K, which is the point of intersection of the vertical line through H with the midmost curve of optimum-b; given $a = a_H$, the value $b = b_K$ can get a simple majority against any other.

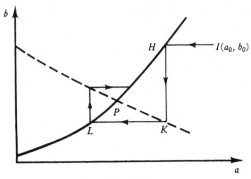

Fig. 138

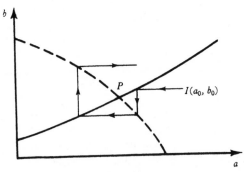

Fig. 139

In fact the course of the voting is I, H, K, L, ... as shown in the diagram, these points being reached successively; and it will be seen that the point P is approached by a converging spiral of votes, and would be reached a' the end of an infinite number of votes. Provided the system sta off sufficiently close to P, it is bound to approach always neare it, and, once reached, this position would not be departed from. P is a point of *stable equilibrium*.

On the other hand, for Fig. 139 and the starting point I there would be a spiral of votes diverging from P, and P is a position of *unstable equilibrium.* The conditions for convergence or divergence have been investigated in the monograph referred to.

A committee voting as between different values (a, b) simultaneously. Let us next consider a committee which again uses a simple majority, but which (instead of selecting a value of a, followed by a value of b, etc., as above) selects a value (a, b) from the various values put forward.

When a and b are discrete variables, the motions can be taken as (a_1, b_1), (a_1, b_2), ... and are finite in number; and the problem becomes the one which we have investigated earlier, in chapter VI.

When a and b are continuous variables, there are an infinite number of values a, each represented by a point on the horizontal axis; and an infinite number of values b, each represented by a

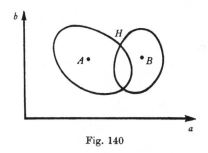

Fig. 140

point on the vertical axis; and the problem can be investigated geometrically. Which value (a, b), if any, will be able to get a simple majority against any other? Or, in other words, how do we pick out a majority motion?

We will deal only with the case of a committee of three members A, B and C say. Let us consider the conditions that must be satisfied by any point H in the plane, if H is to be a majority motion. Through H draw the indifference curves of the members A and B. Then if these contours are as in Fig. 140, they enclose a common area. Every point in this area is preferred by A to the point H, since it lies inside A's indifference contour through H; and similarly every point in the common area is preferred by B to the point H. Therefore any point in the area which is common to their indifference contours can get the votes of both A and B against H; and H cannot be a majority motion. Indeed, for any point H in the plane to be a majority motion the indifference curves of A and B passing through H must have no area in common, i.e.

they must touch at H. Thus the majority motion, if any, must lie on the locus of points of contact of the indifference contours of these two members. In Fig. 141 it must lie on the locus AB.

Likewise when we introduce the third member C, the majority motion, if any, must lie on the locus AC and on the locus CB. Thus

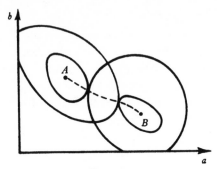

Fig. 141

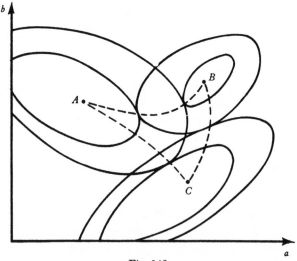

Fig. 142

a *necessary* condition for the existence of a majority motion is that it should be a point common to the three curves of contact of contours.

For the contours of Fig. 142 the three curves of contact have no point in common and there can be no majority motion.

[138]

Indeed, with smooth convex contours this condition can only be satisfied if the peak value of one member lies on the curve of contact of the contours of the other two members. Moreover, when this occurs it is a sufficient condition for the existence of a majority motion. For example, in Fig. 143 the peak value of the member C lies on the locus AB. The point C gets the votes of A and C against any point outside A's contour through C, and the votes of B and C against any point lying outside B's contour through C. That is, C can defeat any other point in the plane and is a majority motion.*

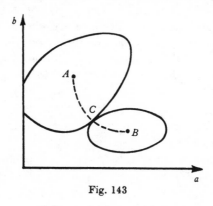

Fig. 143

When a and b are continuous variables, therefore, the conditions that must be satisfied before there can be any majority motion are highly restrictive. The frequency of occurrence of a majority motion as a fraction of the total number of cases possible (i.e. the probability of the existence of a majority motion), is infinitesimally small or 'practically zero'. And no doubt if the treatment were extended to three, four, ... variables, the probability of the existence of a majority motion would become still more negligible. It would also seem (though I cannot prove this) that the probability declines still further with an increase in the number of members in the committee.

* The case when the contours are other than smooth convex curves is dealt with in the monograph referred to, p. 131 above.

CHAPTER XVII

INTERNATIONAL AGREEMENTS, SOVEREIGNTY AND THE CABINET

Two advantages of a symbolic treatment. During recent years the public's knowledge of the nature of international agreements has been vastly extended by the displays and debates before the League of Nations and U.N.O.; and by this time most people have come to have an appreciation of the underlying realities of diplomacy. But the knowledge got in this way is intuitive and difficult to put into words; and on that account, difficult to communicate to others. We might hope, therefore, that the use of a symbolism would at least help to make explicit what people already know intuitively. If the symbolism were no more than a new mode of expression, finding readier terms for what we already know, it might still be worth getting.

Also since the end of the First World War there have been innumerable investigations by lawyers and historians on international relations, and a vast mass of factual information has been compiled. The difficulty about this information is that it lacks a general theoretic scheme to hold it together and in terms of which it could be interpreted; and for this reason again it seems worth while to see if anything can be achieved by a formal approach; it may help to explain the existing information and show what additional information ought to be collected.

International conferences and their procedure. In the theory we give we shall disregard international organizations, which sometimes reach their decisions by a simple majority or a two-thirds majority, and concentrate on the case of international conferences. At an international conference agreement is reached only by a unanimous decision. Any country that dissented from the terms would be altogether unlikely to ratify them. We may take it, therefore, that the requirement in our committee is that there should be unanimity.

We may also assume that steps have been taken before the conference to find the amount of common ground between the nations. There may have been an exchange of notes, or exploratory discussions between the diplomats, which have revealed a desire on the part of the nations concerned to arrive at a common agreement on some particular issue. For this purpose the nations have met round the conference table.

During the conference, if we go by the usual practice, no hard-and-fast procedure will be in use to decide the order in which proposals will be discussed. It will rather be a matter of the countries bargaining among themselves, by twos and threes, and so on, in the search for some proposal that would be acceptable to all. And the chairman will be happy to place before the meeting any proposal that seems likely to get unanimous agreement.

If, in spite of repeated attempts, no proposal seems likely to be adopted, the chairman may put forward the proposal that appears to command more support than any other. Rejection of it may be taken as the signal that no agreement is possible, and that the search for a solution should, meantime, be abandoned.

That is the factual information we have about international conferences. We also know that international discussion is the stage for power politics; that behind the scenes there are promises and threats; and that 'horses are traded', or bargains struck, which do not call for mention in the conference room. The general effect is that the lesser nations swim in the wake of certain great powers, some attached to one and some attached to another; and the ostensible reaction of any small nation will be that of the great power to which it is attached.*

It will, therefore, be a close enough approximation to reality if we suppose that we have, say, four great powers A, B, C and D round the conference table, trying to sift the various proposals that have been put forward and to agree to accept one of them.

The requirement of unanimity ensures that all of the major powers 'benefit' from any change made. The proposal that the conference should be held may have been made for any of a variety

---

* For example, E. H. Carr in discussing the League Assembly quotes as a true description of the facts the remark of Signor Grandi that he 'never saw a dispute of any importance settled otherwise than by an agreement between the Great Powers' (*The Twenty Years Crisis*, p. 133). Pitman B. Potter, in the same connexion, ventures the opinion that 'the present situation—formal equality with actual inequality according to actual power and influence—is the best for all concerned' (*An Introduction to the Study of International Organisation*, p. 393). And Martin Wright, after considering a number of specific instances of international settlement, says 'The method throughout was the same: the Great Powers acting as a directorate' (Royal Institute of International Affairs pamphlet, *Power Politics*, p. 60).

of reasons. It may be that there has been a shift in the balance of power as between the countries A, B, C and D and that some of these countries, climbing to power, consider that the interests of their own nationals deserve fuller recognition than formerly; or, with the balance of power remaining unaltered, new topics arising out of, say, industrial development or technical invention, may seem to call for new regulations, and so on.

With nations climbing to power and demanding new treaties, or changes in the existing treaties, it seems fairly clear that *they* expect to draw benefit from such arrangements as are made; and also that they will not accept the new arrangements unless they consider that they further their own interests. (We take it without discussion that countries are in the main concerned with their own individual interests. While this is not invariably the case, it is a sufficient approximation to the truth for our present purposes.)

The requirement of unanimity at the conference before agreement can be reached, however, ensures that not only some but *all* the major powers shall draw benefit from whatever agreement is arrived at. To see this let us suppose that one of the countries concerned has declined in importance relatively to the others. While it may regret that the old order has changed, it will still be true that if it accepts any alteration in the pre-existing treaties or regulations, it does so because it expects to draw benefit from them.

It is complementary motions and circumstances which are at issue. Let us denote the new international environment by e_1, the old by e_0; and let us denote some new regulation by a_h. The nation might prefer (e_0, a_0) to (e_1, a_h), but may prefer (e_1, a_h) to (e_1, a_0). It is the value e_1 that it expects to be in force, not e_0; and because of this it would in these circumstances prefer a_h to a_0.

If, as we take it, the country is largely concerned with its private interests, it expects to benefit more from a_h than from a_0, though the 'benefit' may consist only of the avoidance of loss—e.g. the absence of hostile action and the non-observance of treaties on the part of the countries which are rising to power—and not in the reaping of fresh gains. The country's concurrence in the agreement is a form of adaptation to its new environment; it realizes that clinging too obdurately to the pre-existing treaties and regulations would unnecessarily worsen its own position in the future.

We conclude that each of the great powers that becomes a signatory to a treaty expects to draw benefit from it, either by obtaining fresh advantages or else by avoiding harm and weakness to its own position.

The theory in terms of straight-line schedules. Let us suppose that the conference has before it the five proposals which are represented by a_1, a_2, a_3, a_4 and a_5, while the existing state of affairs on the topic is designated a_0.

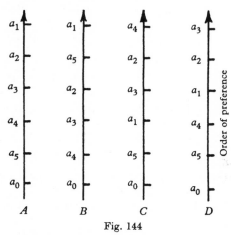

Fig. 144

Preference Matrix for Fig. 144

		(against)			
		a_1	a_2	a_3	a_4
	a_1	0	(2, 2)	(2, 2)	(3, 1)
(for)	a_2	(2, 2)	0	(3, 1)	(3, 1)
	a_3	(2, 2)	(1, 3)	0	(3, 1)
	a_4	(1, 3)	(1, 3)	(1, 3)	0

Fig. 145

Now no nation will accept a proposal unless it prefers it, albeit from force of circumstances, to the existing state of affairs, and the only proposals which it is worth our while discussing are those which all prefer to a_0. We may therefore take it that each of the proposals $a_1, \ldots, a_5$ stands higher on the preference schedule of each nation* than does a_0. This would be the case if the preference schedules of each nation were as in Fig. 144, in which the five proposals $a_1, \ldots, a_5$ stand above a_0 on each schedule; and the problem is: Which of these proposals, if any, will be adopted?

---

* The assumption is that the delegation for each nation has a definite schedule of preferences.

The proposal a_5 stands lower on each schedule than a_1. Rather than accept it each nation would accept a_1. We may therefore eliminate a_5 from consideration.

The attitudes of the nations towards the various proposals are further brought out in the preference matrix. There are two nations that prefer a_1 to a_2, two that prefer a_1 to a_3, and so on. Whatever the proposal under consideration, at least one of the nations would prefer some other proposal. Each nation will try to get the others to accept its view of what a reasonable solution would be. In economic language, each nation wants to attain the most-preferred position which is technologically open to it; and until it is persuaded that it is impossible for it to get its own first choice, its own second choice, etc., adopted, it will be unwilling to accept any other. The technological obstacles which exist to prevent a nation achieving a highly preferred position are imposed not by the laws of Physics or Chemistry, but by the wills of the other nations.

The process of reaching agreement will be one of compromise: new proposals will be put forward which stand at intermediate levels on the schedules; and some nations may give up their more-preferred solutions.

The geometrical treatment. The nature of the process of compromise and of arriving at agreement may become more intelligible from the geometrical treatment. Let us assume that, as in Fig. 146, each of the four nations has a single-peaked preference curve in relation to whatever proposals are put forward, when these proposals are ranged in a certain order on the horizontal axis.

For any agreement to be possible all four nations must prefer one or more of the proposals put forward to a_0, the existing state of affairs; and this condition will only be satisfied, with single-peaked curves, provided all of the curves, when drawn through a_0 as a point on the horizontal axis, rise on the same side of a_0. It would be satisfied in Fig. 146.

Since all four preference curves are down-sloping from O_1 leftwards, all four of the nations would prefer O_1 to any value lying to the left of O_1. Thus the agreement accepted cannot lie to the left of O_1; rather than accept any such agreement, all of them would accept O_1. Similarly, the agreement reached cannot lie to the right of O_4. The agreement reached, if any, therefore, must lie in O_1O_4. Each nation would prefer any point in this segment to the existing arrangement a_0 because over this segment each nation's preference curve is above the horizontal axis, whereas at a_0 it cuts the horizontal axis.*

Again, however, the earlier difficulty arises. Which point inside O_1O_4 is to be accepted? Each nation has its own most-preferred solution. Why should one of them, or a pair of them, give way to the others, and move away from the solutions which they prefer, to accommodate the others? Why should the solution be inside O_1O_2 rather than O_3O_4? After all, whichever proposal is adopted, every nation is going to benefit; and the statesmen attending the conference, in addition to their own ambitions, have behind them the pressure of public opinion in their own countries which expects them to be successful.

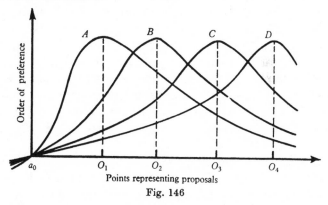

Fig. 146

Nor do these difficulties in bargaining arise only out of selfishness. We might have four nations which were complete altruists and acting from the highest of motives, one of them believing that O_1 is the genuinely best solution for all concerned, another believing that O_2 ought to be adopted, and so on. Each would feel in duty bound to promote a particular solution; and bargaining among a group of altruists might be scarcely less hard and hazardous than among a group of selfish nations—though admittedly it would take a different outward form and be accompanied by fewer of the signs of duplicity.

The real root of the difficulty in international relations is not that the nations are selfish, but that the solution to the problem is

* If, when drawn with a_0 as a common point, the curves rise from left to right, but x_1, the first point of intersection of a down-sloping curve with the horizontal axis, lies within O_1O_4 ($O_1 < x_1 < O_4$), the possible range of agreements becomes O_1x_1 (cf. Fig. 82).

indeterminate. Each nation knows that some of the solutions which it most prefers would also be an improvement on the existing state of affairs from the point of view of each of the other nations; it is a question not of which is going to benefit (in the sense explained above), but of which are going to reap the greater benefits and which the less; and a nation will not readily accept the view that it should reduce its claims in order that some of the others should benefit more. On the contrary, obstinacy, the forcing of others to give way, and duplicity in making concealed bargains with some of the other nations, become part of the attempt to obtain a more favourable solution.

The mathematical indeterminacy in the matrix and in the diagram, is the theoretical correlate of the real indeterminacy which exists at the conference table.

Compromise. Even without bargains being struck behind the scenes, agreement very often is reached, and this through compromise. In arriving at a compromise solution new proposals are put forward which, on the scales of the various nations, stand at levels intermediate to those of the earlier proposals; and this implies the suggestion that concessions be made by all of the nations.

To illustrate from Fig. 146, if the proposals most seriously under discussion are those corresponding to O_1 and O_2 and a compromise proposal a_h is put forward which we may imagine to leave the shape of the preference curve of each nation unaltered when a_h is represented by a point between O_1 and O_2 $(O_1 < a_h < O_2)$, this amounts to the proposal that A should yield some ground to B, C, and D while at the same time B, C and D yield ground to A.

If there is to be progress towards a compromise solution, all the nations must in fact be willing to reduce their claims. A picture of this part of the process might be that a nation signifies its willingness to accept any solution in the range ab, then in the range cd, and so on (Fig. 147). The nation concerned would in fact only speak of its willingness to accept a proposal at one extremity of this range, say the proposal d; but since it is indifferent as between the proposals c and d, which stand at the same level on its preference curve, from the point of view of theory this would entail a willingness to accept any proposal in the range cd.

So the search for a solution may go on, with fresh compromise proposals being put forward and with the efforts of the nations in

[146]

each of the groups whose interests are opposed, to induce those in the other group to extend the ranges within which they are willing to accept a compromise. And as soon as there is a single point of overlap between the compromise ranges for all of the nations concerned, agreement will have been reached.

Obstinacy and gambling for high gains. On the other hand, even for a situation such as that of Fig. 146, it is quite possible that no agreement will be reached. There are prizes to be won; and if they do not fall readily to skilful diplomacy, they may still be compelled by obstinacy. A nation may refuse to move from its more-preferred positions, in the hope that it may thereby force the others to make the concessions. They would get something from the agreement, it may argue, though less than they had hoped for. Conversely, it knows there are prizes to be lost by being too accommodating.

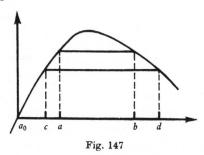

Fig. 147

But if two or more nations remain obstinate, no agreement at all may be reached. Then, in retrospect, the nation or nations concerned may look back on the conference as a gamble which had failed; but looked at prospectively, and perhaps up to the last minute, the gamble may have seemed worth while.

This gambling element explains a noticeable feature of international conferences, namely, that very frequently no agreement is reached until a conference has run almost its full term; and then in the closing hours, perhaps after weeks of waiting, there is a sudden change in the atmosphere and a series of agreements suddenly springs into being. This, one may presume, corresponds to the stage when some of the gambles are called off and a series of cross-bargains struck between the nations.

The two-dimensional treatment: two nations. To elaborate the above picture a little we now assume that each proposal,

L

instead of being valued as a single entity, is valued rather as something having two different aspects (as, for example, the proposal to lend a sum of money to a backward area, coupled with a proposal about the way in which the money will be spent). The valuations of any nation will then become a function of two variables instead of one.

When the conference is between only the two nations A and B, let their preferences be as shown by the indifference contours of Fig. 148, A being the optimum for one nation and B the optimum for the other, and AB the curve of contact of contours. Then the bargaining between them must take place along AB.

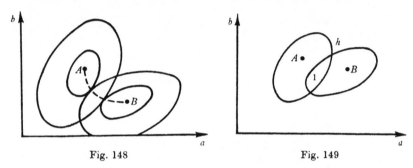

Fig. 148   Fig. 149

To show this let us suppose that the agreement reached between the two nations did not lie on the curve of contact, but lay instead at some other point h. Draw the contour for each nation passing through h (Fig. 149). These contours have the area 1 in common and each nation prefers any point in 1 to h. That is, both prefer any point in 1 to h, and h could not be the agreement reached. Thus any agreement reached must occur on the curve of contact of contours.

Now let us suppose that the existing state of affairs, before they begin to bargain, is represented by the point $I(a_0, b_0)$, and through I draw the contour for each nation. Then any agreement between the nations must lie in the segment $\alpha\beta$ shown in Fig. 150; for it must lie on the curve of contact of contours, and the only points on this curve that present an advantage to both A and B are those in $\alpha\beta$. The agreement will lie nearer to α or nearer to β, according as the bargaining power of A or of B is the greater.

Of course it is still possible that no agreement will be reached between the two nations; for either, or both of them, may think that the other is not giving up enough ground.

[148]

The two-dimensional treatment: three nations. In extending the treatment to three nations, let the existing state of affairs be denoted by $I(a_0, b_0)$ and draw the indifference contour through I for each nation. Before any agreement can be reached all three nations must benefit; and for this to be possible the three contours through I must have an area in common. For the configuration of Fig. 151. for example, no agreement is possible. But for Fig. 152 any point in Δ, the area of overlap between their contours, is preferred by all three nations to I; and so far as this goes, any point in Δ represents a possible pact between them.

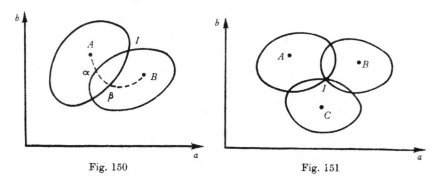

Fig. 150   Fig. 151

For the particular diagram we have drawn, Δ is traversed by the segment $\alpha\beta$ of the curve of contact AB; and whatever point in Δ we name, not lying in $\alpha\beta$, there is some point in $\alpha\beta$ which both A and B prefer to it.

Now let C's indifference curve of lowest preference passing through any point on $\alpha\beta$ be $\gamma\gamma'$ as shown (Fig. 153). Then the agreement reached, if any, must lie in a region of Δ bounded by $\gamma\gamma'$, the region named δ in Fig. 153, because there are points in this region, namely, those lying in the segment $\alpha\beta$, which are preferred by all three nations to any point in Δ which lies outside δ. The particular agreement reached will again depend on the bargaining strengths, obstinacies, etc., of the nations concerned. It may be that represented by the point P, say, which is less preferred by A and B than some points in $\alpha\beta$, but perhaps preferred by C to any point in $\alpha\beta$.

For other diagrams that may be drawn for the case of three nations, the area of possible agreements can similarly be localized. For the case of 4, 5, ... nations we would again begin by looking for the area of overlap between the indifference contours drawn through the point that represents the existing state of affairs.

Probability analysis. Because of the gambling element in international affairs, another important type of analysis would be that in terms of probability and uncertainty. Here, however,

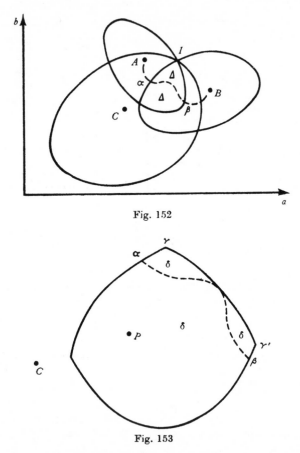

Fig. 152

Fig. 153

Politics has to take its cue from Economics, and even in Economics the techniques of probability analysis are rather undeveloped and have been able to give little information that was both new and helpful. Advance along this line must await further development in Economics.

Suggested reform of the manner of reaching international agreements. We have pointed out that when a number of nations

[150]

attend an international conference the outcome of their bargaining is indeterminate; and it was to this indeterminacy that we traced the difficulty which undoubtedly exists in reaching international agreements.

To some people it has appeared that the source of the difficulty is the requirement of unanimity; and they have suggested that this requirement should be replaced by the use of a simple majority or of a two-thirds majority. This, however, would only partly relieve the difficulty of indeterminacy and would at the same time create other sources of trouble.

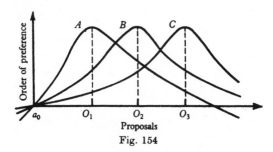

Fig. 154

To show some of the difficulties that would still remain even though the requirement were only that of a simple majority, we may consider the case of Fig. 154 in which there are three nations, each with a single-peaked preference curve. Agreement will emerge if A and B or if B and C can agree to adopt some proposal, but this by no means gets rid of higgling, for the country with the median optimum would presumably investigate with which of the others it is able to drive the best bargain. An increase in the number of countries concerned would intensify the bargaining leading up to the announcement of the proposal that had been agreed by a majority of the countries.

If this seems at variance with our everyday experience of committee working in which a simple majority is used, it is because ordinary committee procedure is an automatic mechanism which is bound to yield a definite result, since only one motion can survive the series of votes; and this is a different matter from a simple majority showing a willingness to accept one out of a number of proposals that have been put forward.

With any requirement other than unanimity, more of the pressure of bargaining would be thrown on to the stages preceding the conference, when the countries would try to discover which proposals might command the necessary majority; and their acceptance of an invitation would depend on what they expected the outcome to be. Under this system the conferences held would be less representative of all of the nations than with the present requirement of unanimity.

The main argument in favour of unanimity, of course, is that it ensures that whichever proposal is adopted will be preferred by every nation to the pre-existing state of affairs, and the great powers have shown no inclination to abandon this guarantee where their major interests were concerned. No requirement short of unanimity could provide this guarantee, and it has been on this objection that proposals for alteration in the size of majority have foundered in the past and are likely to do so in the future.

The sovereignty of a state in its external relations. The above theory should enable us to avoid some of the errors which have been made in discussing the nature of sovereignty, by making clear the limits of the extent to which a state is self-determining or free in its dealings with others.

To compare first the state with the individual, if in civil life the individual performs certain actions such as burglary, he comes into conflict with the law and has to submit to certain consequences which, if he could, he would avoid. Similarly, by acting in certain ways a nation may make probable certain undesirable consequences of a positive kind, e.g. the breaking-off of diplomatic relations by other nations or warlike action against it; or the undesirable consequences may be of a negative kind, e.g. the failure on the part of other nations to carry out certain actions which it desires. The country, like the individual, has a choice, but from a limited range of actions.

As regards its negotiations with other countries, a great power can make suggestions as to what the terms of an agreement should be, and it need not accept any agreement with others unless it prefers this agreement to the existing state of affairs; and to this extent it is self-determining. But at the same time when a great power sits in conference, the only agreements practically open to it are those which are preferred to the existing state of affairs by the other major powers concerned. Further, out of this set of possible agreements, the one accepted by all the nations will be reached by a process of higgling in which the more preferred is the position attained by one nation, the less preferred becomes the result for some of the others; and this higgling narrows down the effective choice for each of them.

Thus the sovereignty or freedom of action even of a great power is restricted in three ways: by the limitation on the actions from which it can make its choice; because it can only reach agreements with other great powers in so far as its interests coincide with theirs; and in so far as it must higgle with these other powers as to which of the agreements that all of them prefer to a_0 will be accepted.

The action of a small country, it is generally agreed, will be largely dictated by the great power on which she is dependent, and in dealing with others her scope for self-determination is at a minimum.

The nature of international law. International law is the body of relations which are observed by nations in their intercourse with one another and which are applied in the settlement of disputes that arise; and we may point to the view of it which is most consonant with the above reasoning.

If we envisage a state of affairs where there is no international law, each dispute between the nations would give rise to discussion in which there could be no appeal to accepted principles; it would bring the need for higgling, with pressure and bluff in the foreground. Not only would each dispute be more acrimonious but, in the absence of definite rules of the game, the number of disputes would be multiplied. While some nations may derive more benefit than others from the particular rules of international law adopted, it is likely to be to the interest of every party to have some definite rules rather than none. But since no one has seriously suggested that the world should do without an international law of one kind or another, this aspect of the matter is of little or no practical importance.

More to the point is that the rules of international law are either set out in conventions between the nations or else give the force of law to already existing customs. In so far as the rules spring from conventions, they will reflect the preponderance of the strongest nations and will tend to favour the nationals of these countries; and in so far as they spring out of custom they will tend to be based on the actions that the more powerful nations have taken in the past to protect the interests of their own nationals. It is fairly

[153]

safe to take it that the motive force behind international law has to a good extent been self-interest. But there is also the factor that until 1939 at any rate, the more powerful nations were maritime nations, thriving on freedom of intercourse; and probably there was little conflict between the interests of their nationals and those of the others. Here, as elsewhere, the 'invisible hand' was carrying out its benevolent work of coordination.

A deeper understanding of the content of international law than a mere knowledge of its rules would require an examination of the historical path by which these rules have come into existence, and of the power factors, cultural factors and moral factors in the environment in which they had their origin. This is the view that a Historical Jurisprudence would seek to give.

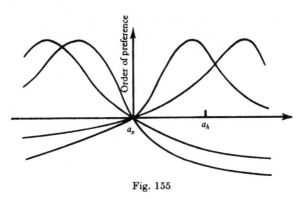

Fig. 155

A forecast of the future content of international law might be made to a first approximation, on the basis of a forecast of the future distribution of power among the nations, conjoined with an estimate of the interests that the countries climbing to power would seek to serve. The different views taken of international law at the Danube Conference of 1948, by Britain and France on the one hand and by the eastern European countries on the other, reflects a shift in the balance of power and a corresponding shift in the interests that international law is likely to support in the future.

The cabinet. The theory of countries arriving at an international agreement applies also to a number of individuals who are arriving at unanimous agreement in a cabinet. At first sight the cases might seem dissimilar, for whereas the country, if a great power, will insist on drawing 'benefit' from each international agreement, some members of a cabinet may accept a decision which they consider less desirable than the existing state of affairs on the topic concerned. Their preference curves drawn through a_0 may rise some on one side of a_0 and some on the other (Fig. 155), and yet those members whose curves are rising from a_h to a_0 may accept a_h as the cabinet decision.

But if we take into account complementarity of valuations, the same theory covers both cases. The country might be unwilling to accept particular clauses of an agreement in isolation, but valuing them along with other clauses it may be willing to accept *the agreement as a whole*. Its freedom, if it is a great power, extends to acceptance or rejection of the agreement; and acceptance necessarily implies that it regards it as an improvement on the state of affairs which, in the absence of the agreement, would exist—for otherwise it would reject it, as it is free to do. Similarly the cabinet minister's valuations are complementary. Without regarding the government's action on every individual issue as being better than the state of affairs which would otherwise exist, he may regard *its policy as a whole* as being preferable to any alternative policy. So long as he is satisfied on this score, he is unlikely to have qualms about retention of his cabinet membership. If he finds himself unable to concur in a decision which seems to him of high importance, he may resign, just as a country might withdraw from an international conference.

As in the case of nations round the conference table, different ministers will carry very different weights in the decisions arrived at by the cabinet; in formulating general policy the Prime Minister, Foreign Secretary and Chancellor of the Exchequer may be the chief powers and a decision may be determined in the main if there is a fair measure of agreement among them. The sense of freedom for the other members of the cabinet, however, will be greatly increased by the fact that each of them will have the power of initiative, and to a large extent the power of decision (that is, little need to compromise), in matters that relate to his own department are of most concern to him.

PART II

HISTORY OF THE MATHEMATICAL THEORY OF COMMITTEES AND ELECTIONS (EXCLUDING PROPORTIONAL REPRESENTATION)

CHAPTER XVIII

BORDA, CONDORCET AND LAPLACE*

1. Jean-Charles de Borda† (1733–1799)

Borda's two justifications of the method of marks. Systematic theorizing on elections was part of the general uprush of thought in France in the second half of the eighteenth century. The first thinker to develop a mathematical theory of elections was Borda, a member of the Academy of Sciences. In the course of a busy life in which he was successively an officer of cavalry and a naval captain, Borda made a number of contributions to Mathematical Physics, and also showed considerable talent in the improvement of scientific instruments. He is commemorated by a statue in his native town of Dax, near Bordeaux, and by a Borda Society.

The paper of Borda's which we possess is his 'Mémoire sur les Élections au Scrutin', *Histoire de l'Académie Royale des Sciences,*

* Part II of the present book omits any discussion of the history of the mathematical theory of proportional representation (the author's view being that such a theory would be immensely difficult to obtain and that even today a serious beginning to it has scarcely been made). A historical account of the main theorizing on P.R. is given in chapter IX of Hoag and Hallett's *Proportional Representation.*

† For an account of his work and all that is known of his life, see Jean Mascart, *La Vie et les Travaux du Chevalier Jean-Charles de Borda (1733–1799)*: *Épisodes de la Vie Scientifique au XVIII Siècle* (pp. 821, Lyon, 1919). This book is excessively long and digressive, though in the present connexion pp. 128–34 are valuable. A lively and penetrating estimate of his work, written by one who had known him, has been left by S. F. Lacroix, *Éloge Historique de Jean-Charles Borda* (pp. 40, Paris, 1800). See also Isaac Todhunter, *A History of the Mathematical Theory of Probability from the time of Pascal to that of Laplace* (1865), pp. 432–4.

1781.* He commences with an arithmetical example to show that
the single vote may select the wrong candidate. His data in this
example are expressed in literary form, and are shown in our
Fig. 156, where eight electors have the candidate A, seven B and
six C as their first preference. For his purpose there is no need
to specify how the second and third places on the schedules of the
eight electors are filled, whether by B or C.
On the single vote A would be elected,
although, as he says, the electors would
prefer B or C to A by a majority of 13
against 8. And so at this stage in his argument Borda is really making use of what
we have termed the Condorcet criterion.

A	B	C
	C	B
	A	A
8	7	6

Fig. 156

One might have expected that Borda,
having made use of it, would go on to develop the Condorcet
criterion, but he does not do so. Instead, he says that this defect
in the single vote can be remedied by either of two methods:
(i) by the elector assigning places, first, second, etc., to all the
candidates, according to the degree of merit that he assigns to
each, i.e. 'election by order of merit'; or (ii) by having a series of
'particular' elections among all the candidates taken two at a time.

In considering the first method he supposes that an elector
ranks the three candidates A, B and C in the order A, and this is

$$B$$
$$C$$

Borda's own notation. Then he continues in the strain of thought
that was later to be caught up by Laplace.

I say that the degree of superiority that this elector has given to A
over B should be considered the same as the degree of superiority that
he has accorded to B over C. Indeed, as the second candidate B is
equally susceptible of all the degrees of merit comprised between the
merits of the other two candidates A and C, there is no reason to hold
that the elector who has decided this order of the three candidates has
wanted to place him nearer A than C, or, what comes to the same
thing, that he has attributed any greater superiority to the first over the
second than to the second over the third. I next state that, because of
the supposed equality between all the electors, each place given by one
of the electors must be deemed to be of the same value and to assign
the same degree of merit as the corresponding position given to another
candidate, or to the same candidate by any other elector whatsoever.

* *Op. cit.* pp. 31–4 and 657–65.

It follows from what I have said that if we want to represent by a the merit that each elector attaches to the last of the three places, and by $a+b$ the merit that he attaches to the second place, we must represent by $a+2b$ the merit that should be attributed to the first place; and likewise for the places given by the other electors, each last place shall be represented by a, each second place by $a+b$ and each first place by $a+2b$.*

Similarly, if there are four candidates, the merit attributed to the lowest, next lowest, second-top and top candidates on an elector's list of preferences will be a, $a+b$, $a+2b$, and $a+3b$ respectively. It is easy to see that a and b can be taken to be any given quantities without altering the result of the election, and he chooses to take $a=1$ and $b=1$.

He applies this scheme in an example where the data are as in Fig. 157, and employs the useful notation to which we have alluded; but instead of say, placing the figure 7 below the scale A to show that

$$C$$
$$B$$

7 electors rank the candidates in this way, he repeats each scale as often as it occurs.

A	A	B	C
B	C	C	B
C	B	A	A
1	7	7	6

Fig. 157

With this group of schedules A with 8 first places and 13 last places, will be attributed a merit of $8 \times 3 + 13 \times 1 = 37$; while B gets 42 and C 47. On method (i), therefore, C will be elected.

In method (ii) he gives each candidate a mark equal to the sum of the votes that he gets when he is put against each of the other candidates individually. This will give the same result as method (i); for, when the candidates in a particular election are A, B and C, if A is placed first in the preferences of any given elector, on method (ii) he will defeat B and C and will secure 2 votes. Or, if A stands second in the elector's preferences, on method (ii) he will defeat one candidate and secure 1 vote. His scoring is the same as it would be on method (i), when, as is legitimate, we give a and b the values $a=0$ and $b=1$. Method (ii) is a particular case of method (i) and must give the same result. With the group of

* *Op. cit.* pp. 659–60.

schedules of Fig. 157, A when placed against B would get 8 votes and when placed against C would get 8 votes, and so would get 16 marks in all; similarly, B would get 21 and C 26 marks; and the differences between these figures are necessarily the same as those between the figures 37, 42 and 47 obtained on method (i).*

In the last brief paragraph of his paper he suggests that his method of arriving at a just decision in an election would apply in regard to any sort of committee decision:

It remains for me to add, as I finish this paper, that all that we have said about elections applies equally to the discussions of corporate bodies or companies; these discussions are in fact only types of elections between different opinions put forward and they are therefore subject to the same rules.†

The value of Borda's work. Of the paper as a whole we can say that it is short, clearly expressed and suggests the possible lines of development that a theory of elections might take. A specific defect is that it fails to distinguish between two separate lines of thought—the criterion which it advocates explicitly and another criterion (that of Condorcet) of which, earlier, it had made implicit use. A more important deficiency is that, to be satisfactory, a theory of elections must give a real insight into the nature of group decisions; and Borda's paper cannot be said to do this. It is a good first step towards a more significant type of theory, but no more than that.

2. Marie Jean Antoine Nicolas Caritat, Marquis de Condorcet‡ (1743–1794)

Introductory. Condorcet was a mathematician, philosopher, economist and social scientist. He became a member of the Academy of Sciences in 1769 and its permanent secretary in 1777 and was elected to the French Academy in 1782. He was one of the *encyclopédistes* who paved the way for the Revolution and later became a member of the Legislative Assembly; but his independent attitude led to his proscription and he died in prison.

---

* Two slips in Borda's arithmetic, *op. cit.* p. 663, confuse the appearance of his argument.   † *Op. cit.* p. 665.

‡ For an account in English of Condorcet's life and thinking, though it excludes his thought on elections and Political Science, see J. S. Schapiro, *Condorcet and the Rise of Liberalism* (1936). This book gives adequate bibliographical notes. See also the essay in John Morley's *Critical Miscellanies*, vol. II, pp. 163–255.

His voluminous writings cover many different tracts of human interest. His non-mathematical works which have been collected occupy in one edition twenty-one volumes and in a later edition twelve volumes, while his mathematical works are scattered and have neither been collected nor reprinted. In both his literary and mathematical writings Condorcet devoted much attention to the problem of elections. His deepest and most sustained thought on the subject is to found in the *Essai sur l'Application de l'Analyse à la Probabilité des Décisions Rendues à la Pluralité des Voix** (Paris, 1785); and we will confine ourselves to the consideration of the views he puts forward in this remarkable document.

The *Essai* is divided into two sections, the text, which is largely mathematical, and a long *Discours Préliminaire* intended to give a non-mathematical account of the argument. Condorcet fails to keep the two discussions quite parallel, but the introduction has the merit of picking out the factors which are more significant for practice and clearing up some of the obscurities of the text. The theory of elections is to be found at pp. 119–36 and 287–96 and pp. lxi–lxx and clxviii–clxxix of the introduction, and forms only one-tenth of the whole work.

The mathematicians and the *Essai*. The only people who might have been in a position to understand the theory of elections of the *Essai* were the mathematicians and it has frequently come to their notice.

Montucla, in his early book on the history of Mathematics, mentions that Condorcet had proposed several new methods of election, but gives no clue as to what his theory was. He dismisses them without discussion on the ground of their impracticability.†

In the biography presented to the Academy of Sciences, Arago, one of Condorcet's successors as perpetual secretary, pays tribute to Condorcet as a mathematician. He commends, in somewhat general terms, the boldness of his work on assemblies, without specifically mentioning the theory of elections.‡

---

* Referred to for the remainder of this chapter as *Essai*.

† Cf. J. F. Montucla, *Histoire des Mathématiques* (Paris, 1802), tome III, p. 421. Montucla, *ibid.*, mentions a work of the mathematician S. A. Lhuilier, *Examen du mode d'élection proposé en février 1793 à la Convention nationale de France, et adopté à Génève* (1794 in 8⁰). I have been unable to locate any copy of Lhuilier's book.

‡ Cf. *Oeuvres de Condorcet*, edited by A. Condorcet O'Connor and M. F. Arago (1847–9), tome I, pp. ix–xxvii.

The first history of the calculus of probabilities, Charles Gouraud's *Histoire du Calcul des Probabilités depuis ses Origines jusqu'à nos jours* (Paris, 1848), bestows the highest praise on Condorcet, as on all other authors it mentions, for the book is quite undiscriminating. It contains no mathematical discussion and deals only in broad generalities.

Todhunter in his classic *History of the Mathematical Theory of Probability* (1865) devotes a chapter to the theory of probability of the *Essai*. He repeatedly objects to the tedium and obscurity of the book and found his own patience and good-humour sorely tried. Only a sense of duty as the historian of the science wrung from him some sixty pages before he finally felt free to break off;* and it is fortunate for us that he persisted, for he has contributed more to an understanding of the *Essai* than anyone else has done, or is likely to do for a good many years to come. But the theory of elections fares badly at his hands. He has only gone a short distance when he exclaims in regard to one of its more obvious and entirely well-founded theorems:

Unfortunately these propositions are not consistent with each other.
Condorcet treats this subject [of elections]...at great length.... His results however appear of too little value to detain us any longer.†

The mathematician Bertrand discusses the theory of juries and assemblies, as developed by Condorcet, though he does not consider the theory of elections which Condorcet developed as a particular branch of it. Of the *Essai* he says: 'None of its principles is acceptable, none of its conclusions approach the truth';‡ and this condemnation is wide enough to include the theory of elections along with the rest of the book.

Czuber§ gives a far more closely reasoned estimate of the theory of juries than any other author, though it is a branch of the theory of probability that he himself finds distasteful. His estimate

---

* The more amusing of his exasperated remarks are to be found in *op. cit.* pp. 441–2.
† *Op. cit.* p. 375.
‡ J. Bertrand, *Calcul des Probabilités* (1888), p. 319.
§ Emanuel Czuber, 'Die Entwicklung der Wahrscheinlichkeitstheorie und ihrer Anwendungen', *Jahresbericht der Deutschen Mathematiker-Vereinigung,* vol. vii (1899), pp. 132–49.

of the theory of elections, as one part of the theory of juries, is that:

It can be said of those applications of the theory of probability which deal with the evaluation (*Beurteilung*) of the decisions of council meetings, of law courts, election committees—in brief, with decisions taken by a majority of votes—that in the long run they were unable to stand up to criticism and can nowadays claim no more than a historical interest.*

Netto, who writes the chapter on probability in Cantor's *Vorlesungen über Geschichte der Mathematik*, is cool and non-committal about the value of the *Essai* as a whole.

Death prevented that man of genius [Daniel Bernoulli] from applying the theory of probability to civil, moral and economic conditions, as he had intended. Condorcet is said to have carried through Bernoulli's intentions after seventy-two years. Other critics consider Condorcet fantastic rather than rigorous, enthusiastic rather than scientifically exact.†

In the theory of elections, he says, Condorcet 'fails to solve the complete contradiction which may occur' in elections where no candidate is able to secure a majority over each of the others; and when the candidates are taken in pairs, the relations between the various votes may be quite irreconcilable.‡

In a paper which we will deal with later,§ E. J. Nanson accepts the criterion of choice proposed by Condorcet. He clearly has benefited from his study of Condorcet, though he neither indicates what his system is, nor is concerned to estimate its value.

If, therefore, we exclude Gouraud, who fails to establish his credentials, and consider the mathematicians who have assessed the value of Condorcet's work, it can be said that not one of them has expressed approval of the theory of elections of the *Essai*. Indeed, I have searched in vain for evidence that any of them, Nanson apart, had really understood it. And, if they had failed, who was to understand it? We will suggest, as we go on, that one reason for the failure of the mathematicians was that Condorcet's theory seemed to belong to one branch of Mathematics and really

---

* *Op. cit.* p. 141.   † *Op. cit.* vol. IV (1908), p. 257.
‡ *Op. cit.* p. 255.
§ 'Methods of Election' in the British Government blue book *Miscellaneous No. 3 (1907)*, Cd. 3501, dealing with *The Applications of the Principle of Proportional Representation to Public Elections*. Nanson's paper had originally been read before the Royal Society of Victoria in 1882.

belonged to another; and besides this, even after allowing for the difficulty of the thought, his exposition is unduly obscure.

Its relationship to the theory of probability. The intention of the *Essai* as a whole is to develop what may conveniently be referred to as the jury problem, as a branch of the theory of probability, and to do it in such a way as to obtain a Science of Politics. A theory that would sufficiently cover the jury problem would also be adequate, Condorcet thinks, to deal with assemblies of any sort, e.g. parliamentary or local-government bodies.

For the benefit of readers who may not be acquainted with it, we may indicate the nature of the jury problem. The probability of throwing 'six' with a single die is $\frac{1}{6}$; and the probability of n 'sixes' when n dice are thrown is $(\frac{1}{6})^n$. Likewise if the probability of each out of n judges making an error is $\frac{1}{6}$, the probability that all of them will concur in a wrong judgement is $(\frac{1}{6})^n$. More generally, the probabilities of the various possible outcomes will be given by Bernoulli's theorem.

Ostensibly at least, Condorcet develops his theory of elections as another application of the theory of probability. Each elector is assumed to have a certain probability of giving a correct judgement and a certain probability of giving a wrong judgement, in relation to the candidates as between whom he is choosing.

Now whether there be much or little to be said in favour of a theory of juries arrived at in this way, there seems to be nothing in favour of a theory of elections that adopts this approach. When a judge, say, declares an accused person to be either guilty or innocent, it would be possible to conceive of a test which, in principle at least, would be capable of telling us whether his judgement had been right or wrong. But in the case of elections no such test is conceivable; and the phrase 'the probability of the correctness of a voter's opinion' seems to be without definite meaning.

Truly this is an unpromising start. How is it that from premisses so clearly inapplicable, Condorcet was able to extract a theory of elections which, as we believe, was far superior to anything that had gone before or has been attempted since? The answer is not far to seek. The premisses that he states as providing the basis of his theory are not his real premisses and can be detached from his theory without affecting it. His real theory is a system of formal reasoning which is quite independent of the theory

M

of probability. Indeed, at the only places where he does introduce the theory of probability, he explicitly rejects its findings in favour of what he calls 'straightforward reasoning' (see pp. 170–2 below). There is little wonder that his theory of elections, which was presented as part of a theory of probabilities, was misunderstood.

The probability formulae of the *Essai*. To give an account of his theory, however, it is necessary to set out the main positions from which, in appearance, it is derived. Let us accept the idea that in some context in which the members of a committee are making a judgement of the 'Yes or No' type, each member makes a correct judgement in the proportion v of all the cases dealt with, and a wrong judgement in the proportion e of the cases. Then v and e can be taken as each member's probability of being right and wrong respectively. (Condorcet chooses the symbols v and e because of the words *vérité* and *erreur*; and of course $v + e = 1$.)

In accordance with Bernoulli's theorem, the probabilities of the different possible outcomes when $h + k$ members are reaching a decision,* are given by the different terms in the expansion of

$$(v + e)^{h+k}.$$

The probabilities that $h + k$, $h + k - 1$, ... members will give a right judgement are given by the terms containing v^{h+k}, v^{h+k-1}, ... respectively; and the probabilities that $h + k$, $h + k - 1$, ... members will give a wrong judgement by the terms containing e^{h+k}, e^{h+k-1}, ... respectively.

The probability that h members will give a right judgement is

$$\frac{(h+k)!}{h!\,k!}\, v^h e^k,$$

and the probability that they will give a wrong judgement is

$$\frac{(h+k)!}{k!\,h!}\, v^k e^h.$$

Thus when a verdict has already been reached by h members ($h > k$), its probability of rightness is to its probability of wrongness as $v^h e^k : v^k e^h$.

The probability that the judgement taken by the h members is right, therefore, is

$$\frac{v^h e^k}{v^h e^k + v^k e^h} = \frac{v^{h-k}}{v^{h-k} + e^{h-k}}.$$

* *Essai*, pp. 10–11; and Todhunter, *History of...Probability*, pp. 356–7.

Likewise the probability that the judgement of the h members is wrong is

$$\frac{e^{h-k}}{v^{h-k} + e^{h-k}}.$$

If we put $X = \dfrac{v^{h-k}}{v^{h-k} + e^{h-k}}$, it can be shown that when v and e are taken as constant and $h + k = $ the given number of voters $ = $ a constant,

$$\frac{\partial X}{\partial h} = 2X^2 \left(\frac{e}{v}\right)^{h-k} \log \frac{v}{e},$$

which is positive for $v > e$, so that X is continuously increasing as h increases.

Similarly, if we take h and k as constant, we find

$$\frac{\partial X}{\partial v} = X^2(h-k) \frac{e^{h-k-1}}{v^{h-k-1}} (v+e).$$

Since $h - k - 1 \geqslant 0$, this expression is always positive, being equal to zero when $v = 1$. For $v = 0$, $X = 0$; and for $v = 1$, $X = 1$. Thus when h and k are given, as v increases X increases continuously from zero to unity.

These results will be used at one or two points in the subsequent argument.

The notation of the *Essai*. In any mathematical account much hinges on the notation used, and it is a pity that Condorcet does not arrange the candidates in a vertical column to show the order in which they are ranked by the voter. Often he gives a literary statement of the data straddled over several paragraphs, and the only way to get a clear picture is for the reader to translate it into symbols.

At other times he has a notation of his own, making use of the signs $>$ and $<$. If, out of three candidates A, B and C, an elector votes for A in preference to either B or C, Condorcet regards him as affirming two propositions:

A is better than (*vaut mieux que*) B, which he denotes by $A > B$ or $B < A$, and

A is better than C, denoted by $A > C$ or $C < A$.

But it is consistent with Condorcet's own use* of these symbols to put a minimum interpretation on them: where a single elector is concerned $A > B$ may denote simply that he votes for A against B;

* See, for example, *Essai*, pp. 119–20.

or, where there is a group of electors $A > B$ may denote that A gets a majority of votes against B. That is, he *defines* $A > B$ to mean that the single elector believes that A is better than B and therefore votes as he does, or that the majority of electors believe that A is better than B and therefore support A against B; but he sometimes drops the prior proposition and uses $A > B$ to express simply a statement about the voting facts.

The argument. Condorcet's general method is to examine the case of three candidates and then extend the results to that of n candidates.

He shows that the single vote may lead to the election of a candidate against whom each of the others would be able to obtain a majority, and concludes that if the single vote is used at all, a candidate should be required to get at least half the votes cast. Even then the single vote would sometimes *fail to make a choice* where there was a majority candidate.* Voters ought to give the order in which they place the candidates.

When each voter indicates his order of preference as between three candidates A, B and C, he must affirm one out of each of the following three pairs of propositions:

either $A > B$ either $B > C$ either $C > A$
or $B > A$ or $C > B$ or $A > C$

It follows that (the case of a tie apart) a majority of the voters will affirm one out of each of the above three pairs of propositions. When we choose the majority proposition from each pair there will in all be $2^3 = 8$ possibilities:

(1) $A > B$	(2) $A > B$	(3) $A > B$	(4) $A > B$
$A > C$	$A > C$	$A < C$	$A < C$
$B > C$	$B < C$	$B > C$	$B < C$
(5) $A < B$	(6) $A < B$	(7) $A < B$	(8) $A < B$
$A > C$	$A > C$	$A < C$	$A < C$
$B > C$	$B < C$	$B > C$	$B < C$

One of these eight *sets* of propositions will express the results of the voting. Six† of the sets are internally consistent and leave no doubt as to which candidate should be elected. The remaining two, namely, the sets (3) and (6), he calls 'contradictory', since any two

* *Essai*, p. lx.
† The number of ways of making an ordered selection of three things is $3! = 6$.

of the propositions in the set yield a proposition which is 'in contradiction' with the third.

The term is unfortunate. When the individual's valuations are intransitive and he prefers A to B, B to C and C to A, we might in a normal use of language speak of them being contradictory. But when the valuations of the electors are transitive and the voting yields

$$A > B \qquad B > C \qquad C > A$$

no contradiction either in logic or in valuation is involved. The danger is that describing these results as 'contradictory' or 'inconsistent' might suggest that the group has a scale of valuations

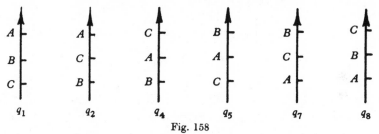

Fig. 158

Matrix for Fig. 158

(against)

		A	B	C
	A	0	$(q_1+q_2+q_4:q_5+q_7+q_8)$	$(q_1+q_2+q_5:q_4+q_7+q_8)$
(for)	B	$(q_5+q_7+q_8:q_1+q_2+q_4)$	0	$(q_1+q_5+q_7:q_2+q_4+q_8)$
	C	$(q_4+q_7+q_8:q_1+q_2+q_5)$	$(q_2+q_4+q_8:q_1+q_5+q_7)$	0

Fig. 159

which is the same in kind as that of the individual, which would be false: the individual values, the group does not; it reaches decisions through some procedure in voting.

Condorcet himself nowhere falls into the error we mention, but the term is none the less unhappy. For the sake of expounding his theory, however, we will continue to use it.

Three candidates: preliminary consideration of the contradictory case. He supposes* that in an election the voters have the schedules shown in Fig. 158. In this all the consistent scales of valuation as between three candidates occur; q_1 voters have the first scale, q_2 the second, and so on. The results of the voting are shown in the matrix. (Condorcet himself uses the symbols

* *Essai*, p. lxi.

$q_1, q_2, \ldots$ but of course uses neither straight-line schedules nor the matrix notation.)

The election may yield a set of contradictory propositions. The propositions will be contradictory and of type (3) whenever the following inequalities hold:

$$q_1 + q_2 + q_4 > q_5 + q_7 + q_8,$$
$$q_4 + q_7 + q_8 > q_1 + q_2 + q_5,$$
$$q_1 + q_5 + q_7 > q_2 + q_4 + q_8;$$

or, rewriting these, whenever

$$(q_1 - q_8) + (q_4 - q_5) - (q_7 - q_2) > 0,$$
$$(q_4 - q_5) + (q_7 - q_2) - (q_1 - q_8) > 0,$$
$$(q_7 - q_2) + (q_1 - q_8) - (q_4 - q_5) > 0.$$

When is it impossible for the contradictory case to arise? Obviously it cannot arise if one of the three candidates is required to get more than half of the first-preference votes before he is regarded as obtaining a majority. Nor can it arise if a majority does not count unless it amounts to 'a third'* (i.e. if the votes for must exceed the votes against by at least a third of the total number of electors). Proof of this would be that the three above majorities add up to

$$(q_1 - q_8) + (q_4 - q_5) + (q_7 - q_2) \leqslant (q_1 + q_8) + (q_4 + q_5) + (q_7 + q_2)$$
$$\leqslant n,$$

where n is the number of electors.

Which candidate to elect when the propositions are contradictory is a difficult question. He says rather inconsequentially that 'it might be supposed' that it would be sufficient to choose the candidate with the largest number of votes in his favour when put against each of the others† (i.e. Borda's solution). Later he is going to reject this or any other method of marks and meantime goes on to lay the basis for his own theory.

Three candidates: when the voting yields a set of consistent propositions. Voting will then lead to one of the following results:

either	$A > B$	or	$B > C$	or	$C > A$
	$A > C$		$B > A$		$C > B$

* *Essai*, p. lxviii.　　　　　† *Essai*, p. 121.

But even though each of the p ositions in a pair, say $A > B$ and $A > C$, gets a majority, it by no means follows automatically that the candidate A should be elected. On Condorcet's premises that candidate ought to be elected who has the greatest probability of being the right candidate; and in such circumstances this need not be the candidate A. He proves this* by means of an example which we summarize in Fig. 160.

Matrix

		A	(against) B	C
	A	0	(18, 15)	(18, 15)
(for)	B	(15, 18)	0	(32, 1)
	C	(15, 18)	(1, 32)	0

Fig. 160

In accordance with the formulae given earlier (pp. 164–5), the probabilities of the various propositions being true are:

$$A > B, \quad \frac{v^3}{v^3 + e^3},$$

$$A > C, \quad \frac{v^3}{v^3 + e^3},$$

$A > B$ and $A > C$,

$$\frac{v^6}{v^6 + 2v^3 e^3 + e^6} = Y_1, \text{ say,}$$

$$B > C, \quad \frac{v^{31}}{v^{31} + e^{31}},$$

$$B > A, \quad \frac{e^3}{v^3 + e^3},$$

$B > C$ and $B > A$,

$$\frac{v^{31} e^3}{v^{34} + v^{31} e^3 + v^3 e^{31} + e^{34}} = Y_2, \text{ say.}$$

When we put $v = 1$, $e = 0$, we get $Y_1 = 1$, $Y_2 = 0$; and as v approaches or reaches its maximum value $Y_1 > Y_2$. The range of values of v, however, is $\frac{1}{2} < v \leqslant 1$; and if at the lower end of this range we put $v = \frac{1}{2} + x$, $e = \frac{1}{2} - x$ and disregard powers of x higher

* *Essai*, pp. 122–4 and pp. lxiii–lxv.

than the first, we find that for values of v just above $\frac{1}{2}$, $Y_1 < Y_2$, because

$$Y_1 \sim \frac{1 + 12x}{4},$$

$$Y_2 \sim \frac{1 + 56x}{4}.$$

In fact for a certain value of v between $v = \frac{1}{2}$ and $v = 1$, Y_1 will be equal to Y_2; for values of v below this $Y_1 < Y_2$, and for values above this $Y_1 > Y_2$.

The values of Y_1 and Y_2 at intervals of $0 \cdot 01$ and $0 \cdot 1$ of v are shown in the table of Fig. 161.

v	0·50	0·51	0·52	0·53	0·54	0·55	0·60	0·70	0·80	0·90	1
Y_1	0·25	0·281	0·319	0·347	0·380	0·418	0·595	0·860	0·969	0·999	1
Y_2	0·25	0·365	0·406	0·401	0·379	0·353	0·229	0·073	0·015	0·001	0

Fig. 161

The situation is decidedly awkward for Condorcet's approach. Even in so simple a case as one candidate securing a majority over each of his two opponents (and assuming $v > \frac{1}{2}$, $e < \frac{1}{2}$), we still cannot say definitely that this is probably the right candidate to choose.

In noticing this Condorcet must have felt a strong impulse to abandon the assumptions whose consequences were so disconcerting. The calculus of probabilities had failed to make a definite choice in one of the simplest of cases.

The course which he takes at this point leads him out of the difficulty—and out of the calculus of probabilities. Will it sometimes be necessary to reject a majority candidate such as A? No, he replies, we ought to choose A, as can be shown by 'straightforward reasoning' (*simple raisonnement*). There seems to be no case at all in favour of C and the choice is between A and B. The argument in favour of B would have to run; we have reason to believe both that B is better than C and that B is better than A. The second of these propositions, however, is untrue, or at any rate has a probability of less than $\frac{1}{2}$ in its favour; and this leaves the case for B very weak. Since we are making a choice between these two candidates and the proposition 'A is better than B' is more probable than the proposition 'B is better than A', we ought to elect A.

Thus, if, out of three candidates, one is able to get a majority over each of the others, he ought to be elected. And *in general the right candidate to elect is the majority candidate.*

The 'straightforward reasoning' by which this conclusion is reached is still an argument in probabiiity; but not in that scheme of probability from which Condorcet had explicitly set out to deal with this and all other cases.*

Three candidates: when the voting yields a set of inconsistent propositions. Let us take the set of inconsistent propositions (3) of p. 166 above: $A > B \quad B > C \quad C > A.$

The larger the majority got by any proposition, the greater the probability that it is true. We do not know the numerical values of v and e—although we assume $v > \frac{1}{2}$ and $e < \frac{1}{2}$—and so cannot measure the probabilities; but we are able to *rank* the probabilities of the different propositions according to the relative sizes of their majorities.

Let us denote the probabilities of the three propositions getting a majority, by p_1, p_2 and p_3, where $1 > p_1 > p_2 > p_3 > \frac{1}{2}$. And let us assume that the proposition with the largest majority in its favour and therefore with the probability p_1, is $B > C$. Two cases must be distinguished. First let us further assume that $C > A$ gets the next largest majority and $A > B$ gets the smallest majority. These propositions will have the probabilities p_2 and p_3 respectively; and we can set out the complete data in the form of the probability matrix of Fig. 162.

Probability matrix

	A	B	C
Probability that A is better than	0	p_3	$(1-p_2)$
Probability that B is better than	$(1-p_3)$	0	p_1
Probability that C is better than	p_2	$(1-p_1)$	0

Fig. 162

Thus, searching for the best candidate, we have

Probability in favour of $A = p_3(1 - p_2)$,

Probability in favour of $B = p_1(1 - p_3)$,

Probability in favour of $C = p_2(1 - p_1)$.

Each factor in the probability in favour of C is less than the corresponding factor in favour of B. We must therefore reject C and the choice lies between A and B.

* His rejection of his previous theory is made particularly clear at p. lxv.

Similarly, each factor in the probability in favour of B is greater than the corresponding factor in favour of A. Hence B ought to be elected.

Secondly, let the least probable proposition be $C > A$. This gives the matrix of Fig. 163.

Probability matrix

		(against)		
		A	B	C
(Probability in	A	0	p_2	$(1-p_3)$
favour of)	B	$(1-p_2)$	0	p_1
	C	p_3	$(1-p_1)$	0

Fig. 163

$$\text{Probability in favour of } A = p_2(1-p_3),$$
$$\text{Probability in favour of } B = p_1(1-p_2),$$
$$\text{Probability in favour of } C = p_3(1-p_1).$$

Each factor in the product in favour of B is greater than the corresponding factor in favour of C, who is rejected. But, this time, in comparing the claims of A and B, either of the relationships

$$p_2(1-p_3) \gtrless p_1(1-p_2)$$

may hold; and the reasoning gives no definite answer as to whether A or B ought to be elected.

Here again Condorcet falls back on 'straightforward reasoning'. To elect B we would have to admit the proposition $B > A$ with the probability $(1-p_2)$, whereas the weakest link in A's claim has the probability $(1-p_3)$ of being true. He therefore holds that A ought to be elected.

Granted that we have only three candidates, all cases can be dealt with by symmetry with the two that we have considered. The answer in each case, he points out, will be given by the simple rule: *of the three propositions with majorities in their favour, delete the one with the lowest majority and take the straightforward interpretation of the other two.** In the first of the above cases, for instance, when we delete the proposition $A > B$, we are left with $B > C$ and $C > A$, and elect B. In the second case, deleting $C > A$ we are left with $A > B$ and $B > C$, and elect A.

In vacuo it is not easy to judge the value of the method that Condorcet proposes; but we can construct examples which throw

* *Essai*, pp. lxvii and 126.

doubt on it. For instance, let us take the preference schedules of 101 electors to be as in Fig. 164, for which the corresponding voting matrix is shown.

On Condorcet's system A would be elected. To common sense, however, it might well seem that the choice should fall on B. Condorcet's rule, in fact, makes its final selection from the last pair of candidates according to the weakest element in either of their claims, and permits no compensation from strength on the positive side of a candidate's claim.

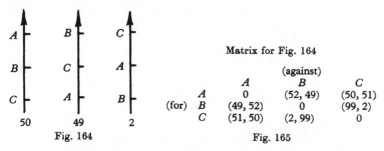

Fig. 164

Matrix for Fig. 164

		(against)		
		A	B	C
(for)	A	0	(52, 49)	(50, 51)
	B	(49, 52)	0	(99, 2)
	C	(51, 50)	(2, 99)	0

Fig. 165

When a candidate is elected in this way, he mentions, the probability that the choice is right is in the first case equal to $p_1(1-p_3)$, and in the second to $p_2(1-p_3)$. Each of these expressions is the product of two factors of which the first is less than 1 and the second less than $\frac{1}{2}$. Thus in any such case the chance that we have selected the best candidate is less than $\frac{1}{2}$.

He also deals with the case in which there is an equality of votes for two of the candidates and a proposition of the form $A = B$ results.*

Any number of candidates: preliminary. With n candidates, the number of pairs of propositions of the type $A > B$ will be equal
$$B > A$$
to the number of combinations of 2 things chosen out of n, i.e. $\frac{1}{2}n(n-1)$. A set of propositions is formed by choosing one from each of these pairs; and the number of sets will therefore be $2^{\frac{1}{2}n(n-1)}$. The number of sets of consistent (transitive) propositions will be the number of ways of making an ordered selection of n objects, i.e. $n!$. The number of sets in which the propositions are inconsistent will be $2^{\frac{1}{2}n(n-1)} - n!$.

As the number of candidates increases, the inconsistent sets will

* *Essai*, pp. 128–9.

form a rapidly increasing proportion of the whole as is shown in the table of Fig. 166.

Any number of candidates: consistent propositions. The order in which the candidates have been ranked by the majorities will show which one ought to be chosen;* and if we want to elect 2, 3, ... candidates, the top 2, 3, ... should be chosen.†

Condorcet adds that if we are not forced to make an election, before choosing the top candidate we can insist that the probability that he is the best candidate should be greater than $\frac{1}{2}$. But if we have no practical means of reckoning v and e, we cannot calculate the probability that he mentions.

	No. of sets of propositions	
No. of candidates	Consistent	Inconsistent
2	2	0
3	6	2
4	24	40
5	120	904

Fig. 166

Any number of candidates: inconsistent propositions. The inconsistencies may be such that we are still able to pick out the best candidate, or the best and also the next-best, etc. For instance with the five candidates A, B, C, D and E, the voting may yield the set of ten propositions:

$$A > B \quad A > C \quad A > D \quad A > E \quad B > C$$
$$B > D \quad B > E \quad C > D \quad E > C \quad D > E$$

Contradiction only arises between the last three propositions. There is no contradiction between the first four, which show that A is the best candidate; and there is no contradiction between the first seven propositions, which show that while A is the best, B is the next-best candidate.‡

But the contradictions may be such that no candidate is seen to be better than all of the others in this way. Here Condorcet gives the instruction that we should make out the list of propositions that result from the voting, then remove from it those propositions that have the smallest majorities in their favour, and adopt the decision that follows from the first consistent set of propositions

* *Essai*, p. 126.　　† *Essai*, p. clxxii.　　‡ *Essai*, pp. clxxi–clxxii.

remaining.* He gives no argument for the rule beyond that it accords with his procedure in the case of three candidates. And he states that if we admit this method a different result may follow according as we begin with the set of propositions

$$
\begin{array}{lll}
A \gtrless B & \text{or} \quad B \gtrless A & \text{or} \quad C \gtrless A, \\
A \gtrless C & B \gtrless C & C \gtrless B, \\
A \gtrless D & B \gtrless D & C \gtrless D, \\
\cdots & \cdots & \cdots
\end{array}
$$

and so on.†

As Nanson says 'The general rules for the case of any number of candidates as given by Condorcet are stated so briefly as to be hardly intelligible...and as no examples are given it is quite hopeless to find out what Condorcet meant.'‡ The following three interpretations, however, might be suggested.

(i) We might write down the list of propositions for A in relation to each of the other candidates, those for B, etc., as shown; and then deem the largest size of minority to be a majority, then the next largest minority, and so on, until all of the propositions relating to one of the candidates become majorities (either true or deemed) and elect him.

(ii) It would be more consistent with Condorcet's words, though not with his lists of symbols, to take into account all of the propositions derived from the voting and disregard the proposition $G > H$, say, which has the smallest majority in its favour, and the corresponding $H < G$. Then if propositions of the type $H > I$, $I > G$ existed, we would deem $H > G$. Proceeding to delete the smallest, next-smallest,...majorities, we would select that candidate who was the first to secure a majority or deemed majority over each of the others.

(iii) It would be most in accordance with the spirit of Condorcet's previous analysis, I think, to discard all candidates except those with the minimum number of majorities against them and then to deem the largest size of minority to be a majority, and so on, until one candidate had only actual or deemed majorities against each of the others.

Contrary to what Condorcet says, however, each of these three interpretations would give rise to the choice of a definite candidate (ties in the voting apart), so that none of them may be what he had

* *Essai*, pp. 126 and lxviii.   † *Essai*, p. 127.
‡ British Government blue book *Misc. No. 3 (1907)*, Cd. 3501, p. 137.

in mind. It is a pity that on this crucial question his argument should be so fragmentary. His brief comment on the matter, as we shall see later, is in marked contrast to the attitude of C. L. Dodgson who came to regard just this point—the correct treatment of the contradictory case—as being the problem in the theory of committees which was most worth investigation.

As an afterthought, Condorcet attempts to provide some justification for his proposal in the *Discours Préliminaire*.* He points out that although when the propositions are contradictory, the probability that the candidate selected is better than any of the others is necessarily less than $\frac{1}{2}$, nevertheless, the probability that this

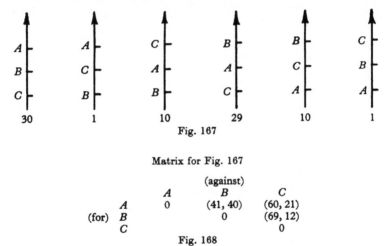

Fig. 167

Matrix for Fig. 167

		(against)		
		A	B	C
	A	0	(41, 40)	(60, 21)
(for)	B		0	(69, 12)
	C			0

Fig. 168

candidate is better than any other individual candidate may be greater than $\frac{1}{2}$. Let us suppose, for example, that out of six candidates the probability in favour of the one who is selected is $\frac{5}{12}$, and that in favour of the others $\frac{2}{12}$, $\frac{2}{12}$, $\frac{1}{12}$, $\frac{1}{12}$ and $\frac{1}{12}$ respectively. Then there is a probability of either $\frac{5}{7}$ or $\frac{5}{6}$ that the candidate chosen is better than any other individual candidate. The difficulty remains, however, that so far as we know the candidate with the probability of $\frac{5}{12}$ in his favour need not be the one selected by Condorcet's method (whatever it may be).

He also suggests that where an election must be made, there should be a preliminary vote, to make sure that each of the candidates allowed to stand is of sufficient calibre. Then a candidate

* *Essai*, pp. clxxiv–clxxv.

elected without a clear set of majorities would nevertheless be satisfactory.*

The refutation of any single set of marks. He shows† that it is impossible to devise any one list which gives a definite mark for a top place, a definite mark for a second-top place, ..., so as to select the majority candidate, i.e. the candidate who ought to be elected.

His example is that of Fig. 167 in which A is the majority candidate. Let the mark for a candidate at the top of a schedule be f, at second place g and at third place h. Then if A is to be elected rather than B, we must have

$$31f + 39g + 11h > 39f + 31g + 11h,$$

$$8g > 8f,$$

$$g > f,$$

and we would require to attribute more credit to a second place on a schedule than to a first—which is impossible.

Very justly, however, Condorcet observes that Borda's method would lead to a wrong result in only a small number of cases. It is much superior to the single vote and has the practical advantages of being extremely simple and of always giving a definite result.‡

A possible objection considered. Right at the end of his reasoning Condorcet introduces a point of fundamental importance. Suppose that an elector believes that A is better than B and B is better than C. Should the propositions

$$A > B \quad B > C \quad A > C$$

be treated as being equally valid? Or should not the proposition $A > C$ be given more significance than either of the others and treated as being more probably true, because it can be reached by the person concerned both by the immediate comparison of A with C, and through the comparison of A with B and B with C?

His answer is worth reproducing in full, both for its own importance and as an illustration of his manner of writing.

But one can reply thus [to this question], 1° that one can, in a very great number of cases, consider as equally probable two propositions

---

* *Essai*, p. 127 and p. lxvi.

† *Essai*, pp. 295–6, clxxvii–clxxix. To avoid confusion, in the example that follows we have replaced Condorcet's symbols a, b and c by f, g and h.

‡ *Essai*, p. clxxix.

which pronounce upon the difference between two objects, although the difference asserted by the two propositions is not the same; 2° if the comparison is made only in relation to the same quality...it does not seem that the probability need increase, because the comparison of A with B and of B with C does not furnish us proofs of the superiority of A over C that the immediate comparison of A with C does not already furnish us with; 3° if the comparison is made in relation to two or more qualities, the same observation again holds good. For example, if A is judged superior to B in the matter of one of these qualities, and over C in regard to the other, and thereafter comparing B and C, I find in the one superiority in the first of these qualities and in the other in the second, my judgement in favour of B will only be the preference accorded by me to the first of these qualities; and the probability that this preference is a just one increases the probability of the greater amount of the difference between A and C, but not the existence of this difference in favour of A; 4° lastly the two propositions $A > B$ and $A > C$, if they have been made separately without comparing B and C, do not necessarily for that reason become more probable whatever may be the result of the comparison between B and C.

We therefore believe that it is better to look upon all these propositions in general as being equally probable which have an equal majority, because the difference in their probability, often nil or very small, can only be estimated in a very arbitrary way.*

We get no help in the interpretation from the parallel passage in the *Discours Préliminaire*,† for its language is no less stilted and artificial than this, being based, as is the style of the whole book, on the Roman and Greek models rather than the spoken French. The meaning must be pondered over and weighed before it can be grasped. In these jerky sentences Condorcet raises the most sceptical objection that can be brought against his system, namely, that it may not be satisfactory to treat valuation as being merely relative; perhaps some relative valuations correspond better to the facts than others. He is aware of the psychological and logical issues that arise; and his conclusion is an endeavour to cut a path through the difficulties.

The relationship between Condorcet's and Borda's theories. Borda read a paper 'Sur la Forme des Élections' before the Academy of Sciences on 16 June 1770.‡ Four members were charged with making a report on it, but this was never done, and

---

* *Essai*, pp. 294–5. † Pp. clxxv–clxxvii.
‡ Condorcet's connexion with the Academy had begun in 1769, but he was not present at this meeting.

it is unlikely that the Academy considered elections again during the succeeding fourteen years.*

At the meeting of the Academy of 17 July 1784, Bossut and Coulomb presented a report on Condorcet's manuscript *Essai*, and accompanied their account with high commendation. At the very next meeting, 21 July 1784, Borda again read a paper on elections and completed its reading at the meeting held a week later.

Borda's paper was printed in the *Histoire de l'Académie* dated 1781, but published in 1784. He says in a footnote: 'The ideas contained in this memoir have already been presented to the Academy fourteen years ago.'†

Condorcet in the *Essai* explains that, though indirectly, he is indebted to Borda and says, after discussing the method of marks:

Although the famous applied mathematician (*Géomètre*) to whom one is indebted for this method has published nothing on this subject, I have thought it necessary to mention him here, 1º because he is the first who noticed that the method of election in common use was faulty; 2º because the method that he proposed to substitute for it is extremely ingenious and would be very simple in practice. Besides although it is not exempt from those defects which ought to make us discard the ordinary method, nevertheless these defects in it are far less pronounced: it is even very probable that it would only very rarely lead us into error on the true decision concerning the majority of votes.

In a footnote added to this passage, it seems, when the *Essai* was already in type, Condorcet says:

This work had been printed in its entirety before I had any acquaintance with this method [of Borda], apart from the fact that I had heard several people speak of it (*si ce n'est pour en avoir entendu parler à quelques personnes*). It has since been published in the *Mém. de l'Acad.* 1781.‡

Throughout their lives the two were close friends, and during Borda's prolonged absences from Paris they corresponded much on scientific matters.§ From Condorcet's acknowledgement—for they are the words of one who in all the relationships of life was most

---

* We examined the minutes of the Academy for the years 1779–83, without finding any reference to the theory of elections.

† *Op. cit.* p. 657.   ‡ *Essai*, p. clxxix.

§ Arago, *Oeuvres de Condorcet*, tome I, p. iv, and J. Mascart, *La Vie...de Borda*, pp. 95–6.

generous—we may infer that he owed his knowledge of Borda's views not to correspondence or personal discussion, but to the persistence at the Academy of an oral tradition that had taken its rise from Borda's paper of 1770.

Soon after hearing Borda's paper in 1784 the Academy adopted his method in elections to its membership. It remained in use until 1800, when it was attacked by a new member and was modified soon afterwards. The new member was Napoleon Bonaparte.*

3. Pierre-Simon, Marquis de Laplace† (1749–1827)

His theory of elections. Laplace's theory of elections was given‡ within a decade of that of Condorcet. It is put forward in his style of simple elegance and seeks to reduce the matter to a theorem in mathematical probability. In passing to his pages from those of Condorcet, we move from turbulence and excitement into tranquillity.

To show how he poses the problem we will first present a simplified version. Let us consider a single voter in, say, four different elections, each with three candidates. In each of these elections, we may suppose, he attributes a certain measurable merit to the candidate of his first choice, some lesser (measurable) merit to the candidate whom he places second and some lesser merit again to the candidate whom he places lowest. This state of affairs would be depicted by a diagram of the type of Fig. 169, which shows the merit that the voter attributes to each candidate in each of the elections, the elections being ranged in the diagram from left to right in accordance with increasing merit attributed to the first-choice candidate. The two intervening points marked on each of

* J. Mascart, *op. cit.* pp. 128–34.

† See E. T. Bell, *Men of Mathematics*, chapter XI; and for an unconventional view of his character, 'Laplace, being Extracts from Lectures delivered by Karl Pearson', *Biometrika*, vol. XXI, 1929.

‡ 'Leçons de Mathématiques, données à l'École Normale en 1795', which appeared in the *Journal de l'École Polytechnique*, tome II, septième et huitième cahiers (Paris, June 1812). This material was reproduced, with minor verbal alterations, in the *Essai Philosophique sur les Probabilités*, which, after appearing separately (1814), was made the introduction to the second edition of the *Théorie Analytique des Probabilités* (1814). It was also in the second edition of the *Théorie Analytique* that his mathematical theory of elections first appeared. The relevant passages are to be found at pp. XC–XCIV and 277–9 in the *Oeuvres Complètes* (Academy edition), tome VII (1886).

the ordinates show the merits attributed to the candidates of his second and third choice.

To get Laplace's view of the problem, let us now assume that the number of elections in which this voter participates becomes indefinitely multiplied so as to become infinite, while the number of candidates in each still remains three. Let the maximum merit that he attributes to any candidate in one of these elections be, say, h; and let us take it that the maximum merit that he attributes to the candidate of his first choice in these elections ranges

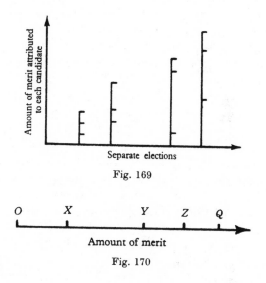

Fig. 169

Fig. 170

from the infinitesimally small to h in such a way that all merits between these limits are equally likely. And let all merits attributed by the elector to his second and third choices, between the infinitesimally small and that attributed to his first choice, again be equally likely. Then the problem of finding the merit attributed on the average to a first-, second- and third-choice candidate becomes that of finding what, on the average, are the lengths cut off on a straight line OQ by three points X, Y and Z respectively, chosen at random, given that $OX < OY < OZ \leqslant OQ = h$ (Fig. 170). It can be shown* that on the average of an infinite number of cases, X, Y and Z divide the line OQ into four equal segments, so

* M. W. Crofton, article 'Probability', *Encyclopeadia Britannica*, ninth edition (1885), vol. XIX, p. 780, § 43, and Todhunter, *History of...Probability*, pp. 546–8.

that $OY = 2OX$, $OZ = 3OX$; the merits attributed to the three candidates stand in the ratios $1:2:3$.

If there are n candidates, the corresponding conclusion applies; on the average the elector will attribute merits to the candidates of his last, ... second and first choice in the ratios

$$1: \ldots : n-1 : n.$$

Now the candidate who ought to be elected, Laplace postulates,[*] is that one to whom most merit is attributed by the group of voters. From this he deduces that a just form of election would give a candidate 1 mark for each lowest place that he has on a ballot card, 2 marks for a second-lowest place, 3 marks for a third-lowest place, and so on; and the candidate with the highest number of marks would be elected. Starting from slightly different premisses he arrives at the same set of marks as Borda.

If the assumptions are widened so as to let the different voters attribute different maximum merits to the candidates of their first choice, say, h, h', h'', ..., the same conclusion still follows.

The only obstacle which Laplace foresees to the use of the scheme is that its working might be frustrated by electors placing the strongest opponents to their favourite candidates at the foot of their list. This would give a great advantage to candidates of mediocre merit, for while getting few top places they would also get few lowest places. The same difficulty had been foreseen by Borda, who, when confronted with it, had replied 'My scheme is only intended for honest men.'[†]

That Laplace's justification of the method of marks (like that of Borda) is untenable. Borda in one of his two proofs used probability theory at the common-sense level to obtain his set of marks; and Laplace by a more sophisticated route arrives at the same result.

The approach of these two authors, however, seems to require assumptions which are quite untenable. It supposes, for instance, that a voter considers the relative worths of two candidates to stand in some definite ratio to each other, such as $5:4$ or $6:1$ or some other. But we may feel quite sure that the human mind does not work in this way. There are definite ratios of exchange for goods in the market, and a purchaser may value equally two units

---

* *Oeuvres*, tome VII, p. 278.

† S. F. Lacroix, *Éloge Historique de J.-C. Borda*, pp. 37–8 and J. Mascart, *La Vie...de Borda*, p. 130.

of one and three units of another; but the same is not true of the elector's valuation of candidates.

Next the scheme assumes the merit attributed by one elector to be exactly the same in kind as that attributed by another. The difficulties of making interpersonal comparisons of merit have already been examined by economists under a slightly different guise, in connexion with making interpersonal comparisons of utility. Just as we would be reluctant to adopt an economic theory of this type, so we would be unwilling to adopt a political theory which assumed the merit attributed by voters to be measurable and the same in kind as between one voter and another.

On the other hand, in defence of the approach of Laplace (or Borda) against that of Condorcet (or the present book) it might be said that the essential difference between the two is that Laplace's system rests on a theory of absolute valuation, Condorcet's on a theory of relative valuation; and that not everything is in favour of the theory of relative valuation. Here the main considerations seem to be these. A theory of relative valuation affirms nothing about reality which is untrue; people do make relative valuations. This, however, is not the entire matter, for while we judge that one candidate is preferable to another, we may also judge that we much prefer him, that his selection would do a great deal of good, would give us considerable pleasure, and so on. The theory of relative valuation tells no lie, but it fails to take into account some of the features that characterize valuation in reality, and in this way fails to tell the whole truth. On the other hand, a theory of absolute valuation, such as that used by Laplace, in attempting to take into account the features which are disregarded by the theory of relative valuation, makes crude assertions about reality which we know to be untrue and incorporates elements of error. This line of defence, therefore, may throw doubt on the completeness of Condorcet's system, but doing so does not validate the system of Laplace.

4. Conclusions

The academicians. The second half of the eighteenth century in France was one of the outstanding epochs of scientific thought. Science had felt its strength and its impulse and did not know what barriers it might not cross.

                                        ...it may be
         Beyond that last blue mountain barred with snow...
         There lives a prophet who can understand
         Why men were born.   Flecker, *Hassan*

The hope had sprung up to carry the methods of rigorous and
mathematical thought beyond the physical and into the realms of
the human sciences. But after a brilliant start, its fate was to be
misunderstood and forgotten.

The initial step was taken by Borda, who, like the others of the
triumvirate we have considered, had already achieved distinction
as a mathematician and had for the centre of his life the Academy
of Sciences. It was no doubt elections to the Academy, membership of which was for him the most valuable of all privileges, and
not the wider problems of politics that first directed his mind to
the theory. In it he showed the same eye for the significant fact
and for the simplifying assumption as in his other researches,* and
he broached the subject in a new way. His work has the robust
good sense of the practical man.

It is not only the same strand of reasoning on which both Borda
and Laplace rely and the same conclusion that they adopt, but it
is also the same spirit that actuates the work of both of them. By
a straight and untortuous line of reasoning they proceed from
premiss to conclusion; and no one, whether mathematician or
politician, can fail to feel the attraction of their theory. It com-
bines a logical with a practical appeal and its virtues are much
more visible than its defects: the real phenomena involved in
elections are far more complex, tortuous and indecisive than it
represents.

Condorcet, on the other hand, saw the complexities. He had a
deep intuitive vision of the truth and tried to impart it, more,
perhaps, by the use of symbols than by a strict Mathematics. His
symbolism purported to belong to the mathematical theory of
probability, but would now be regarded as a primitive topology,
though this branch has only been developed quite recently; and it
was misunderstood by the mathematicians. Without help from
them, the student of politics lacked the means of approaching the
theory. Not that all of the faults were on the part of the readers,
for the root of the trouble lay in the presentation of the theory.

* S. F. Lacroix, *Éloge Historique de J.-C. Borda*, pp. 13 and 16 and J. Mascart,
La Vie...de Borda, p. 67.

It was buried away at various parts of a long and difficult book and its meaning must be wrung from Condorcet's stilted and crabbed sentences. He presents no clear view of the phenomena whose nature he had so deeply scrutinized. Not, by any means, that it is easy to do so, for the phenomena themselves are interlacing and unexpected and difficult to depict; they do not conform to the rules which we observe external objects to obey, nor to the Mathematics of physical objects on which we have been brought up. A new type of connexion exists and the laws stating the relationships between the objects will be novel. When they are set down, the mind that is familiar with the existing laws of Physics, say, or even of Economics, finds them incongruous and grotesque.

Borda and Laplace discuss the matter no further than is necessary to establish that one form of election is good and the others, *ipso facto*, defective. Condorcet set out with a wider end in view and his theory of elections is a fragment of a systematic discussion of the justice of the decisions reached by political bodies. In this chapter we have not shown the wider context in which he places his theory, but we trust that we have shown that his theory gives a far more vital account of the nature of elections and of group decision-taking than any other. If our estimate of this part of his work is accepted, it implies that a revaluation should be attempted of the whole of Condorcet's theory of Politics.

CHAPTER XIX

E. J. NANSON AND FRANCIS GALTON

The English mathematicians. The interest in elections of Todhunter and Crofton was purely incidental to their work in the theory of probability. Isaac Todhunter* (1820–84, Fellow of St John's College, Cambridge), in his magistral work *A History of the Mathematical Theory of Probability* (1865), mentioned Borda's conclusions in regard to elections and examined the views of Condorcet and Laplace falling within the calculus of probabilities. As an aid to understanding Condorcet's book, Todhunter is indispensable, though he himself failed to understand its theory of elections.

* Alexander MacFarlane gives a short biography in *Ten British Mathematicians*, pp. 134–46.

M. W. Crofton (1826–1915, Fellow in the Royal University of Ireland) gave an ingenious proof of Laplace's rule for allocating marks.*

The only other mathematicians, so far as we know, who have devoted some attention to elections are E. J. Nanson, Francis Galton and Rev. C. L. Dodgson (Lewis Carroll); and we will deal with Dodgson's contributions at some length in the following chapter.

E. J. Nanson. Just before the centenary of Condorcet's *Essai* E. J. Nanson (1850–1936, Fellow of Trinity College, Cambridge, and Professor of Mathematics at Melbourne from 1875 till 1922) wrote his memoir on elections.† By reason of its subject-matter Nanson's paper is broken up into rather a large number of sections and makes difficult reading. Yet the only mathematics it employs is elementary algebra and the argument is expressed clearly. The truth seems to be that it is the *ideas* involved in the theory of elections that are difficult to grasp, even when properly stated; and they will remain so until some more advanced mathematical technique enables us to work out automatically the consequences of stated assumptions in this field.

Nanson's paper is needlessly obscure only where he uses one of Condorcet's fundamental ideas without explaining the structure of the thought from which it had been derived.‡ This sets out the 'contradictory' case in which, with three candidates A, B and C, the voting yields the result

$$A > B \quad B > C \quad C > A.$$

What had baffled Todhunter could scarcely be intelligible, without explanation, to the ordinary reader.

Nanson also states the conclusions of Borda (or Laplace) and Condorcet as to the best method of voting, without indicating the systems of thought from which these conclusions had sprung. Another essay on the works of these authors, which he was well qualified to write, would have been needed to fill this gap in the account.

He opens his paper by saying that the majority candidate ought to be elected and seems to think that this position, once it has been

* 'Probability', *Encyc. Brit.* 9th ed. (1885), vol. XIX, p. 780, § 43.
† 'Methods of Election' in Brit. Gov. blue book, *Misc. No. 3 (1907)*, Cd. 3501.
‡ *Op. cit.* p. 130.

stated, is self-evident. He then shows* that Borda's method 'leads to an erroneous result' in that it may yield a different answer.

He goes on to examine the working out of a number of other systems of voting, the single vote, double election, exhaustive voting, etc., in relation to the criterion he has chosen. When he finds them defective he shows how, by a system of attributing marks at various rounds of voting, the majority candidate can be selected.†

An interesting feature of Nanson's system of marking occurs in the case of three candidates, no one of whom is able to get a majority over each of the others. Let the result be

$$A > B \quad B > C \quad C > A.$$

Condorcet had suggested that in these circumstances we should delete the proposition with the smallest majority, say $C > A$, and choose the candidate given by the remaining two propositions, in this case A; and Nanson shows‡ that his system of marking would, in these circumstances, also choose the candidate A. He believes, however, that where there are more than three candidates and inconsistent propositions result, his own method and Condorcet's will select different candidates. But in any event it is impossible to say how Condorcet's system would work out in this case.§

The real defects in Nanson's method of election are of a practical kind. It proceeds by a series of eliminations and, requiring a new set of marks at each round, works out very laboriously. Nanson himself says: 'There can be no doubt...that the method would be tedious if the number of electors were very large, unless the number of candidates was very small indeed.'‖ And although it can deal with the case in which an elector brackets two or more candidates at the same level of preference, it needs rather complicated markings to do so. Even apart from this, the method would not be intelligible to the average elector; and the requirement of intelligibility must be insisted on if we are to foster democratic government.

The last paragraph of Nanson's paper contains some good

* *Op. cit.* p. 124.
† *Op. cit.* pp. 129–32, 134–41.
A short mathematical proof of his method is given by C. G. Hoag and G. H. Hallett, *Proportional Representation*, pp. 492–3.
‡ *Op. cit.* p. 130.   § *Op. cit.* p. 137 and pp. 174–6 above.
‖ *Op. cit.* p. 136.

remarks on proportional representation and a criticism of Hare's system. The pamphlet* which he published seventeen years later, however, was no more than a conventional description of the working of that system.

Another method of picking out the majority candidate was devised by George H. Hallett, Jr., but the twenty-four rules that he gives† are much more complicated even than those proposed by Nanson and are quite unusable.

Francis Galton. Galton (1822–1911) made only a small contribution to the theory of committees and one which no doubt was made independently by many other people, but we mention it in view of the interest that attaches to Galton as one of the originators of modern statistical methods. He notices the property of the median optimum when the variable under consideration is measurable (provided the voters' preference curves can be taken as single-peaked):

A certain class of problems do not as yet appear to be solved according to scientific rules, though they are of much importance and of frequent recurrence. Two examples will suffice. (1) A jury has to assess damages. (2) The council of a society has to fix on a sum of money, suitable for some particular purpose. Each voter, whether of the jury or of the council, has equal authority with each of his colleagues. How can the right conclusion be reached, considering that there may be as many different estimates as there are members? That conclusion is clearly *not* the *average* of all the estimates, which would give a voting power to 'cranks' in proportion to their crankiness. One absurdly large or small estimate would leave a greater impress on the result than one of reasonable amount, and the more an estimate diverges from the bulk of the rest, the more influence would it exert. I wish to point out that the estimate to which least objection can be raised is the *middlemost* estimate, the number of votes that it is too high being exactly balanced by the number of votes that it is too low. Every other estimate is condemned by a majority of voters as being either too high or too low.‡

Some of Galton's statistical work is related, at one or two removes, to the theory of elections and has been commented upon by Karl Pearson.§

* *Electoral Reform, an Exposition of the Theory and Practice of Proportional Representation* (Melbourne, 1899).

† C. G. Hoag and G. H. Hallett, *Proportional Representation*, pp. 496–508.

‡ 'One Vote, One Value', *Nature*, vol. LXXV, 1907, p. 414; cf. also 'Vox Populi', *ibid.* p. 450 and 'The Ballot Box', *ibid.* p. 509 and Galton's *Memories of My Life*, pp. 278–83.

§ Karl Pearson, *The Life, Letters and Labours of Francis Galton*, vol. II, pp. 400–14.

CHAPTER XX

THE CIRCUMSTANCES IN WHICH
REV. C. L. DODGSON (LEWIS CARROLL)
WROTE HIS THREE PAMPHLETS

Publications on committees, elections and proportionate representation. The Rev. Charles Lutwidge Dodgson (1832–98), whose stories and verse appeared over the pseudonym Lewis Carroll, at one stage in his life wrote extensively on committees, elections and proportionate representation. Owing to the importance of Dodgson's work and the interest attaching to his character, his three main pamphlets are reprinted in the following appendix. We will list his main publications on the subject, all now either scarce or very rare. Fuller bibliographical details will be found in the *Handbook of the Literature of the Rev. C. L. Dodgson (Lewis Carroll)* (Oxford, 1931), by Sidney Herbert Williams and Falconer Madan (late Bodley's Librarian), a work which is the product of the most ripe scholarship and love of its subject and which is a perfect model of its kind.

(1) *A Discussion of the Various Methods of Procedure in Conducting Elections.* (Preface dated 18 Dec. 1873: pp. 15 + 1.)†

Dodgson considers various methods of election which are in use, including the single vote and the method of marks (which we have described above in connexion with Borda) and shows their deficiencies. His own suggestion is that a modification of the method of marks should be employed, which treats the possibility of 'no election' as if it were the name of a candidate, and assigns marks so as to discourage the elector from bracketing candidates together. He considers that the originality of his paper lies in these two modifications.

---

* The present chapter may not seem in keeping with the earlier ones, for it gives a description of the circumstances in which the Rev. C. L. Dodgson wrote his three papers on elections and committees, whereas the earlier chapters recount only the theories of the authors concerned. The discrepancy, however, is apparent rather than real, for the writer did attempt to discover any circumstances which might have had an influence on the theories of Borda and Condorcet; but even a fairly sustained attempt yielded no more than the meagre details recorded above. In the case of Dodgson the same inquiry met with a better fortune.

† Only a single copy of this is known to exist, that in Princeton University Library. This copy has Dodgson's own additions and amendments.

(2) *Suggestions as to the Best Method of Taking Votes, Where More than Two Issues are to be Voted on.* (Preface dated 13 June 1874: pp. 7 + 1.)

This brief pamphlet consists of only between six and seven hundred words and no symbols. Dodgson has now hit on what we have referred to as the Condorcet criterion, but realizes that very often no motion will exist which is able to satisfy it. He recommends that if this criterion fails to pick out any motion as having the best claim to adoption, then his modified method of marks should be used.

(3) *A Method of Taking Votes on More than Two Issues.* (Written 23 Feb. 1876, dated March 1876: pp. 20.)

The first pamphlet had referred to elections, the second has in mind mainly, but not exclusively, a committee choosing a motion, and the third again refers mainly to elections.

There is evidence that Dodgson knows a great deal about the nature of cyclical majorities; as in his second pamphlet he makes use of the Condorcet criterion, but now employs in connexion with it a matrix notation; he suggests a way of dealing with cyclical majorities where they occur; and he alludes briefly but clearly to the possibility of complementary valuation on the part of the members and indicates how, for the case which interests him, provision may be made for taking this into account.

Dodgson intended to write a book on elections and immediately sent out this pamphlet, interleaved with blank pages, to a number of friends and colleagues at Christ Church, for their criticisms and suggestions.

(4) 'The cyclostyled sheet', dated 7 Dec. 1877.

This is merely a stereotyped letter which Dodgson sent to various people, along with his pamphlet *A Method...* (1876), in a further attempt to elicit criticisms and also 'an account of any rules, written or unwritten' adopted in the various colleges 'to settle difficulties arising in elections'.

(5) Nine letters or articles on elections and proportionate representation appearing in *The St James's Gazette*, an evening newspaper, the first on 4 May 1881 and the last on 4 Dec. 1885.*

* Their dates are given by Roger Lancelyn Green in 'Lewis Carroll and *The St James's Gazette*', *Notes and Queries*, 7 April 1945. One of the dates which

(6) *The Principles of Parliamentary Representation.* (First edition, 1884: pp. 8 + 48.)

This booklet, of which the preface is dated 5 Nov. 1884, contains Dodgson's own scheme for securing proportionate representation, which had already been fairly fully worked out in the letters to *The St James's Gazette.*

It gives a neat algebraic treatment of a few problems in voting, but the scheme of P.R. which it suggests is entirely dependent on the assumption that there are only two political parties in the country concerned. At the time when Dodgson was writing there was a certain amount of justification for this extreme assumption, for in the period 1868–85 'the two-party system was... more clear-cut than ever before'.* The effect of this assumption, however, is to reduce the problem to one of relatively little interest; he is dealing with a special problem and not with the general problem.

Also the solution that Dodgson suggests permits the candidates themselves to hand over the surplus votes which they get over and above the quota needed for election, to other candidates who have not yet obtained the quota; and most people would consider this undesirable.

(7) *The Principles of Parliamentary Representation.* (Second edition,† 1885: pp. 8 + 48.)

The preface is dated 1 Jan. 1885. The ordering of the argument is altered from the first edition, but certainly not for the better, and a few minor improvements and corrections are made.

(8) *The Principles of Parliamentary Representation: Supplement.* (Dated Feb. 1885: pp. 7 + 1.)

(9) *The Principles of Parliamentary Representation: Postscript to Supplement.* (Dated Feb. 1885: pp. 4.)

In these last two items Dodgson defends the *Principles* against the criticism, put forward seemingly by some acquaintance, that

Mr Green gives, 30 Dec. 1881, should be omitted from his list, for in the letter concerned Dodgson is dealing entirely with church matters.

Excerpts from the letters of 4 May 1881 and 5 July 1884 are given in Stuart Dodgson Collingwood, *The Life and Letters of Lewis Carroll*, pp. 232–6.

* John S. Hawgood, 'The Nineteenth Century', in *The British Party System*, edited by Sydney D. Bailey, p. 32.

† Williams and Madan believe that the only extant copy is that in the Princeton University Library (*op. cit.* p. 106). A second copy, however, is to be found in the Harcourt Amory Collection at Harvard.

his system is inferior to the orthodox scheme of the Proportional Representation Society—this being the same as the one which the Society still advocates.

His scheme of proportionate representation is of less significance than his theory of elections and committees and will not be dealt with further in this book.

The originality of Dodgson's work on elections. Dodgson had gone up to Christ Church as an undergraduate in 1849, and within a few years had become a Senior Student, equivalent to a Fellow, in this college, and its Mathematical Lecturer. He remained unmarried, and from his undergraduate days to his death was resident at Christ Church, leaving it only during vacations to stay with his family or to holiday at the seaside or, on one occasion, to make a trip abroad.

He gained fame as 'Lewis Carroll' with the appearance of *Alice's Adventures in Wonderland* (1865), to be followed by *Through the Looking-Glass, and what Alice found there* (1872) and *The Hunting of the Snark* (1876). In addition to the *Elementary Treatise on Determinants* (1867) he was the author of a stream of writings on elementary Mathematics, and of pamphlets, broadsheets and letters relating to a wide variety of subjects concerning Christ Church and the university.

There would have been nothing surprising about a mathematical lecturer in the 1870's writing on the subject of elections and committees as a development of the work of other mathematicians with which he was acquainted. But it is unlikely that Dodgson's work did begin in this way, for although he worked hard throughout his entire life he read very little, except in general literature; and after he had brought out his book on Determinants his reading in Mathematics became more and more confined to Euclid and schoolboy Mathematics. As has been remarked* Dodgson's natural preference was to investigate some topic on which, so far as he knew, little or nothing had previously been done; and had he known that others had already worked in the theory of elections, the effect would only have been to turn him away from the subject.

One book, however, which referred to elections, Dodgson probably had read while he was an undergraduate or soon after—the *Essai philosophique sur les probabilités* of Laplace. The *Essai* is

* Florence Becker Lennon, *Lewis Carroll*, p. 267.

literary and non-mathematical, and there is a close parallelism between Dodgson's statement of the method of marks in the first pamphlet and a passage in the subsection 'Des choix et des décisions des assemblées'. Dodgson himself makes no reference to Laplace or any other author in any of his writings on elections or proportionate representation, and says in the preface to his first pamphlet 'I conclude by describing a Method of Procedure (whether new or not I cannot say)'. The construction of the pamphlet suggests that Dodgson simply regards the method of marks as one with which the reader will be familiar from its use in practice, and not one that he associates with any particular book. We should judge that he had at some time read Laplace's *Essai* and forgotten it and is now unconsciously reproducing the substance of its argument. But the point is unimportant since there was nothing to be gleaned from Laplace that would assist him in making his real contribution, which was that of the second and third pamphlets.

For them assistance might have been got from Todhunter's *History of the Mathematical Theory of Probability* which had appeared in 1865, for it summarized the views of Borda and Condorcet and gave references to their works. Certainly every mathematical lecturer in the country ought to have studied Todhunter's book closely and Dodgson was sufficiently dutiful to place it in his library,* but as Dr E. T. Bell says,† did not read it.

Now although it seems unlikely, on general grounds, that Dodgson would be at all interested in the work of earlier writers on elections, and although he had not *read* Todhunter, there is still the possibility that, thumbing through Todhunter's book, he might have come on the item 'Elections' in the index and got a summary of the views of Borda and Condorcet and (a somewhat remote possibility), that this might have led him to examine the writings of these authors when he was working on the subject. As it happens we can prove almost beyond doubt that he was unacquainted with the works of these two authors, because when we examined the volume of the *Histoire de l'Académie Royale des Sciences* for 1781, containing Borda's article, in the Christ Church Library, we found that its pages were still uncut; and this is surely the copy, if any, which Dodgson would have consulted. And it seems clear enough that

* *Catalogue of the furniture...and library of...C. L. Dodgson* (1898), p. 31.
† Lennon, *op. cit.* p. 266.

if he did not read Borda neither did he read Condorcet, for the two authors hang together in Todhunter's account. In any case while there was no copy of Condorcet's *Essai sur l'Application de l'Analyse...* in the Christ Church Library, we found that in the copy in the Bodleian one of the pages of a section on elections was uncut. It is fairly definite, therefore, that Dodgson had not seen the work of either Borda or Condorcet; and it seems most unlikely that he had noticed the item 'Elections' in Todhunter's index. His work owes almost nothing to his predecessors.

Dodgson as a mathematician and logician. The key to understanding Dodgson's contribution to the theory of elections lies not in his mathematical reading but in the situation at Christ Church in his own day and in Dodgson's meticulous, logical and hairsplitting mind and, not least, in his somewhat curious temperament.

Dodgson's studies at Oxford had been in Philosophy, the Classics and in Mathematics. In spite of the encouragement that he had, as a lecturer on the subject, to devote himself to a study of the Higher Mathematics, he lacked both the aptitude and the inclination. When, by resignation from his lectureship twenty-five years after he had taken it up, the compulsion to work on Mathematics was removed, he gave himself over to other studies, notably Formal Logic.

In this respect Sir Thomas Muir's assessment of the *Elementary Treatise on Determinants* (1867), Dodgson's one attempt at making a solid contribution to Mathematics, is of some interest. Sir Thomas says:

This is a text-book quite unlike all its predecessors. Professedly its aim is logical exactitude. In pursuance thereof all definitions, conventions, axioms, propositions and corollaries are carefully formulated, labelled and numbered: every step in a train of reasoning is kept scrupulously separate from its antecedent and consequent, and in order to guard against possible contamination of the reasoning illustrative examples are relegated to the footnotes. Clearness is also sought to be promoted by the use of more than the ordinary variety of printers' type, and precision by the introduction of new terms and symbols.... The consequence is that the pages, though broad-margined and well-printed, present an unwonted and bizarre appearance.*

* Sir Thomas Muir, *The Theory of Determinants in the Historical Order of Development*, vol. III, p. 24.

Dr E. T. Bell puts a great deal of truth into a single sentence:

As a mathematical logician, he was far ahead of his British contemporaries. If he had lived in Germany, instead of in England, the story would have been quite different: he had in him the stuff of a great mathematical logician.*

The Christ Church background. Dodgson entered Christ Church at the time when it was just about to begin changing from a medieval into a modern institution. We are told that about 1830

the Dean and Canons in rotation nominated young men to Studentships. In many cases these nominations were mere matters of favour, and were bestowed on the sons of Canons, or some other of their relations and friends, without regard to merit. But the Dean and some of the Canons had begun of late to nominate Commoners of the House on the recommendation of the Censors and Tutors.†

Until after the middle of the century there was little encouragement to academic work and the standing of the college in the university visibly declined.

The Dean under whose aegis the college had lost ground, Thomas Gaisford, was himself a fine scholar who enjoyed the goodwill and respect of his fellows, and Dodgson regarded the man who had welcomed him to Christ Church with a certain amount of affection. Gaisford disdained all change, and when in 1850 a Royal Commission was established to inquire into the state of the university and colleges of Oxford and to recommend changes in their administration and studies, he ignored its communications and treated it as if it did not exist. Yet he was compelled to witness the first stirrings of the new age; and in 1855 the Dean and Canons were forced to give up their immemorial right of nomination to Studentships. Their parting shot was an aggrieved comment not without its element of truth, though scarcely relevant in their own defence, on the undesirability of making awards on 'mere intellectual merit'.

At this time, the middle of the century, the college was still administered, as three centuries earlier, by the Dean and the Cathedral Chapter. The new governmental organization for the college was created by an Ordinance of 1858 and by the Christ Church (Oxford) Act of 1867. Now all the main issues, educational

---

* Cited in Lennon, *op. cit.* p. 276.
† H. L. Thompson, *Henry George Liddell, a Memoir*, p. 15.

policy and the management of the properties and revenues (except as regards the Cathedral) were brought under the control of a Governing Body which was to consist of the Dean, the Canons and the Students; and in it the Students would form the majority.

When Gaisford died his successor was, by contrast, one who had stood in the vanguard of reform and had in fact been a member of the Royal Commission. H. G. Liddell, joint-author of 'Liddell and Scott', the famous *Greek Lexicon*, and father of the still more famous ' Alice', became Dean in 1855 and his reign extended to 1892. Now that the college had been aroused from its torpor there were bound to be extensive educational changes; in particular it was necessary to arrive at a new definition of the rights and duties of the Students who had been given a main voice in the formation of policy. A strong-natured man like Liddell would inevitably hasten and amplify these changes and make them more thorough-going. But, as it happened, Liddell was to make his mark in his own generation and to leave visible evidence of it for later generations, by a trait of character which could scarcely have seemed of much account at the time of his election. As a young man he had conceived a deep interest in art and architecture, which might never have found any outlet more significant than the artistic 'doodling' that he accomplished during committee meetings; but once at Christ Church he found and made new opportunities for his artistic impulses and embarked without delay on a series of improvements and transformations of the college buildings. Starting with his own house, he converted the Deanery into a gracious place of residence; then the ancient cathedral was extensively improved and in the course of time the quadrangle and belfry were to change their appearance, Fell's Buildings were to be demolished and the new Meadow Buildings rise in their place.

Dodgson's loyalty to Christ Church. One reason then why Dodgson was attracted to the theory of committees (one of the subjects in which his abilities as a logician are demonstrated) was the changes that were taking place in the structure of government of Christ Church and the significance for the life of the college of the decisions that were being taken by the Governing Body. Every Student of Christ Church was vitally interested in these matters; and Dodgson, it may be felt, approached the whole subject in the manner that was natural to a logician of his calibre. Yet this explanation, which might on the face of it seem sufficient, would, as it happens, miss out a quite essential element, for Dodgson's contribution to the theory of committees was no less due to his state of mind at the time when he was writing. This can best be understood by pointing to the two motives, each largely of an unconscious nature, from which his work derives.

Even the most casual study of Dodgson's biography will make it clear that as a boy and a young man and indeed throughout his entire life, he was devoted in a quite extraordinary degree to his own family. From the family circle he had gone up as an undergraduate to Christ Church where he was to remain for the rest of his life. Now, minor divergencies apart, Christ Church reproduced the same formal pattern as his own family circle. It was a closed society occupying its own house—in fact, the college is always referred to by its members as *the House*.* It was his father's old college, and his feelings of esteem and loyalty had been awakened before ever he set eyes on it. At its head Dean Liddell swayed its policies with the same appearance of reasonableness and the same dominance as his father did at home, and the Liddell daughters were a refined and aristocratic version of his sisters.

Without any change towards the circle at home, the same attitude that Dodgson had towards his own family came to be extended to Christ Church—an attitude of reverence and solicitude, in which he was always asking himself how he could help. His nature made it difficult for him to conform altogether to the general pattern of college life, but if we judge loyalty by the test of being driven inevitably to protect its interests, Christ Church has had no more loyal son. And we will find that at least his first two pamphlets on committees gave expression to the desire to protect and serve his college.

Dean Liddell and Alice. The other main motive or unconscious drive from which these pamphlets spring is of a less admirable nature. Here again we can only state our view rather baldly but the reader may be referred for a fuller consideration of the subject to two recent biographies.† It seems that during the period within which these pamphlets were written, Dodgson's relations with the Liddell family were highly peculiar and that he had in some sense or other fallen in love with his old child-friend Alice Liddell,

* The rendering into English of its proper legal title, *Aedis Christi*.

† Alexander L. Taylor, *The White Knight*, chapters VII and VIII, and Derek Hudson, *Lewis Carroll*, chapters VII, X and XI.

though without the normal desire to marry her, and that about this time he had come to feel the most intense animus against the Dean and Mrs Liddell.

The evidence that chiefly concerns us is to be found in some of the pamphlets which he published on Christ Church affairs at practically the same time as he was writing on elections and mainly in *The New Belfry* and *The Vision of the Three T's*. Before this he had expressed himself freely, mainly in humorous skits, on numerous matters relating to college and university policy. He had resigned the office of Public Examiner in Mathematics for the university as a protest against the change in regulations permitting science students to give up Classics after passing Moderations (*The New Examination Statute*, 1864); he had taken part in the Jowett controversy (*The New Method of Evaluation as Applied to π*, 1865) and had written humorously (1865) on Gladstone, the Member for Oxford University, and protested (1867) against converting the Parks into cricket fields. These and other broadsheets and pamphlets had all Carroll's fondness for play upon words and contained much good fun. But with the appearance of *The New Belfry* (June 1872) and *The Vision of the Three T's* (April 1873) there was a change to a different key.

With his general concern for Christ Church we can easily imagine that Dodgson felt some anxieties, among other things, about the completed design of the college buildings after the many alterations that Liddell had in mind had been carried through; and it would not be altogether unexpected that a person of Dodgson's conservative tendencies should dislike some of the changes that were being made in the ancient fabric. But in writing about the matter Dodgson went beyond the reasonable bounds of polemics, and his humour in some of the Christ Church pamphlets of the period with which we are concerned is sometimes savage and repellent.*

A really astonishing example of this is where, in *The Vision of the Three T's*, he allows himself, when ostensibly dealing with college architecture, to speak of the Liddell daughters under the guise of birds, as 'King-fishers' with an eye for the 'Nobler kinds' [of undergraduates] and 'Gold-fish' (i.e. wealthy undergraduates). In a dialogue concerning the fish that may be got from the pool in the

* See the comment of John Francis McDermott in his edition of *The Russian Journal and other selections from the works of Lewis Carroll*, pp. 26–7.

middle of the Great Quadrangle of Christ Church, an angler gives some explanations:

I will say somewhat of the Nobler kinds, and chiefly of the Gold-fish, which is a species highly thought of, and much sought after in these parts, not only by men, but by divers birds, as for example the Kingfishers: and note that wheresoever you shall see those birds assemble, and but few insects about, there shall you ever find the Gold-fish most lively and richest in flavour; but wheresoever you perceive swarms of a certain gray fly, called the Dun-fly, there the Gold-fish are ever poorer in quality, and the King-fishers seldom seen.*

The ambitions of the Liddells for their daughters were well known, and Christ Church was the traditional place of education for the sons of many of the noble families. Prince Leopold, the youngest son of Queen Victoria, was also in residence at this time. Dodgson's meaning is clear enough and is put beyond doubt by Falconer Madan, who had himself known the ageing Dodgson and who remarks that the passage 'gave some offence at the Deanery'.†
Some of the rest of the 'fun' of the other tracts of this period is in little better taste than the passage we have quoted.

Whatever the allowance we make for Oxford's fondness for pamphleteering at this time, it is certainly strange to find a college don writing in such disrespectful terms about the family of his Dean. We cannot here consider in detail the reasons for Dodgson writing as he did, for this would require a fairly lengthy study; but we will simply state what appears to us to be the almost inescapable conclusion. It is that by about 1872, when Alice Liddell, a girl of outstanding beauty and charm, reached twenty, surrounded by some of the most eligible young bachelors in England, and Dodgson reached forty without much reputation in Christ Church, he realized that Alice Liddell, who had meant so much to him, was slipping out of his life. Even while Alice was still a child Mrs Liddell had not concealed her distaste for Dodgson: the Dean considered him an impractical person whose opinion on business matters had often been a hindrance and rarely a help; and for years before this he had been discouraged from calling at the Deanery. Dodgson felt frustrated and humiliated.

His reaction amounted to the attempt to triumph over Liddell and lower the stature of the Dean. By his pen, the instrument of

* *The Lewis Carroll Picture Book*, edited by Stuart Dodgson Collingwood, pp. 122-3. † Williams and Madan, *op. cit.* p. 54.

his genius, he would alter the direction of architectural policy, and college policy, the objects at the centre of the life which he still shared with the Liddells and the objects which conferred or took away college reputation. And only the most warped of judgements could have allowed him to speak disrespectfully of the Liddell daughters.

The disreputable part he **was** playing would have been impossible to Dodgson unless he **had** believed his motives to be quite other than they really were. He was aware that he felt concern for Christ Church and that he disapproved of the Dean's architectural plans. But the emotional impetus behind these various pamphlets is altogether disproportionate to the college matters to which ostensibly they refer, and his exacerbated and ragged feelings had their source nearer the heart. The model child in his own family and the favourite of his father had been rejected in his new family and he was in revolt against Dean Liddell and all his works, whatever they might be. The years 1872–6 were for Dodgson the years of turmoil. They were also the last years of his period of high artistic creation.

'A Discussion...' (1873). At the same time as he was writing cantankerously about Christ Church architecture (or really, as we have suggested, about Dean Liddell), Dodgson commenced working on the theory of elections and committees; and we must deal in some detail with the circumstances affecting his main writings on the subject, namely, his first three pamphlets.

We may regard Dodgson as having begun to approach the subject of elections a couple of years before his first pamphlet appeared. And the briefest way of setting out the sequence in which things happened may be to give the dates of the main events, including those mentioned in the recently published *Diaries*,* which seem to be connected with his work on elections and committees.

March 1871. He printed a broadsheet 'Suggestions for Committee appointed to consider the expediency of reconstituting Senior Studentships at Christ Church', advocating that Studentships be granted 'for educational purposes, or to promote the interests of learning; but that none be given as sinecures' and specifying the conditions of their tenure.

* *The Diaries of Lewis Carroll*, edited and supplemented by Roger Lancelyn Green, in two volumes.

He was still engaged with this* in May 1871.

June 1871. He prepared for the use of the Governing Body of Christ Church a digest of the new schemes relating to Studentships being introduced by other colleges.

He was still working on this† in February of the following year.

June–July 1872. He took steps to attend a meeting in the Commons and one in the Lords on the Ballot Bill.‡ These appear to have been the only occasions when he attended the debates in parliament.

The first pamphlet, *A Discussion*... (1873), was written quickly for the meeting of the Governing Body that was to make the first appointment to the Lee's Readership in Physics at Christ Church and also an election to a Senior Studentship; and its preface, dated 18 Dec. 1873, explains:

The following paper has been written and printed in great haste, as it was only on the night of Friday the 12th that it occurred to me to investigate the subject, which proved to be much more complicated than I had expected.

We know from the minutes of the Governing Body that on the 12th, the day when he commenced the pamphlet, Dodgson had attended a *viva voce* examination of some candidates, but no significance seems to attach to this.

The diary entries for the following days are:

Dec: 13. (S). Began writing a paper (which occurred to me last night) on 'Methods of Election', in view of our election of a Lee's Reader in Physics and a Senior Student next Wednesday.

Dec: 18. (Th). Election of Baynes and Paget: we partly used my method.

Dec: 29. (M)....I have been engaged writing about Elections very constantly lately.

Alongside this we may place the minute of the Governing Body for the date 18 Dec. 1873:

Mr Francis Paget, B.A., Jun. Stud., was elected to a Clerical Senior Studentship.

Mr Robert Edward Baynes, B.A. of Wadham College, was elected to the Lee's Readership in Physics.

* *Diaries*, vol. II, entry for 4 May 1871, and Black, 'Discovery of Lewis Carroll Documents', *Notes and Queries*, Feb. 1953, p. 78.

† *Diaries*, vol. II, entries of 7 and 15 June 1871 and of 26 Feb. 1872. No copy of this digest is known to exist.

‡ *Diaries*, vol. II, entries of 28 June and 8 July 1872.

In view of Dodgson's preface and the minute of the Governing Body, it had seemed, even before the appearance of the *Diaries*, that Dodgson's method of marks might have been used in the elections of that day; and when the present writer explained this view to Mr J. O. Urmson, secretary of the Governing Body, and Mr Geoffrey Bill, archivist of Christ Church, they instituted a search, and one of the first documents which emerged from a bureau which had traditionally been the property of the secretary of the Governing Body, was the piece of paper on which the voting had been noted on the day in question. On the one side this was marked 'Election of R. E. Baynes (Analysis of Votes), Dec. 18. 1873', and on the other side was a record of the voting. This showed that Dodgson's method of marks had been used at the first stage in making the appointment to the Lee's Readership in Physics: but when two of the three candidates practically tied for first place—Baynes 47 marks and Becker 48 marks—their names had again been put to the meeting and this time Baynes (11 votes) defeated Becker (9 votes).*

Now although Dodgson both in the preface to his pamphlet and in the *Diaries* speaks of the importance of the elections to be held that day, he also knew that a further item of business was the proposal to be put forward by his friend Vere Bayne, that a sub-committee should be appointed to deal with the building of the belfry, and this proposal was adopted.

A Committee of eight (4 elected by a majority of those present, 2 nominated by the Dean, 2 by the proposer (Mr Bayne)) was appointed with full power to choose a plan for the completion of the Belfry and to report the estimate to the Gov[erning] Body with a view to proceeding with the work. (Minute of the Governing Body, 18 Dec. 1873).

Dodgson's pamphlet *The New Belfry* shows how keenly affected he was by this topic, and further evidence of his interest is afforded by his attendances at the meetings of the Governing Body. The record shows that for a period of several years after this date he might 'cut' other meetings, but was almost invariably present if the discussion was to be on architectural business (the belfry and the quadrangle) or Studentships.

It seems likely, therefore, that the stimulus to Dodgson's first

* There is no record of Dodgson's method having been used in the election of Paget to the Senior Studentship.

pamphlet was not only the impending elections, but also the important decision which he knew was to be taken that day in regard to the belfry, about which he had expressed opinions which must have been disagreeable in the extreme to Dean Liddell.

The preface to Dodgson's first pamphlet on elections is dated 18 Dec. 1873, and it must have been printed that day, for on the same day the meeting of the Governing Body used the method of procedure it suggests. This was done, although all the evidence, including that which can be gleaned from its minutes, is that Dodgson was far from being an influential member of the Governing Body; on the contrary his opinion carried little weight and he was practically never appointed to a subcommittee. Nor were his friends in the college numerous, though he was less isolated at this period than he was to become at a later stage in his life.

The explanation of the almost instantaneous adoption of Dodgson's method of marks lies in the atmosphere in which the suggestion was put forward. For many years around this period Christ Church was facing a crisis: its finances had been seriously strained by its building policy, and it was open to question whether it could wisely undertake all the reconstruction on which it was engaged; resources had been drained away from the strictly educational side and not all the permitted number of Studentships had been filled; even apart from this the educational side was in process of being transformed from an archaic pattern to a modern one. Now it is common experience in any institution that interest is greatest when the future is most insecure, and that times of near-crisis evoke maximum discussion of the possibilities that lie open and of the plans that may be formulated. In this atmosphere any view and any plan will secure a hearing and will be judged on its merits. It was in such circumstances making for open-mindedness and a heightened critical faculty that Dodgson (as we know from the *ipsissima verba* of his pamphlets)* was able to explain in the Common Room and elsewhere the views which he was putting forward. And if his audience was specially prepared by circumstances to consider seriously the views of Dodgson or of any other, it happened also to be one which was unusually well qualified to do so in virtue of its high level of intellectual attainment, though any more exact pronouncement on this point must await the appearance of a history of Christ Church at this period.

* *A Method...* (1876), §3, pages 227–30 below.

Thus when he placed the first of his pamphlets in the hands of members of the Governing Body, although, as he himself says, he was 'no orator', and although he carried little weight in its councils, his scheme was adopted. It had been explained to his colleagues in the days before the meeting and had commended itself to a sufficient number of them in the Common Room.

'Suggestions...' (1874). A result of the use of his method must have been to draw Dodgson's attention to the main weakness of it; using the method of marks a candidate had been selected who failed to get a simple majority when put against one of the other candidates. This was an odd outcome and must have set Dodgson thinking about the next development in his theory.

After the Christmas vacation the Belfry Committee began its meetings and its intentions were no doubt a frequent subject of conversation. We can piece together fairly well the history of this committee from a document which may be referred to as the 'Vere Bayne Memorandum Book'.* In this notebook at various dates between 4 February 1874 and 14 December 1891, and more particularly for the early period, Vere Bayne, the secretary of the Governing Body, made rough jottings of minutes for some of the ancillary committees to which also he acted as secretary—the Belfry Committee, the Quadrangle Committee and the Committee on the Election of Senior Students in some cases without Examination. Indeed, it may have been to keep together the complexities of the Belfry and Quadrangle Committees that Vere Bayne started his record.

Running through all the entries for the early months there is the note of difference of opinion and perplexity as to the choice of design for the belfry. The first entry in the 'Memorandum Book' is the copy of a letter to Sir George Gilbert Scott, the architect who had already been responsible for the improvements in the structure of Christ Church Cathedral:

The Committee being dissatisfied with all suggestions hitherto made for completing the Belfry and feeling the great importance of having a larger choice of designs in a matter of so much consequence, have resolved to apply to a limited number of Architects to furnish Sketch Plans; and they hope that Sir G. G. Scott will not object to be included in the number of those invited to compete.

* This document came to light along with those referred to in Black, 'Discovery of Lewis Carroll Documents', *Notes and Queries*, Feb. 1953.

Eight architects were approached, of whom three agreed to compete, then five others were approached of whom two, including Mr George Bodley, entered the competition; and later Scott, who at first had declined, also agreed to submit plans. Soon Scott appeared before the committee to enquire 'in what point or points the previously submitted plans failed to satisfy?'—a question not easy to answer since different people wanted different things.

Vere Bayne's entry in his notebook is itself a little confused.

We gave him the answer copied in the following letter:

Ch. Ch.
11 Mar. 1874

My dear Sir,

The three drawings shall be sent to your office to-morrow; meanwhile you may like a memorandum of the only answer we were able to give to your questions today. I also enclose the suggestions framed to help us in comparing the various drawings, that you may avail themself [sic] of them with regard to the plan you may think fit to recommend.

When the Committee laid the plans before the G[overning] B[ody], the G[overning] B[ody] did not accept any of them, but the reasons given were very various, and expressed in many cases the opinions of individuals. It seems then to the Committee that they are not in a position to give such an answer to Sir G. G. Scott as might be taken to represent the opinion of the G[overning] B[ody].

Dodgson meantime gave vent to his feelings on Oxford architecture and other matters, by bringing out late in May* his *Notes of an Oxford Chiel*,† which gathered within the same covers his three sharply worded tracts *The New Belfry*, *The Vision of the Three T's* and *The Blank Cheque* (this last, of February 1874, referring to a university and not a college matter—but Liddell was at the time Vice-Chancellor) and some other Oxford pieces.

The Belfry Committee met on 20 May, 22 May and 8 June, and eliminated some designs that had been submitted and certain general proposals, such as to have a belfry constructed of wood and lead; and on the last of these dates and again on 12 June its report was considered by the Governing Body. Dodgson was present at

* Or at the beginning of June, see *Diaries*, vol. II, p. 330, for he made few entries in these months.

† Reprinted with explanatory notes by Lewis Sergeant in *The Lewis Carroll Picturebook*, ed. S. D. Collingwood, pp. 41–159, and in Alexander Woollcott's Nonesuch edition of *The Complete Works*, pp. 908–20, 1121–76; and five of the six papers are given in J. F. McDermott, *A Russian Journal*, pp. 124–89.

the first of these meetings and probably also at the second, for which no list of those present is given.

June 8. When the Dean stated certain conclusions at which the Belfry Committee had arrived; and the meeting was again adjourned till Friday (12th), but no business was then transacted. (Minute of the Governing Body).

The question of the belfry was again to be raised at the stated general meeting to be held on 18 June, and the evidence is overwhelming that acute difference of opinion existed among the members, with agreement only on the need that a decision should be taken. It was as a sudden preparation for this next meeting of the Governing Body that Dodgson wrote his second pamphlet, *Suggestions...* (1874). In his preface he alludes somewhat breathlessly to the circumstances:

In the immediate prospect of a meeting of the Governing Body, where matters may be debated of very great importance, on which various and conflicting opinions are known to be held, I venture to offer a few suggestions as to the mode of taking votes.

At various times during the past six months his mind had turned to elections, among many other subjects: he had had glimpses of a wider theory, but had not worked it out systematically; and the impending meeting about the belfry and the divided opinion of the members forced the pamphlet from him before he was ready to write on the subject. It gives only a suggested procedure to arrive at a decision with no attempt to show *why* this procedure might be considered satisfactory.

His proposal is that, for a start, all of the issues before the Governing Body should be listed and the first-preference votes for each of them should be counted; and if any motion is the first preference of an absolute majority of the members it should be adopted. But even though no proposal is able to get a majority of first-preference votes, it may be that there is some motion which can get a majority against each of the others which have been put forward; and, if so, this motion will be a satisfactory decision.

The minute of the Governing Body of 18 June reads:

These proposals were voted upon, all four at the same time, with this result:

1. To adopt Mr Jackson's Tower .... 9 votes in favour
2. To take Mr Bodley's Gateway as a basis ...... 2 votes in favour

3. To ask Mr Bodley for a fresh design,
                         wholly in stone .... 7 votes in favour
4. To adopt Mr Deane's Arcade .... 5 votes in favour

As this gave no absolute majority a vote was then taken, Bodley *v.*
Jackson; For Bodley 17, For Jackson 9. Bodley had also a slight
majority over either Deane or Scott. And it was carried by 16 *v.* 4 to
get Bodley and Deane to work together if possible in preparing a design.

A final vote was then taken as to proceeding at once, with Bodley and
Deane in combination if possible, else with Bodley: 19 Aye *v.* 6 No.

Dodgson's prognostication had been correct. No proposal could
get a majority of first-preference votes, but nevertheless the proposal that Bodley be entrusted to produce a fresh design could
claim to have the support of a majority against each of the other
proposals which had been put forward.

The only other information we have about the meeting is that
it lasted for five hours; and it would be interesting to know after
what disputes Dodgson's method was resorted to. He had per-
formed a signal service to his college in enabling it, in circumstances
where opinion was divided and each member was attached to his
own favourite scheme and feeling ran high, to arrive at a decision
of manifest reasonableness. He had also in a curious way placed
himself above Liddell, temporarily, as it were, usurping the
functions of the Dean: for while the Dean presided officially,
Dodgson had chosen the procedure that the Governing Body would
follow. The relish of his triumph was that he owed his ascendancy
to the logic of his ideas and to the appeal to the sense of justice
of his fellows. Both his urges were satisfied, his very real urge to
help his college and his still stronger impulse of hostility to
the Dean.

'A Method...' (1876). Dodgson now intended to write a book
on elections. He must already have accumulated notes and
examples on the subject and probably had some notions about the
general lines which the theory would take. But it seems that the
long vacation of 1874 did not provide time for this work.

The autumn term commenced with the alterations to the quadrangle in full swing and afforded the occasion for perplexity and
irritation. He published in *The Pall Mall Gazette* a rash and out-
spoken criticism of the proposed erection of cloisters, which he
knew was favoured by Liddell and some of his colleagues; and in
a further letter obstinately defended his right to make public

[207]

criticism of this kind, so long as it was done before a decision on the matter had been formally arrived at by the Governing Body.* In point of fact Dodgson's first letter was a strong criticism not only of the proposed building at Christ Church but also of the past building policy and of its educational and financial policy. The tone of the letters is insolent and hostile.

In the meeting of the Governing Body of December 1874, he voiced his disapprobation of the alterations to the quadrangle which a number of members had in mind; and then during the year that follows we are without any evidence of his feelings towards either Christ Church's architecture or its Dean. The diary entry after the statutory meeting of the Governing Body at the end of 1875, however, shows that he still bears in mind his desire to work on elections.

Dec: 18. (Sat). Election of Senior Students. After the usual dispute as to the way in which votes should be taken (a most complicated problem, which I still hope to work out some day) we elected Dalton, of C.C.C., & Payne Smith, of Trinity.†

Early in the following February an event occurred which set up another emotional crisis for Dodgson and was instrumental in leading him to write his third pamphlet. Max Müller, who had been resident at Oxford for twenty-eight years, during most of which he had held one or other of two chairs, latterly that in Comparative Philology, had for some time felt strongly that he should devote the remainder of his life and energies to his self-appointed task of translating and editing some of the sacred books of the East and that he should waste no further time in teaching, 'doing work which others could do as well, or even better; while I had to leave work undone which I could do, and ought to do'.‡ After his intention became known he received the offer of a chair at Vienna which would havè freed him from all lecturing duties and allowed him to devote himself entirely to the task on which he had set his mind. Thereupon, at the thought of losing a scholar who had won such universal esteem and whose name was so closely identified

* *Diaries*, vol. II, pp. 333–4, entries for 29 Oct. and 4 Nov. 1874, where Mr Green quotes part of the first of these letters to *The Pall Mall Gazette*.

† This entry and that for 9 Feb. 1876, do not appear in the published version of the *Diaries* and are given here by courtesy of Miss F. Menella Dodgson.

‡ *The Life and Letters of the Right Honourable Friedrich Max Müller*, edited by his Wife, vol. I, p. 500.

with the university, Oxford opinion was stirred and a plan was very hastily put forward to enable Max Müller to remain; he might be relieved of all his teaching duties and retain half his salary, while the other half was used to engage a successor; and Liddell was to lay this plan before Convocation.

In the same way as Dodgson had disapproved of the architectural changes at Christ Church, so also he disapproved of this plan; and in both cases, without knowing it, his real hostility may have been towards the author or instrument, Dean Liddell, rather than towards the plan itself.

There is no preface to Dodgson's third pamphlet, but its place can be taken by the three broadsheets which he published on the Max Müller affair a few days before the pamphlet was written. Just as before 'conflicting opinions' were held by members of the Governing Body in regard to the choice of a belfry, so now 'There seems to be good reason for believing that there is among Members of Convocation a wide-spread feeling of dissatisfaction with the proposed Decree as it stands';* and, as is made clear by *The Times*† report of the debate that took place in Convocation, there was in fact extreme diversity of opinion.

Dodgson's own feelings were divided and he felt himself tugged in different directions, for this time action against Liddell entailed also action against a valued friend. He reassured himself and others that his motives were entirely praiseworthy: 'an unbroken friendship of years with the Professor makes me feel safe from the imputation of any personal motives of hostility';‡ and this was perfectly true so far as his feelings to Max Müller were concerned.

Yet a reference to architecture reminds one that Dean Liddell too may be concerned: 'It appears incredible, while the University is able to provide so lavishly for the claims of Natural Science, for architectural improvements, &c., that so small a matter as this [provision of a pension quite apart from the emoluments of the chair] should be beyond its power.'§ Again soon after the dispute had arisen he wrote his 'Easter Greeting to Every Child who Loves "Alice"';‖ perhaps his latest act of revolt against Liddell had awakened recollections of the happier times, a dozen years earlier,

* Second broadsheet on 'The Professorship of Comparative Philology'.
† Of 16 Feb. 1876.
‡ Second broadsheet on 'The Professorship of Comparative Philology'.
§ Third broadsheet on 'The Professorship of Comparative Philology'.
‖ Reprinted in part in Lennon, *op. cit.* pp. 92–3.

when amid trips on the river and visits to the Deanery his genius had been loosed and he had been inspired to write his immortal stories. Dodgson's feelings were indeed mixed.

The sequence of events was:

2 February. Dodgson learned of the proposed decree.

3 February. He wrote the first broadsheet on 'The Professorship of Comparative Philology' which was clear in logic and expression and stated the issue impersonally.

12 February. He wrote his second broadsheet (and the same day his 'Easter Greeting'). Personal considerations are now arising in his mind and he speaks of his long friendship with Max Müller.

This broadsheet is a little woolly in statement but penetrates to a principle which might be of great importance in regard to the decision to be taken in Convocation.

...partly from the fear of being left in a small, and therefore conspicuous, minority, it seems likely that many of the dissatisfied will abstain from voting, and that a clause...may thus be passed '*multis dissentientibus sed nemine contradicente*'....

I propose then, if thirty names at least are sent me, by 4 p.m. on Monday, of Members of Convocation prepared to vote against this Decree, to print the names I receive (excepting any who may express a wish to the contrary) in alphabetical order, and to circulate the paper on Monday evening or Tuesday morning. Such a paper would be an assurance to all wishing to vote against the Decree that they will not be singular in so doing.

15 February. His third broadsheet was distributed at the door of Convocation House to inform the other dissentients that as a result of the appeal he had received twenty-seven names. He repeats the arguments against the proposed decree, but the tone is more irascible and the personal reference fairly clear. It is Liddell he has in mind, for he more than anyone else seems to have been the author of the step now being taken; and he delivers his parting jibes at the Dean.

This transferring of income from one man to another, leaving the funds of the University intact, is at all events one of the cheapest forms of generosity ever yet invented, and reminds one of the celebrated charity-sermon, where one of the congregation was so overcome by the preacher's eloquence that he hastily transferred to the subscription-plate all the loose cash he could find in his neighbour's pocket.

Let me tell one more story, and I have done. A certain parsimonious country-Rector had two Curates enjoying the respective stipends of

£100 and £90. One day the junior Curate resigned: whereupon the Rector sent for the senior, and told him that in consideration of his long and faithful services, etc., he was about to raise his stipend to £110. The Curate could scarcely believe his ears: after a few breathless words of gratitude, he wandered home, saying to himself 'Is it all a dream?' Next day brought an applicant for the junior Curacy: he had met the senior Curate outside, and had been assured by him that, whatever rumour might say to the contrary, the Rector was a man of true generosity of soul. 'Understanding', the stranger began, 'that the stipend you offer a junior Curate is £90 a year —' 'By no means!' interposed the worthy Rector, mildly, but with an unmistakable firmness. '*That* Curacy I have just reduced to £80 a year!'*

The outcome of the affair is given in Dodgson's laconic entry in his diary:

Feb: 15. (Tu)...The advocates of the Decree persisted so much in praising Max Müller, and ignoring the half-pay of the Deputy that I rose to ask them to keep more to the point. The Decree was carried by 94 to 35.†

The Times‡ report of Dodgson's speech to Convocation is:

Mr DODGSON wished that the defenders of the decree would address themselves to the point attacked, which was not the merits of the Professor, but the mode of procedure.

Practically every speaker in Convocation had approached the decree from a different angle, and Benjamin Jowett coming late in the debate had summed up that 'there were many objections to all propositions: there were many to this; but as many to any other'.§ As it was, the decision was mainly determined by the massive persuasion of Dean Liddell, who, after the vote, 'walked up at once to "Parks End" to tell Max Müller that the decree had passed, whilst many other friends crowded in, to congratulate themselves and the University, as they said, on their success'. ||

It was during this very same fortnight, while he was exercised over the proposed decree, that Dodgson had again begun to work on his theory of elections.

Feb: 9. (W). G[overning] B[ody] Meeting. The question of a system for taking votes at an election was again postponed. Afterwards I

---

* 'The Professorship of Comparative Philology', third paper.
† *Diaries*, vol. II, p. 350.
‡ Of 16 Feb. 1876.   § *Ibid.*
|| *The Life and Letters of the Honourable Friedrich Max Müller*, edited by his Wife, vol. II, p. 7. Liddell's speech is reprinted in full, *ibid.* pp. 430–3.

arranged with Bayne that we should try to get information as to the rules adopted in the other Colleges. Lawrence's opinion, given to-day, that 'the greatest number of votes does not necessarily mean an absolute majority', gives us the means of a final settlement of the matter, when there is a 'cyclical majority' that will yield to no other remedy.*

Just eight days after the meeting of Convocation with its excitement and mixed feelings, Dodgson's third pamphlet was written—the one which entitles him to a position in the theory of elections and committees only a little lower than that of Condorcet.

Feb: 23. (W). Spent the afternoon in writing out a new *Method for taking Votes* which I sent to the Press to be set up in slip.†

He got the page proofs back from the printers on 7 March‡ and circulated the pamphlet, interleaved with blank pages for observations and criticisms, to friends and others who might be interested.

What response he got, if any, we do not know, but it is likely to have been negligible. A year and a half later he again sent out the document in the hope of obtaining comments that might help him to clarify his views, this time issuing along with it the appeal contained in 'the cyclostyled sheet', which also we have reproduced along with his three pamphlets in the appendix.

Conclusion. Dodgson had been caught in the grip of the theory of elections and committees and his understanding of the subject was second only to that of Condorcet. After 1876 it was still his intention to write his book. But he lacked the systematic approach of Mathematics on which Condorcet had been able to lean. The contributions he had made were artistic rather than scientific, a curious amalgam of conscious logic and unconscious symbolism; and the struggles which he was symbolizing did not recur—for the main struggle was in his own inner nature and not in the Christ Church committees, and after 1876 this was rapidly changing.

It can safely be said that he kept by him over a period of years, the drafts of some chapters of his projected book, for even apart from the entries in *The Diaries*, the pamphlet of 1876 shows that he has a much more extensive knowledge of the subject, and in particular of cyclical majorities, than he there commits to print.

* Not in published version of *Diaries*. See footnote on p. 208 above.
† *Diaries*, vol. II, p. 350.
‡ A copy in the Harcourt Amory Collection has the stamp of the Clarendon Press with this date.

To the present writer it seems probable that he would add to these MSS after 1876, though perhaps not significantly. So far the inquiries which have been made have failed to bring to light any of these MSS, written before or after 1876, though they may still exist.

As it is we see Dodgson later, among his multifarious activities, using the logic of his theory of committees in his letters and pamphlet* on *Lawn Tennis Tournaments* (1882–3), although in a way which is quite trivial. And at the same stage in his life, when he was Curator of the Common Room, he gave small luncheon parties where the guests were asked to arrange the wines in order of preference and Dodgson arrived at their joint decision by employing the method of marks.†

When in the years 1881–5 he was engaged on the subject of proportional representation and improvements in the administrative arrangements for holding general elections, he was still, by any ordinary standards, a striking and original thinker, but a near-genius now rather than a genius. In *Sylvie and Bruno*, which he completed in 1893 after it had been a quarter of a century in the writing, he is seen to have emerged from the dream world which he had once tenanted: his symbolism now becomes conscious and is far less potent than in *Alice*. So in these later writings on general elections and P.R. there is a solitary flash of brilliance in arriving at the voting formulae, and much good sense and subtlety. But they say only what he means to say, whereas the greatness of his earlier pamphlets had been that they meant much more than he knew. They had dealt with the outer world of committees but also were symbols of the inner world of Dodgson's personality and of his own divided nature—a different type of reality, fraught with far more significance and far more difficult of approach.

* The Nonesuch edition of *The Complete Works of Lewis Carroll*, pp. 1201–11.
† See also *The Principles of Parliamentary Representation: Postscript to Supplement, passim*, where he touches on the subject of cyclical majorities.

TEXT OF DODGSON'S THREE PAMPHLETS
AND OF 'THE CYCLOSTYLED SHEET'

EDITOR'S NOTE. This reprint of *A Discussion*...is made by courtesy of the Princeton University Library in which is the only known copy. It had been Dodgson's own copy and the small emendations which he jotted on the text have been incorporated in the present version.

A short time after *A Discussion*... had been printed he wrote § 6, 'The Method of Nomination', and had it printed as a separate sheet, intending it to come at the end of chapter I (see S. H. Williams and F. Madan, *Handbook of the Literature of the Rev. C. L. Dodgson*, p. 55). In the reprint 'The Method of Nomination' is given the position that Dodgson had in mind (pp. 218–19 below) and we have added the corresponding entry in the list of contents (p. 215 below).

In his copy Dodgson had marked the three paragraphs 'This Method...having none"' (p. 219 below), 'Here again...instead of *C*"' (p. 220) and 'The conclusion...of a candidate' (p. 220) which he was going to incorporate in his third pamphlet *A Method...*, where they reappear (pp. 231–2 below).

The editor's footnotes in the reprint have been enclosed in square brackets.

A DISCUSSION OF THE VARIOUS METHODS OF
PROCEDURE IN CONDUCTING ELECTIONS

[Imprint by E. B. Gardner, E. Pickard Hall and J. H. Stacy, Printers to the University, Oxford.]

[PREFACE]

The following paper has been written and printed in great haste, as it was only on the night of Friday the 12th that it occurred to me to investigate the subject, which proved to be much more complicated than I had expected. Still I hope that I have given sufficient thought to it to escape the commission of any serious mistake.

I commence by considering certain known Methods of Procedure, in the case where *some* candidate *must* be elected, proving that each Method is liable, under certain circumstances, to fail in giving the proper result.

I then consider the question of 'Election or no Election?' proving that the two ordinary Methods of deciding it are unsound.

And I conclude by describing a Method of Procedure (whether new or not I cannot say) which seems to me not liable to the same objections as have been proved to exist in other cases.

C. L. D.

Cн. Cн., Dec. 18, 1873.

Contents

Chapter I

On the failure of certain Methods of Procedure, in the case where an Election is necessary

Chapter II

On the failure of certain Methods of Procedure, in the case where it is allowable *to have 'no Election'*

Chapter III

On a proposed Method of Procedure

Chapter IV

Summary of Rules

[1 This has been inserted, as explained on p. 214. Ed.]

Chapter I

On the failure of certain Methods of Procedure, in the case where an Election is necessary

§ 1. *The Method of a Simple Majority*

In this Method, each elector names the *one* candidate he prefers, and he who gets the greatest number of votes is taken as the winner. The extraordinary injustice of this Method may easily be demonstrated. Let us suppose that there are eleven electors, and four candidates, *a*, *b*, *c*, *d*; and that each elector has arranged in a column the names of the candidates, in the order of his preference; and that the eleven columns stand thus:

Case (α)

a	a	a	b	b	b	b	c	c	c	d
c	c	c	a	a	a	a	a	a	a	a
d	d	d	c	c	c	c	d	d	d	c
b	b	b	d	d	d	d	b	b	b	b

Here *a* is considered best by *three* of the electors, and second by all the rest. It seems clear that he ought to be elected; and yet, by the above method, *b* would be the winner—a candidate who is considered *worst* by *seven* of the electors![1]

§ 2. *The Method of an Absolute Majority*

In this Method, each elector names the *one* candidate he prefers; and if there be an absolute majority for any one candidate, he is taken as the winner.

Case (β)

b	b	b	b	b	b	a	a	a	a	a
a	a	a	a	a	a	c	c	c	d	d
c	c	c	d	d	d	d	d	d	c	c
d	d	d	c	c	c	b	b	b	b	b

[[1] On the blank page facing the text Dodgson, no doubt at the time when he was preparing his third pamphlet, wrote the following example and comment. The interesting feature of the example is that it yields the identical matrix with the above case (α). Ed.]

a	a	a	a	a	a	a	b	b	b	b
c	c	c	c	c	c	c	d	c	c	c
d	d	d	d	d	d	d	a	a	a	a
b	b	b	b	b	b	b	c	d	d	d

agrees with opposite, both in marks, & in votes on pairs.

Here a is considered best by nearly half the electors (one more vote would give him an absolute majority), and never put lower than second by any; while b is put last by *five* of the electors, and c and d by three each. There seems to be no doubt that a ought to be elected; and yet, by the above Method, b would win.

§ 3. *The Method of Elimination, where the names are voted on by two at a time*

In this Method, two names are chosen at random and proposed for voting; the loser is struck out from further competition, and the winner taken along with some other candidate, and so on, till there is only one candidate left.

Case (γ)

a	a	a	a	a	b	b	c	d	d	d
c	c	c	c	d	a	a	b	b	b	b
b	d	d	d	c	c	c	a	a	a	a
d	b	b	b	b	d	d	d	c	c	c

Here it seems clear that a ought to be the winner, as he is considered best by nearly half the electors, and never put lower than third; while b and d are each put last by *four* electors, and c by *three*. Nevertheless, by the above Method, if (a, b) were put up first for voting, a would be rejected, and ultimately c would be elected. Again, if (a, c) were put up first, c would be rejected, and if (a, b) were put up next, d would be elected—but if (a, d), b would be elected.

Such preposterous results, making the Election turn on the mere accident of *which* couple is put up first, seem to me to prove *this* Method to be entirely untrustworthy.

§ 4. *The Method of Elimination, where the names are voted on all at once*

In this Method, each elector names the *one* candidate he prefers: the one who gets fewest votes is excluded from further competition, and the process is repeated.

Case (δ)

b	b	b	c	c	c	d	d	d	a	a
a	a	a	a	a	a	a	a	a	b	c
d	c	d	b	b	b	c	c	b	d	d
c	d	c	d	d	d	b	b	c	c	b

Here, while *b* is put last by *three* of the electors, and *c* and *d* by *four* each, *a* is not put lower than second by any. There seems to be no doubt that *a*'s election would be the most generally acceptable:[1] and yet, by the above rule, he would be excluded at once, and ultimately *c* would be elected.

§ 5. *The Method of Marks*

In this Method, a certain number of marks is fixed, which each elector shall have at his disposal; he may assign them all to one candidate, or divide them among several candidates, in proportion to their eligibility; and the candidate who gets the greatest total of marks is the winner.

This Method would, I think, be absolutely perfect, if only each elector wished to do all in his power to secure the election of *that candidate who should be the most generally acceptable*, even if that candidate should *not* be the one of his own choice: in this case he would be careful to make the marks exactly represent his estimate of the relative eligibility of *all* the candidates, even of those he *least* desired to see elected; and the desired result would be secured.

But we are not sufficiently unselfish and public-spirited to give any hope of this result being attained. Each elector would feel that it was *possible* for each other elector to assign the entire number of marks to his favorite candidate, giving to all the other candidates zero: and he would conclude that, in order to give his *own* favorite candidate any chance of success, he must do the same for him.

This Method is therefore liable, in practice, to coincide with 'the Method of a Simple Majority', which has been already discussed, and, as I think, proved to be unsound.

§ 6. *The Method of Nomination*[2]

In this Method, some one candidate is proposed, seconded, and the votes taken for and against. This Method is fair for those electors *only* who prefer that candidate to *any* other, or else *any*

[1 Dodgson had made the following marginal note. Ed.]

        a beats *b* by 8 to 3.

        ,,   ,, *c* ,,   do.

        ,,   ,, *d* ,,   do.

[2 Printed separately later, as explained above, p. 214. Ed.]

other to him. But any other elector might say 'I do not know whether to vote for or against a till I know *who* would come in if he failed. If I were sure b would come in, I would vote against a: otherwise, I vote *for a*'.

If this Method leads to a *majority* of votes being obtained for the proposed candidate, it is identical with 'the Method of an absolute Majority', which was discussed in § 2. If a *minority* only is obtained, it may be thus represented:

b	b	c	c	d	d	a	a	a	a	a
a	a	a	a	a	a	b	b	c	c	d
c	c	b	b	b	b	c	c	b	b	b
d	d	d	d	c	c	d	d	d	d	c

Here there seems no doubt that a ought to be elected; and yet, by the above Method, he would be rejected at once, and, *whichever* candidate came in, *nine* of the electors would say 'We would rather have had a'.

CHAPTER II

On the failure of certain Methods of Procedure, in the case where it is allowable to have 'no Election'

§ 1. *The Method of* commencing *with a vote on the question 'Election or no Election?'*

This Method has the strong recommendation that if 'no Election' be carried, it saves all further trouble, and it *might* be a just method to adopt, provided the electors were of two kinds only—one, which prefers 'no Election' to *any* candidate, even the best; the other, which prefers *any* candidate, even the worst, to 'no Election'. But it would seldom happen that *all* the electors could be so classed: and any elector who preferred certain candidates to 'no Election', but preferred 'no Election' to certain other candidates, would not be fairly treated by such a procedure. He might say 'It is premature to ask me to vote on this question. If I knew that A or B would be elected, I would vote to *have* an election; but if neither A nor B can get in, I vote for having none'.

Let us, however, test this Method by a case—representing 'no Election' by the symbol '0'.

Case (ε)

a	a	b	b	c	c	0	0	0	0	0
0	0	0	0	0	0	a	a	b	b	c
c	c	a	a	b	b	d	d	c	c	b
d	d	d	d	d	d	b	c	a	a	a
b	b	c	c	a	a	c	b	d	d	d

Here there seems no doubt that 'no Election' would be the most satisfactory result: and yet, by the above Method, an Election would take place, and, *whichever* candidate came in, *nine* of the electors would say 'I would rather have had no Election'.

§ 2. *The method of* concluding *with a vote on the question 'Shall* X (*the successful candidate*) *be elected, or shall there be no Election'?*

Here again a voter who preferred certain candidates to 'no Election', but preferred 'no Election' to certain other candidates, would not be fairly treated. He might say 'If you had taken *A* or *B*, I would have been content, but as you have taken *C*, I vote for no Election', and his vote might decide the point: while the other electors might say 'If we had only known how it would end, we would willingly have taken *A* instead of *C*'.

But let us test this Method also by a case.

Case (ζ)

b	b	b	b	b	0	a	a	a	a	a
a	a	a	a	a	b	0	0	0	0	0
c	c	c	c	c	a	b	b	b	b	b
d	d	d	d	d	c	c	c	c	c	c
0	0	0	0	0	d	d	d	d	d	d

Here there seems to be no doubt that the election of *a* would be much more satisfactory than having no Election: and yet, by the above Method, *b* would first be selected from all the candidates, and ultimately rejected on the question of '*b* or no Election?' while *ten* of the electors would say 'We would rather have taken *a* than have no Election at all'.

The conclusion I come to is that, where 'no Election' is allowable, the phrase should be treated exactly as if it were the name of a candidate.

Chapter III

On a proposed Method of Procedure

The Method now to be proposed is, *in principle*, a modification of No. 5, viz. 'The Method of Marks', since it assigns to each candidate a mark for every vote given to him, when taken in competition with any other candidate.

Suppose that, in the opinion of a certain elector, the candidates stand in the order a, b, c, d: then his votes may be represented by giving a the number 3, b 2, c 1, and d 0.

Hence all that is necessary is that each elector should make out a list of the candidates, arranging them in order of merit.

If 'no Election' is allowable, this phrase should be placed somewhere in the list.

If the elector cannot arrange all in succession, but places two or more in a bracket, a question arises as to how the bracketed names should be marked. The tendency of many electors being, as explained in Chap. I, § 5, to give to the favorite candidate the maximum mark, and bracket all the rest, in order to reduce their chances as much as possible, it is proposed, in order to counteract this tendency, to give to each bracketed candidate the same mark that the *highest* would have if the bracket were removed. This plan will furnish a strong inducement to avoid brackets as far as possible.

In order to illustrate this process, let us apply it to the various 'Cases' already considered.

	α	β	γ	δ	§ 6[1]	ϵ	ζ
a	25	27	23	24	27	21	37
b	12	18	15	15	17	21	33
c	20	11	14	14	14	20	16
d	9	10	14	13	8	10	5
0						38	19

It will be seen that in each case the candidate, whose election is obviously most to be desired, obtains the greatest number of marks.

[[1] Dodgson wrote § 6, 'The Method of Nomination' after *A Discussion*... had already been printed; and he added the column of figures headed '§ 6' in manuscript alongside the table in his own copy. We have placed the figures inside the table and corrected a slip in his arithmetic. Ed.]

Chapter IV

Summary of Rules

1. Let each elector make out a list of the candidates, (treating 'no Election' as if it were the name of a candidate), arranging them as far as possible in the order of merit, and bracketing those whom he regards as equal.

2. Let the names on each list be marked with the numbers, 0, 1, 2, &c., beginning at the last.

3. Whenever two or more names are bracketed, each must have the mark which would belong to the highest, if there were no bracket.

4. Add up the numbers assigned to each candidate.

The *first* Rule is all with which the electors need trouble themselves. Rules 2, 3, 4 can all be carried out by one person, as it is merely a matter of counting.

SUGGESTIONS AS TO THE BEST METHOD OF TAKING VOTES, WHERE MORE THAN TWO ISSUES ARE TO BE VOTED ON

[Imprint by E. Pickard Hall and J. H. Stacy, Printers to the University, Oxford.]

[PREFACE]

In the immediate prospect of a meeting of the Governing Body, where matters may be debated of very great importance, on which various and conflicting opinions are known to be held, I venture to offer a few suggestions as to the mode of taking votes. On this subject I printed a paper some little time ago, but have since seen reason to modify some of the views therein expressed. Especially, I do not now advocate the method, there proposed, as a good one to *begin* with. When other means have failed, it may prove useful, but that is not likely to happen often, and, when the difficulty does arise, the question what should next be done may fairly be debated on its own merits.   C. L. D.

Ch. Ch., June 13, 1874.

§ 1. *Votes to be taken in writing*

The method here suggested is to divide a sheet of paper into as many columns as there are issues to be voted on, and place the name of each at the head of a column. The paper is then passed round, each voter placing his name in the column he prefers.

The only objection to this method, that I can think of, is that it takes rather more time than voting *vivâ voce*; and even *this* is not always the case, as it is by no means unusual for a doubt to arise as to the result of a *vivâ voce* vote, which makes it necessary to take the votes over again.

Its advantages are, that it enables the division-list to be put on record, which I think should always be done when an important matter is voted on, except in elections of Students, in which case there are obvious objections to the names of the voters being recorded.

At the end of a meeting, it should be settled which of the division-lists, if any, are to be entered on the minutes; and the other lists might then be destroyed.

§ 2. *A list to be made of all the issues to be voted on*

This should be done before *any* vote is taken at all. The list should contain every issue which is proposed, and seconded, for entry on it. The *general negative* issue ('that there be no election', or, 'that nothing be done') should, I think, find a place on this list (provided of course that it be proposed and seconded), and should not be voted on separately—a course sometimes adopted, but which I think I have shown, in a former paper on this subject, to be unsound.

§ 3. *The first vote to be taken on all the issues collectively*

This course is suggested in the hope that it may give an absolute majority (or such a majority as may be previously declared to be binding), so as to settle the question at once.

§ 4. *Failing a settlement by this method, the issues to be then voted on two at a time*

This course is suggested in the hope that by it some one issue may be discovered, which is preferred by a majority to every other taken separately. For this purpose, any two may be put up to begin with, then the winning issue along with some other, and so on. But no issue can be considered as the absolute winner, unless it has been put up along with *every* other.

§ 5. *Failing a settlement by this method also, further proceedings may be then debated on*

If no settlement has been arrived at by § 3 or § 4, it will at least prove that the matter is one on which the meeting is *very evenly divided in opinion.* Such a state of things is of course very difficult to deal with, but the difficulty, though possibly not diminished, will certainly not have been increased by adopting the process I have here suggested.

A METHOD OF TAKING VOTES ON MORE THAN TWO ISSUES

[Written 23 Feb. 1876 and printed at the Clarendon Press, Oxford. The title-page, dated March 1876, is headed 'Not yet published' and bears, beneath the title, the following note.]

(*As I hope to investigate this subject further, and to publish a more complete pamphlet on the subject, I shall feel greatly obliged if you will enter in this copy any remarks that occur to you, and return it to me any time before....*)

§ 1. *Proposed Rules for Conducting an Election*

I

Each elector shall write down the issue he desires ('no Election' being reckoned as an issue) and hand in the paper folded, with his name written outside: and the Chairman, or some one appointed by him, having before him a list of the electors, shall enter these issues against their names.

II

If the Chairman find any issue having an absolute majority of votes, he shall communicate the list to the meeting. This issue shall then be formally moved, and, if none object, the Chairman shall declare it carried.

III

If the Chairman shall find no issue having an absolute majority of votes, he shall communicate to the meeting the list of issues only, without stating who vote for each, and shall return the papers, that each elector may add the other issues, arranged in his order of preference. The Chairman shall enter these on his list, and then communicate the whole to the meeting.

IV

If an issue be found which has a majority over every other taken separately, it shall be formally moved as in Rule II: but if none be found, the majorities being 'cyclical', opportunity shall be given for further debate. In ascertaining which of any pair of issues is preferred to the other, any elector whose paper contains one only of the two shall be reckoned as preferring that one, and any whose paper contains neither shall be considered as not voting.

V

If the issues cannot be all arranged in one cycle, but form a cycle and a set of issues each of which is separately beaten by each of the cycle, it shall be formally moved that this cycle be retained and all other issues struck out, and, if none object, this shall be done.

VI

If, a formal motion having been made that a certain issue be adopted, or that a certain cycle be retained and all other issues struck out, any one object, he may move as an amendment that a division be taken between the issue he desires and the issue so to be adopted, or any one of the cycle so to be retained. If every such amendment be lost on a division, the Chairman shall declare the original motion carried: but, if any such amendment be carried, by some voting contrary to their written papers, they shall be required to amend their papers, and the process shall begin again.

VII

When the issues to be further debated consist of, or have been reduced to, a single cycle, the Chairman shall inform the meeting how many alterations of votes each issue requires to give it a majority over every other separately.

VIII

If, when the majorities are found to be cyclical, any elector wish to alter his paper, he may do so: and if the cyclical majorities be thereby done away with, the voting shall proceed by former Rules: but if, when none will make any further alteration, the majorities continue cyclical, there shall be no election.

§ 2. *The Legal Conditions*

In any election, when there are only *two* issues to vote on—for instance (there being only one candidate), 'shall *A* be elected or not?' or again (there being only two candidates, and it being understood that there is to be an election) 'shall *A* or *B* be elected?'—and when the Chairman is able to give a casting vote, it is clear that there *must* be a majority for one or other issue, and in this case open voting is the obvious course.

But wherever there are three or more issues to vote on, any one of the following three cases may exist in the minds of the electors:

(α) *There may be one issue desired by an absolute majority of the electors.*

(β) *There may be one issue which, when paired against every other issue separately, is preferred by a majority of electors.*

(γ) *The majorities may be 'cyclical', e.g. there may be a majority for A over B, for B over C, and for C over A.*

The words of the Ordinance are **'That Candidate for whom the greatest number of votes shall have been given shall be deemed elected'.**

It seems to me that this may be complied with by either of two modes of election:

In case (α) *If a candidate be declared elected who, when all are voted on at once, has an absolute majority of votes.*

In case (β) *If a candidate be declared elected who, when paired with every other separately, is preferred by the majority of those voting.*

But that it is *not* complied with by the following mode:

In case (γ) *If a candidate be declared elected, though it is known that there is another who, when paired with him, is preferred by the majority of those voting.*

Mode (α) needs no discussion. Failing this, it seems clear that mode (β) would be a satisfactory result, as any one who preferred some other candidate might be allowed to take a division between the two.

If modes (α) and (β) both fail, it shows that the majorities on the separate pairs are 'cyclical', and if, after all possible discussion, this continues to be so, any election that may be arrived at *must* introduce mode (γ). My own opinion is that, under these circumstances, there ought to be 'no Election': two other courses might be suggested, which I will now consider.

§ 3. *Courses that have been suggested for the case of* '*Cyclical Majorities*'

(1) *That all candidates should be voted on at once, and the one who has the greatest number of votes should be elected.*

This might be thought to fulfil the *letter* of the law, if after the words 'shall have been given' we supply the words 'in the final voting'.

Let us suppose that there are 11 electors, and 4 candidates, a, b, c, d; and that each elector has arranged in a column the names of the candidates in the order of his preference; and that the 11 columns stand thus:

a	a	a	a	b	b	b	c	c	c	d
d	d	b	b	c	c	d	b	b	b	c^{*}
c	c	d	d	a	a	c	d	d	d	b^{*}
b	b	c	c	d	d	a	a	a	a	a

Fig. 1.

Here the majorities are cyclical, in the order $a\,d\,c\,b\,a$, each beating the one next following.

Moreover, if we make a table of majorities in the separate pairs, in which the numerator of each fraction represents the number voting for the issue which stands at the top of that column and the denominator the number voting for the issue which stands at the end of that row, and in which every division, where the issue at the top of the column is beaten, is distinguished by placing the fraction in a parenthesis, we have

	a	b	c	d
a		$\frac{7}{4}$	$\frac{7}{4}$	$(\frac{6}{8})$
b	$(\frac{4}{7})$		$\frac{6}{5}$	$(\frac{3}{8})$
c	$(\frac{4}{7})$	$(\frac{6}{8})$		$\frac{6}{5}$
d	$\frac{8}{5}$	$\frac{8}{3}$	$(\frac{6}{8})$	

Fig. 2.

Here a and d each need 4 changes of votes to win, but b and c each need one only: for instance, the interchange of the two issues which are marked * would make b win. It seems clear that a has much less claim to be elected than either b or c (observe that he is put *last* by nearly half the electors, and only needs *one* interchange of votes to cause him to be beaten by *every* other candidate separately), and yet by the above course he would win.

Again, let there be 13 electors and 4 candidates.

a	a	a	a	b	b	b	c	c	c	d	d	d
b	b	b	b	d	d	d	d	a	a	b	b	b
c	c	c	c	c	c	c	a*	b	b	c	c	c
d	d	d	d	a	a	a	b*	d	d	a	a	a

Fig. 3.

Here the majorities are cyclical, in the order *a b c d a*; the table of majorities being:

	a	b	c	d
a		$(\frac{6}{7})$	$\frac{9}{4}$	$\frac{7}{6}$
b	$\frac{7}{6}$		$(\frac{3}{10})$	$(\frac{4}{9})$
c	$(\frac{4}{9})$	$\frac{10}{3}$		$(\frac{6}{7})$
d	$(\frac{6}{7})$	$\frac{9}{4}$	$\frac{7}{6}$	

Fig. 4.

Here *a*, *c*, *d* each need 4 changes of votes to win, while *b* needs only one, for instance, the interchange of the two issues marked *. Yet by the above course *a* would win—a candidate whom this single interchange would cause to be beaten by *every* other candidate separately.

(2) *That all candidates should be voted on at once, and the one who has the smallest number of votes should be struck out, and the process repeated till only two are left.*

a	a	a	a	b	b	b	b	c	c	c
b	b	c	c	c	c	c	c	b	a	a
c	c	b	b	a	a	a	a	a	b	b

Fig. 5.

Here the majorities are cyclical, in the order *a b c a*. Moreover, *a* beats *b* (6 to 5), *b* beats *c* (6 to 5), but *c* beats *a* (7 to 4).

If any one is to be elected, it would seem that *c* has the strongest claim; but by the above method *a* would win—a candidate who is put last by nearly half the electors.

Again, let there be 15 electors and 4 candidates:

a	a	a	a	b	b	b	b	c	c	c	c	d	d	d
d	d	d	d	c	c	c	c*	d	d	d	d	a	a	b
b	b	b	b	d	d	d	d*	a	a	b	b	c	c	c
c	c	c	c	a	a	a	a	b	b	a	a	b	b	a

Fig. 6.

Here there is a cyclical majority, in the order $a\ b\ c\ d\ a$; therefore by above Rule d is excluded: we now have

a	a	a	a	b	b	b	b	c	c	c	c	a	a	b
b	b	b	b	c	c	c	c	a	a	b	b	c	c	c
c	c	c	c	a	a	a	a	b	b	a	a	b	b	a

Fig. 7.

Here there is again a cyclical majority, in the order $a\ b\ c\ a$; therefore c is excluded.

The candidates are now reduced to a and b, and a wins by a majority of 8 to 7.

But if we tabulate the majorities thus—

	a	b	c	d
a		$(\frac{7}{8})$	$\frac{9}{6}$	$\frac{11}{4}$
b	$\frac{8}{7}$		$(\frac{6}{9})$	$\frac{11}{4}$
c	$(\frac{6}{9})$	$\frac{9}{6}$		$(\frac{7}{8})$
d	$(\frac{4}{11})$	$(\frac{4}{11})$	$\frac{8}{7}$	

Fig. 8.

we see that a needs 6 changes of votes to win, b 5, c 2, and d only 1. It seems clear that d ought to win; yet he is the very first to be excluded by the above course.

Lastly, let us take a case in which these two courses bring in different candidates, neither of them being the one that ought to win.

Let there be 23 electors and 4 candidates.

a	a	a	a	a	a	a	b	b	b	b	b	b	c	c	c	c	c	c	d	d	d	d
b	b	c	c	c	c	d	d	d	d	d	d	d	b	b	b	b	b	b	b	b	c	c*
d	d	b	b	b	b	b	a	a	a	a	a	a	a	a	a	a	a	d	a	a	b	b*
c	c	d	d	d	d	c	c	c	c	c	c	c	d	d	d	d	d	a	c	c	a	a

Fig. 9.

Here the majorities are cyclical in the order $a\ d\ c\ b\ a$. The table of majorities is:

	a	b	c	d
a		$\frac{16}{7}$	$(\frac{8}{15})$	$(\frac{11}{12})$
b	$(\frac{7}{16})$		$\frac{12}{11}$	$(\frac{5}{18})$
c	$\frac{15}{8}$	$(\frac{11}{12})$		$\frac{13}{10}$
d	$\frac{12}{11}$	$\frac{18}{5}$	$(\frac{10}{13})$	

Fig. 10.

Now, by course (1) a wins.

By course (2) d is excluded; but we still have a cyclical majority $a\ c\ b\ a$; we then exclude a, and c wins.

But, if we reckon how many changes of votes each needs to win, we find that a needs 5, c needs 6, and d needs 8; whereas b needs only 1—a single interchange, such as the two marked *, would give him a clear victory.

Note also that this single interchange would cause c (who is brought in winner by course (2)) to be beaten by *every* other candidate separately.

The instances I have taken seem to show that neither of these courses can be relied on to give a satisfactory result. But there is a stronger, and as I think a fatal, objection to both; namely, that any elector, who had not consented to this course being adopted, would have a very strong ground of appeal against the election if he were able to say 'A was declared elected, and yet he had not "the greatest number of votes" given for him, since he was beaten when paired against B'.

The conclusion I come to is that, in the case of persistent cyclical majorities, there ought to be 'no Election'.

I am quite prepared to be told, with regard to the cases I have here proposed, as I have already been told with regard to others, 'Oh, *that* is an extreme case: it could never really happen!' Now I have observed that this answer is always given instantly, with perfect confidence, and without any examination of the details of the proposed case. It must therefore rest on some general principle: the mental process being probably something like this— 'I have formed a theory. This case contradicts my theory. *Therefore* this is an extreme case, and would never occur in practice.'

§ 4. *Reasons for beginning with a vote on all issues at once*

One reason for this is that it *may* show an absolute majority for some one issue, and so save all further trouble. But another, and a stronger, reason is that, when a division is taken first of all between a certain pair of issues, there will very often be some of the electors who will not know which way to vote. I am not speaking of electors who are willing to vote contrary to their real opinion, but of electors generally.

An example or two will make this clear.

Suppose there are two vacancies, but that it is not necessary to fill both: and that a division is taken first of all on the question 'Shall both vacancies be filled, or only one?' An elector might reasonably say 'I wish to elect A alone. If I were sure he would come in, I would vote for electing *one* only: but if B is preferred, then, rather than lose A, I would vote for electing *two*'. And another might say '*I* wish to elect A and B, but I strongly object to C. If I were sure A and B would come in, I would vote for electing *two*: but if that would result in A and C coming in, then I vote for *one* only.' How much simpler to allow the one to write down 'A alone', and the other 'A and B'.

Again, suppose it settled that two are to be elected, and a division to be taken between B and D. An elector might reasonably say 'I wish to elect A at any rate: the other to be B or C, I do not care which: but I object to D. I would vote for B, if I were sure that A would be elected as the other. But if I knew that C would beat A on a division, I should wish to get C and A elected, and this *might* be effected by voting for D. I happen to know that C and A can each beat D, so that he has no real chance. My voting for him would not mean that I wish to bring him *in*, but that I wish to keep B *out*, and so to get C and A elected, instead of C and B'. How much simpler to allow him to write 'A, and then B or C'.

§ 5. *Reasons for allowing 'no Election' to be reckoned among the other issues*

Evidently an elector who desires 'no Election' ought to have *some* opportunity of voting on the question. And if it be not reckoned as an issue, it must be voted on, as a separate question, at the beginning or the end of the proceedings.

(1) *The method of* beginning *with a vote on the question* '*Election or no Election?*'

This Method has the strong recommendation that if 'no Election' be carried, it saves all further trouble, and it *might* be a just method to adopt, provided the electors were of two kinds only— one, which prefers 'no Election' to *any* candidate, even the best; the other, which prefers *any* candidate, even the worst, to 'no Election'. But it would seldom happen that *all* the electors could be so classed: and any elector who preferred certain candidates to 'no Election', but preferred 'no Election' to certain other candidates, would not be fairly treated by such a procedure. He might say 'It is premature to ask me to vote on this question. If

I knew that A or B would be elected, I would vote to *have* an election; but if neither A nor B can get in, I vote for having none'.

(2) *The method of* ending *with a vote on the question 'Shall* X *be elected, or shall there be no Election?'*

Here again a voter who preferred certain candidates to 'no Election', but preferred 'no Election' to certain other candidates, would not be fairly treated. He might say 'If you had taken A or B, I would have been content, but as you have taken C, I vote for no Election', and his vote might decide the point: while the other electors might say 'If we had only known how it would end, we would willingly have taken A instead of C'.

The conclusion I come to is that, where 'no Election' is allowable, the phrase should be treated exactly as if it were the name of a candidate.

§ 6.[1] *Reasons for having a preliminary voting on paper and not open voting*

Suppose A to be the candidate whom I wish to elect, and that a division is taken between B and C; am I bound in honour to vote for the one whom I should *really* prefer, if A were not in the field, or may I vote in whatever way I think most favourable to A's chances? Some say 'the former', some 'the latter'. I proceed to show that, whenever case (α) fails to occur, and there are among the electors a certain number who hold the latter course to be allowable, the result *must* be a case of cyclical majorities.

Let there be 3 candidates, A, B, C, each preferred by about one-third of the electors; and suppose that, when a division is taken between A and B, A wins. A division is now taken between A and C, which of course depends on the votes of the B-party; perhaps a majority of them *really* prefer A, and if they voted accordingly A would win under case (β); it might need only two or three to vote contrary to their real opinion to turn the division in favour of C. We have now got 'A beats B, C beats A', and of course a division must be taken between B and C; this depends on the votes of the A-party, and, as before, it may only need two or three to vote contrary to their real opinion to prevent C winning the election. Thus we get 'A beats B, C beats A, B beats C'.

This principle of voting makes an election more of a game of

---

[1] [Dodgson had wrongly numbered this §5. Ed.]

skill than a real test of the wishes of the electors, and as my own opinion is that it is better for elections to be decided according to the wish of the majority than of those who happen to have most skill in the game, I think it desirable that all should know the rule by which this game may be won. It is simply this: 'In any division taken on a pair of issues neither of which you desire, vote against the most popular. There *may* be some one issue which, if all voted according to their real opinion, would beat every other issue when paired against it separately: but, by following this rule, you *may* succeed in getting it beaten *once*, and so prevent its having a clear victory, by introducing a cyclical majority. And this will give, to the issue you desire, a chance it would not otherwise have had'.

Now, it is impossible to prevent such votes being given: and even if a preliminary voting on paper should seem to lead to case (α) or (β), it is impossible, when it comes to the final formal vote, to prevent votes being given contradictory to previous votes.

The advantages of having the preliminary voting taken on paper and not openly are, first, that each elector, not knowing exactly how the others are voting, has less inducement to vote contrary to his real opinion, so that a more trustworthy estimate is arrived at of the real opinion of the body of electors, and cyclical majorities are less likely to occur, than with open voting; and secondly, that if cyclical majorities do *not* occur in this process, they cannot occur in the formal voting except by some one or more of the electors giving votes inconsistent with their written opinions, and I think it desirable that in such a case the body of electors should know who they are that have so voted—a result which this method would secure.

I do not suppose that any one would be so unwilling to have it known that he has so voted that this publicity would *prevent* an artificial cyclical majority—for I am sure that those who do so believe it to be an honourable course to take, and so have no motive for desiring concealment—but I think it would increase the sense of the responsibility incurred by those who thus exercise their right of voting, and so make its occurrence less likely.

These written lists will also be, in many cases, a great saving of time. An example will best show this. Suppose there are 2 vacancies to be filled, and 3 candidates, all recommended on various grounds by the examiners, and that the electors are divided among the following 6 issues, '*A B*', '*B A*', '*A C*', '*C A*', '*B C*', '*A* alone'. These, taken two and two, give 15 pairs: that is, it might require 15 divisions to be taken to get the information which the written lists furnish at once.

'THE CYCLOSTYLED SHEET'

(7 *December* 1877)

Ch. Ch. Dec. 7/77

Would you kindly consider this pamphlet, and let me have it again, with any criticisms that it may suggest to you or others, some time next term?

Also an account of any rules, written or unwritten, adopted in your College to settle difficulties arising in elections, will be very acceptable.

A really scientific method for arriving at the result which is, on the whole, most satisfactory to a body of electors, seems to be still a *desideratum*.

Truly yours,

C. L. DODGSON

NOTES ON DODGSON'S THIRD PAMPHLET
A METHOD... (1876)

Dodgson's three papers are set out with a beautiful simplicity and directness, and only the third, because of the condensed nature of the argument, needs any comment.

The regulation of the Christ Church Ordinances of 1867 which the Governing Body was bound to observe in the election of Students was: 'That Candidate for whom the greatest number of votes shall have been given shall be deemed elected.' At its meeting of 9 February 1876, the Governing Body, taking legal advice, satisfied itself that this clause might be interpreted in more than one way.[1] Dodgson had been taking a renewed interest in elections just before this time and, as we have argued, the Max Müller business had brought him to a state of mind in which he was ripe for further thinking on the matter. The legal opinion

---

[1] Indeed, in adopting Dodgson's method of marks in the first vote at its meeting of 18 Dec. 1873, the Governing Body had already abandoned the interpretation that it must elect the candidate with the greatest number of first-preference votes.

left him free to work out some scheme which might satisfy both the requirements of logic, with which hitherto he had been mainly concerned, and those of the statute. It would serve as a preliminary sketch for the book on elections which he was going to write; meantime his objective was to influence procedure at Christ Church.

The audience for which his pamphlet is intended explains the order in which he sets out the argument. The logical order would have required a statement of the theory, followed by a deduction of the types of election which seemed to have most claim to rationality, and lastly the choice from among these rational modes of election of those satisfying the legal requirements. Dodgson's arrangement is the reverse of this. At the beginning, where it will get most emphasis,[1] he puts his suggested procedure for elections; next he shows that this procedure conforms to the Ordinances of 1867, and lastly he gives his theoretical development.

In this pamphlet Dodgson's recollections of the Max Müller business in Convocation are still lively in his mind. He had considered (see p. 210) that some members might be deterred from expressing an opinion and voting for it, because they believed some other view to have a larger volume of support; whereas their own opinion might have a tacit support more extensive than they realized. Now they are to be encouraged to express whatever opinions they hold and will do so in secrecy: 'Each elector shall write down the issue he desires...and hand in the paper folded' (§ 1, I)—which contrasts with the single sheet divided into columns, on which all sign their names to indicate their first preferences, *Suggestions*..., § 1.

If this does not lead either to the election of a candidate or to the decision to make no election, the papers will be returned and each voter will rank the other issues in order of preference; this again amounts to secret and uninhibited voting, as contrasted with the open voting on pairs of proposals in *Suggestions*..., § 4.

At this stage he takes it for granted that the Condorcet criterion will be accepted, and that if any candidate or the proposal of 'no Election' is able to get a majority over each of the others, the matter is settled. There may have been no need for discussion of this step: the Governing Body was already familiar with the main outline of the procedure, for it was similar to that which, on Dodgson's advice, it had used in the choice of a design for the belfry less than two years earlier; and most members would have heard additional explanations of his views since that time.

Dodgson now turns his attention to the case where the majorities are found to be 'cyclical', and he takes it for granted that the meaning

---

[1] He was no doubt also influenced by his love of drawing up elaborate rules for games of all sorts, beginning with the rules for passengers, guards and others in his childhood game of railways.

of this term will be familiar and does not define it until § 2. He appears to be aware that far from being exceptional, cyclical majorities tend to become the general rule as the number of motions increases: and it seems very likely that he is acquainted with their main properties, such as those we have formulated in chapter VII above.

One would judge that the real disagreement among the members of the Governing Body was about the procedure to be adopted in the event of cyclical majorities arising, for much of the paper deals with this problem. He suggests a procedure (§ 1, V–VIII) which in some circumstances, though not in all, will break a cycle of this kind and secure the election of a candidate in such a way as to conform to the Ordinances. This method will sometimes fail to get rid of a cycle; and in these circumstances, he suggests, no solution exists which is both legal and rational.

Clearly other people at Christ Church had also devoted their attention to such cycles in voting and he goes on (§ 3) to consider two of the methods that had been proposed. He shows that both of them lead to results for which there can be no possible justification, and he also questions their legality.

In this section, as was natural to the author of the *Elementary Treatise on Determinants*, he displays the logic of committee decisions by employing the matrix or determinant notation, which is certainly the most suitable instrument for the purpose; and in this he is without any precursor. (The reader should notice that in dealing with Dodgson's matrix the votes *for* a candidate are got by reading *down* the relevant column.)

§ 4 relates to a committee which is making an election and may fill either one vacancy or two vacancies, and inquires what is then the best method of arriving at a decision? This was in fact a recurrent problem at Christ Church and a letter exists,[1] of a date shortly after that when Dodgson was writing, in which Dean Liddell asks permission from Lord Selborne to make elections to two Studentships instead of one.

'Ch. Ch. Oxford
18 Dec. 1878

My Lord,

The Gov. Body of Ch. Ch. this day held an Election to a Clerical Senior Studentship according to notice. Examiners were appointed to report upon the literary merits of the Candidates, and their Report is enclosed herewith, the names being omitted.

On receiving this Report, some of the Electors, conceiving the merits of the two Candidates in question were pretty evenly balanced, voted for *B*. But the great majority voted for *A*; and he was elected.

---

[1] Supplied to me by courtesy of Mr Geoffrey Bill.

But *B*'s merits appeared so considerable that the majority wished to secure him also for the future service of the House; and no doubt, if the Commission had not been sitting, they would have proceeded to elect him to a second Studentship, as has been done on several former occasions.... The Electors voted by 15 to 6 (2 not voting) that application should be made to the Commission with the view of ascertaining whether they would interpose any objection to the election of B.'

In Dodgson's hands, this problem, which, to most people, might seem very simple, is shown to involve complementarity in valuations. Although the problem is introduced in relation to the election of candidates, it must even more have forced itself on his attention in regard to the building operations that were being undertaken at Christ Church. The choice of design that seemed appropriate to any given individual in regard to say, the belfry, would depend on the architectural changes that he expected in the quadrangle, and vice versa: or the changes that seemed appropriate at one part of the quadrangle, would depend on the changes to be introduced at another part and so on. Often in real life the basic pattern has been fixed by custom and we contemplate change in what we regard as a single element only: our valuations are independent. But if a problem is large and requires to be broken down into several elements for discussion and decision, then our ranking of the choices in one element will depend on what we expect to be done in regard to other elements: our valuations are then complementary. The valuation of complementary objects arose also at Christ Church in another way, for the college had to choose between filling Studentships on the one hand, and discarding or modifying parts of its building programme on the other.

Dodgson was aware of this complexity in the valuations of the members of the Governing Body and he attempted to make provision for it in his theory. He was the first, by a considerable number of years, to discuss complementarity in Politics; and even in Economics, where it is easier to deal with the matter, it was practically never referred to in the English literature until sixty years after the time at which he was writing.

In § 5 he deals with the best way of giving a meeting the choice of making 'no election'. This choice is of the same kind as the choice of a particular candidate and should be treated in exactly the same way, namely by allowing 'no election' to enter the voting just as if it were the name of a candidate. Dodgson had dealt with this topic more fully in *A Discussion*..., from which he incorporates three passages in the present pamphlet.

The final paragraph deals with the best method of taking votes to give effect to his scheme. When some members of the Academy suggested to Borda that his scheme was satisfactory in theory but would not work in practice because people would misrepresent their true valuations in their voting so as to help their own candidate, he had replied 'My scheme is only intended for honest men'.[1] Dodgson's solution is more realistic. To the question Am 'I bound in honour to vote for the one whom I should *really* prefer?' in a series of separate votes between candidates, his answer is No, 'I think it desirable that all should know the rule by which this game may be won. It is simply this: "In any division taken on a pair of issues neither of which you desire, vote against the most popular."' As against this, however, he also suggests that at an early stage each voter should record his schedule of relative valuations on all the issues put forward. Those who in the subsequent votes between pairs of motions (if no majority candidate exists) vote otherwise than in accordance with these lists so as to gain advantage for their own candidates (or so as to get rid of a cyclical majority), will then be seen to have done so; and they are to be asked to rewrite their schedules so that they conform to their voting behaviour. Thus Dodgson insists on the requirement that each member's voting behaviour shall be expressible in terms of a single schedule; and at the same time he opens up the possibility of creating a majority candidate in circumstances where formerly there had been none.

[1] See page 182 above.

INDEX

Lacroix, S. F., 156 n., 182 n., 184 n.

Laplace, P.-S., Marquis de, develops Borda's argument, 157, 180–2; appeal of his theory, 180, 184; criticism of his assumptions, 182–3; limitation of his theory, 185; possibly read by Dodgson, 192–3. *See also* Borda criterion

Lennon, Mrs Florence B., 192 n., 193 n., 195 n., 209 n.

Lhuilier, S. A., 160 n.

Liddell, H. G., 196–200, 203, 205–6, 209–11, 236–7

Liddell, Miss Alice, 197–200, 209–10

MacFarlane, A., 185 n.

Machiavelli, N., 115

Madan, F., 189, 191 n., 199, 214

Majority motion (or candidate), defined, 18; with single-peaked preference curves, chapter IV; with curves either single-peaked or single-peaked with plateaus on top, 25–32; with some other shapes of preference curves, 32–5; picking out, when number of motions is finite, 35–8; with two or more variables (complementary motions), chapter XVI

Marks, method of, *see* Borda criterion

Marshall, A., 105

Mascart, J., 156 n., 179 n., 180 n., 182 n., 184 n.

Matrix, construction of, 35–7; properties of, 37–8; deriving group of schedules to correspond to a given matrix, 119–24

May, Sir T. Erskine, 2

McDermott, J. F., 198 n., 205 n.

Median optimum, definition of $O_{med.}$ 18; theorems on $O_{med.}$ 14–19, 24–5; Galton on, 188

Montucla, J. F., 160

Morley, J., 159 n.

Motion, defined, 1; motions are alternatives, 1–2; representation by symbol or point in plane, 2–3, chapters II and III; number of motions finite, 2; chapter VI; number of complementary motions finite, 125–30; number of motions infinite, 3, 10–11, 14–15; number of complementary motions infinite, 131–9

Motion a_0, defined, 3–4; curves drawn through a_0 as point on horizontal axis, 21–4, 32, 90–5, 144–7, 151, 154–5; position of a_0 in matrix, 36–7

Muir, Sir T., 194

Müller, Sir F. Max, 208–11, 234–5

Nanson, E. J., gives an algebraic development, 186; adopts Condorcet criterion, 162, 186–7; shows how to pick out majority candidate by multiple system of marks, 187; comments on a rule of Condorcet's, 175

Netto, E., 162

Newing, R. A., xi, 35 n., 131 n., 139 n.

O'Connor, A. C., 160 n., 179 n.

Optimum, definition of, 15; numbering of optima, 15

Optimum-a and -b curves, 132–3

Order in which motions are voted on may alter decision, with ordinary committee procedure, 39–41; with special majority, 92–9

Pearson, K., 180 n., 188

Politics compared with Economics, 18–19

Potter, P. B., 141 n.

Preference, two modes of representation of order of, 4–6

Preference schedules, 4–5; incomplete schedules, chapter VIII, 90; partial and complete schedules, 125–7. *See also* Curves, Indifference contours

Probability, 150, 163–5, 168–73, 176–8; of occurrence of majority motion with one variable, 50–1; of majority motion (a, b), 139; of particular motion being selected with simple majority, 39–41; with special majority, 92–9. *See also* Borda criterion

Procedure, ordinary committee with simple majority, procedure (α), 3–4; 21–2, 38–45, chapter VIII; procedures (β), (γ), with simple majority, 22–5, 41–4; ordinary procedure (a) with special majority, 90–9, 151–2; procedure (b) with special majority, 92–9; complementary motions, choosing alternate values of a and b, 127–30, 135–7; choosing value (a, b), 137–9; at international conferences, 140–1

Proportional representation, 72–5, chapter XI, 156 n., 174, 187–8, 190–2, 213

Schapiro, J. S., 159 n.

Schedule of preferences, *see* Preference schedules

61319941R00158

Made in the USA
San Bernardino, CA
16 December 2017